Borrowed Words

Borrowed Words

Translation, Imitation,
and the Making
of the Nineteenth-Century Novel
in Spain

Elisa Martí-López

Lewisburg
Bucknell University Press
London: Associated University Presses

© 2002 by Elisa Martí-López

All rights reserved. Authorization to photocopy items for internal or personal use, or the internal or personal use of specific clients, is granted by the copyright owner, provided that a base fee of $10.00, plus eight cents per page, per copy is paid directly to the Copyright Clearance Center, 222 Rosewood Drive, Danvers, Massachusetts 01923, [0-8387-5520-8/02, $10.00 + 8¢ pp, pc.]

Associated University Presses
440 Forsgate Drive
Cranbury, NJ 08512

Associated University Presses
16 Barter Street
London WC1A 2AH, England

Associated University Presses
P.O. Box 338, Port Credit
Mississauga, Ontario
Canada L5G 4L8

The paper used in this publication meets the requirements of the American National Standard for Permanence of Paper for Printed Library Materials Z39.48-1984.

Library of Congress Cataloging-in-Publication Data

Martí-López, Elisa, 1960–
  Borrowed words : translation, imitation and the making of the nineteenth-century novel in Spain / Elisa Martí-López.
    p. cm.
  Includes bibliographical references and index.
  ISBN 0-8387-5520-8 (alk. paper)
    1. Spanish fiction—19th century—History and criticism. 2. French fiction—19th century—-Translations into English—History and criticism. 3. Spanish fiction—19th century—French influences. 4. Sue, Eugáne, 1804–1857. Mystáres de Paris. 5. Nationalism and literature—Spain. 6. Social problems in literature. I. Title.
PQ6144 .M333 2002
863'.509—dc21
                        2002018406

PRINTED IN THE UNITED STATES OF AMERICA

Als meus pares

Contents

Preface   9

Introduction: The Controversial Literariness of the Misterios   17

1. The Market Conditions in a Peripheral Literary Space   33
   The Progenitorship of the French Novel by the Spanish Publishers   34
   Marginality and Orphanhood of the Autochthonous Novel in Spain   37

2. The Preoccupation with Autochthony   45
   The Foreign Discourse on Spain: The Other of Civilized Europe   45
   The Uncertain Character of Modern Spain: Literary Decadence and the Hope for Redemption   49
   The Decentered Literary Consciousness: Latecomers and the New Cultural Order   53
   The Rise of the Novel in Spain: The "Little Poor Speakers" and Their Conspicuous Thefts   56
   Reclaiming the Image of Spain: The European Languages of Culture   59

3. The Critical Reception of the French Novel   63
   The Progenitorship of the French Novel: The Exemplarity of *Les mystères de Paris*   64
   The Radicalization of a Politics of Reformation: The Condemnation of Sue's Novel-Writing   69

4. From Translation to Imitation   77
   The Naturalization of the Foreign Original: From Romance to History   79
   The Question of Authority over the Text: The Translator Against the Author   88
   Translation as Autochthonous Writing   98

5. Imitation and the Autochthonous Novel: *Los misterios de Barcelona*   101
    From Romance to History   102
    The Mysteries of the City and Provincial Life   120

Afterword   135

Appendix: Plot Summary of *Los misterios de Barcelona*   139
Notes   143
Bibliography   177
Index   191

Preface

AN INCREASINGLY LARGE NUMBER OF SCHOLARS WORKING FROM DIFFERent critical approaches have recently reexamined literary life in nineteenth-century Spain. These studies have placed at the center of their critical endeavors many texts (from a diversity of genres) traditionally obscured and excluded from scholarly consideration. Within the context of this critical revaluation, the emphasis has been placed mostly (though not exclusively) on novels written by women or for women, and on the complex relationships among gender, nation, and strategies of cultural prestige. To this extensive and diverse critical activity I would like to contribute another theoretical approach, another set of questions, and, of course, another group of forgotten works.

In this book I address the apparent paradox at the base of the processes of cultural production and consumption in mid-nineteenth-century Europe, that is, the simultaneous emergence of two, seemingly contradictory phenomena: the dependence of literary markets on the importation of French and English cultural paradigms and a notion of art, specifically literature, as being closely linked to national identity. To explore this issue I have taken as my object of study a group of books whose existence is intimately linked to the functioning of nonsynchronic literary markets: the Spanish translations and imitations of *Les Mystères de Paris* (1842–43) by Eugène Sue. I believe these works, although not an exhaustive selection of mid-nineteenth-century novels, represent quite accurately the writing born in the 1840s under the paradoxical conditions described above.

Before I continue I need to clarify the terms *Spain* and *Spanish*. This books deals with some of the cultural and literary processes that accompanied the establishment of the new liberal regime of Queen Isabella II after the death of her father, the absolutist monarch Ferdinand VII, in 1833. Spain was at that time, following the abolition of the political jurisdictions of the old kingdoms, a centralized monarchy with unified territorial and commercial borders. It was not a nation in the new bourgeois sense of a cultural and spiritual community. The absolutist monarchy stood over profoundly diverse regions organized around strong protonational bounds. The formation of a new nation-state based on the political and economic principles of liberalism and a particular notion and feeling of nationhood was precisely the task that lay ahead, and in the mid nineteenth century most liberals, regardless of regional origin or political leaning (conservative or progressive), were committed to its realization. The new modern state, the new Spain, was a project; its content and forms, however, were vague and often contradictory. It is well known that this project was soon to be challenged by the emergence of regional nationalisms that questioned or opposed that of the state. Thus, in this book, the terms *Spain* and *Spanish* reflect the historical existence of a Spanish monarchy and a Spanish liberal state organizing numerous instances of social and economic life in the regions, the political vision of many mid-nineteenth-century liberals, and the common cultural circumstances that conditioned their literary practices. They are not intended to name a single, unified national reality. Moreover, the expression "Spanish novel" refers both to the novel written in Spain and to the novel written in Spanish. While it is true that in the period studied in this book, and for well-known historical reasons, all novels are written in Spanish, the literary and cultural processes discussed here are also relevant to the later development of the novel in other languages of the state. I have tried not to erase the diversity of historical processes that constituted Spain during those years and that had a decisive effect on cultural and literary production both then and later on. With this purpose, chapters 4 and 5 frame the general processes described in the book within particular local and regional conditions.

In the Introduction I question commonly held views on *folletines* and imitations and present the critical approach I deem appropriate for the Spanish *misterios*. First, I contend that the description of most misterios as *folletín* novel is problematic. Literary modes and cultural discourses other than melodrama found their way into these texts, and their readership was mostly male and middle class. I argue that, contrary to the perception of these novels as escapist and alienating literature, the emergence of the misterios in the 1840s is related to the will of political expression that gave rise to the daily press—a phenomenon inscribed in the process of consciousness-raising set in motion by the middle class outside the boundaries of the prevailing constitutional system. Second, I examine the notion of imitation traditionally associated with the misterios. I undertake the critical evaluation of the concepts of "originality" and "genius," and against them I contend that imitation is a discursive resolution to a crisis that originated in the awareness of a provincial separation from modern cultural processes, and that it is also the driving force shaping the culture of peripheral countries such as Spain in the mid nineteenth century. I propose to replace the irreconcilable opposition between original and imitative writing with the notion of *appropriation*. The term, following Bakhtin's notion of "persuasive discourses," acknowledges the processes of literary borrowings, and analyzes cultural ascendancy as a deep and productive influence able to generate a further creative development of another's discourse in a new context and under new conditions.

In chapter 1, "The Market Conditions in a Peripheral Literary Space," I explore the new structure for the production and consumption of cultural goods in Spain. In particular, I try to answer two questions: how did the new literary market affect the establishment of the Spanish book industry, and how did it condition the writing environment of the Spanish novelists? In my view, in the context of modern cultural production, it is not enough to inquire into the forms of writing; we also need to consider the conditions for the possibility itself of writing. I argue that in the mid nineteenth century all commercial publishing resources were invested in promoting and disseminating the French novel in Spain. The French novel saturated the Spanish literary market and determined the habits and expectations of Spanish readers. These facts transformed the close economic and artistic collaboration between publisher and author—which sustained the emergence of the novel as a new hegemonic genre in nineteenth-century France and Britain—into a strictly economic transaction where the creative energy of the *literatos* was redirected toward translation and imitation. Translation and imitation were the forms of novel-writing brought forth by the peripheral position the Spanish literary market occupied in the new cultural order.[1]

In chapter 2, "The Preoccupation with Autochthony," I explore the reaction of the literatos to the fact that the French had successfully replaced them in two important initiatives: in adapting and re-creating the Spanish literary tradition for contemporary audiences and within modern parameters (that of Romantic poetics); and in creating for European and other foreign audiences the image—and value—of Spain. I contend that the position of the literatos with respect to the cultural hegemony of France over Spain— and, specifically, the role French literature should play in the creation of a modern Spanish novel—was complex and often contradictory. On the one hand, the literatos would not accept the historical dependency and cultural marginality they were condemned to by what was perceived as Spain's slow process toward modernization. They held a grudge against the French for their interference in Spanish literary practices and readership, and firmly opposed the intrusion by proclaiming the irreducibility of Spain's historical conditions to foreign forms of the novel. On the other hand, the literatos were aware that to succeed in Paris, as well as to succeed in one's own national territory, a Spanish author had—and very often sought—to negotiate his or her own alien and odd cultural position (that of a culturally peripheral subject) into the more *familiar* and *admired* grounds provided by the dominant cultural paradigms. To create an autochthonous novel required a decentered literary consciousness—the obligation to deal with an alien discourse and alien world. In this sense the literatos refused to acknowledge the difference between original and imitative writing, and freely misread foreign writings and re-created them as if they were their own.

In chapter 3, "The Critical Reception of the French Novel," I examine the critical fostering of foreign narratives that accompanied, and sanctioned, the publishers' importation of the French novel. To determine the impact contemporary French authors had in the Spanish literary field, I take into account the literatos' critical views on the new hegemonic genre, and their own envisioning of an autochthonous novel. I contend that the scrutiny of the French novel was a political act, and that the central point of contention among the literatos was the social function the novel was expected to perform in the new liberal order established by the *Estatuto Real* (1833). All foreign novels were analyzed and evaluated according to this criterion, and their originally alien nature was actualized or neutralized in conformity with it. I describe how most literatos recognized in *Les mystères de Paris* a writing that transformed the novel from mere moral entertainment into a space of political and moral argumentation where the new liberal society recognized itself. I examine how the potential political radicalism of Sue's writing was soon made apparent by the publication of his second major best-seller, *Le juif errant* (1844–45). Against those Spanish supporters of Sue's novels for whom writing was an exercise in public communication, the conservative literatos commended Cecilia Böhl de Faber (Fernán Caballero), who prescribed a novel that was to be contained within the private home and read as a domestic affirmation of moral amenity and leisure.[2]

In chapter 4, "From Translation to Imitation," I analyze Juan Cortada's translation of *Les mystères de Paris*, *Los misterios de París* (Barcelona: Tomás Gorchs, 1845), as an example of the "half-our and half–someone else's" word which characterized the rise of the nineteenth-century novel in Spain. I contend that translation provided an opportunity for experimentation (although a restricted one) few literatos were willing or able to forego. Through the hermeneutic motions that constitute the act of translation, Cortada tried out imaginary forms to account for both the foreignness and the familiarity of the new novel with respect to the historical and cultural conditions of Spain and, in particular, Catalonia. Cortada's translation compellingly manifests both the opposition and the fluidity—the shock of difference and familiarity—that binds one's own identity with otherness. I explore the sudden, sporadic, and often erratic movements of Cortada's text away from the foreign novel. I argue that Cortada's move away from literality and reliance on paraphrase and imitation has two main significant literary consequences: Cortada's actual supplantation of Sue's authorship, and the emergence of a new text with a distinctive style and imagination.

In some parts of chapter 4, where a Spanish translation of a French text is analyzed, an English translation is not provided because no English translation provides an accurate representation of the linguistic strategies discussed in that part of the chapter. The English translation effects its own set of stylistic deviations and variations from the French original, which differ from those effected by the Spanish text. Adding English translations in these particular instances brings confusion and, more important, makes incomprehensible the points made by the analysis.

In chapter 5, "Imitation and the Autochthonous Novel," I analyze José Nicasio Milá de la Roca's imitation of *Les mystères de Paris*, *Los misterios de Barcelona*. I argue that we recognize some of Cortada's specific hermeneutic motions in Milá's own assimilation of the foreign text. This is not a coincidence. First, imitation represents yet another step in the effort to make the alien character of the bourgeois novel a little less foreign to the sociohistorical conditions of mid-nineteenth-century Spain; second, both Cortada and Milá are addressing the same local audience, that of Catalonia; and finally, these authors supported the same moderado politics. But imitation is a freer exercise than translation; the autochthonous elements of the story take preference over the original, and even the loosest notion of truthfulness to the model is replaced by the necessity to betray it—the inevitable twist of displaced ideas. I argue that, although Milá closely follows Sue's reliance on romance to represent the social violence which accompanies the consolidation of the new capitalist order, and subscribes to the politics of reform characteristic of *Les mystères de Paris*, he takes on the task of providing narrative form to the historical conditions that distinguished Barcelona from Paris. Milá effects a distinctive hermeneutic movement toward history that is absent from his model. It is precisely the particular merging of romance, journalism, and history, and, more specifically, the reliance of *Los misterios de Barcelona* on current events to tell its story that constitutes the half-our half–someone else's word which characterizes Milá's autochthonous writing.

The analyses of both Cortada's translation and Milá's imitation intend to point out tendencies shown by these texts, rather than laws that rigidly constitute them. These analyses do not exhaust the numerous literary and cultural issues these texts bring forth or the diversity of writing shown by other misterios. In this sense, this book presents a set of working hypotheses rather than demonstrated and verified conclusions, and is a contribution to the study of the misterios and the novelistic writing they created.

Two more observations. I have modernized the orthography of the primary texts I quote, but have not modified the punctuation; In the case of personal names, I have decided to maintain their Spanish or Catalan spelling according to the bibliographical record of the works used in this study.

A first version in Spanish of chapter 1 was published in *Bulletin Hispanique* in 1996. Some arguments I elaborate in the Introduction appear in *Siglo XIX (Literatura Hispánica)* (1998) and in the chapter on folletín included in "The Cambridge Companion to the Spanish Novel from 1800 to the Present" (forthcoming).

The material in this book first saw light in the form of a dissertation, and I am grateful to my adviser at New York University, Sylvia Molloy, and the other members of the dissertation committee, Luis F. Cifuentes, James Fernández, Margaret Cohen, and John Coleman, who guided the original project. I would like also to specially thank Franco Moretti who read parts of this manuscript and made invaluable comments, Akiko Tsuchiya who read a first version of the "Introduction," and my colleagues at both the University of Notre Dame and Northwestern University without whose support I could not have transformed my dissertation into a book. Finally, I want to thank Mario Santana who aided in the translation into English of Catalan, French, Italian, and Spanish texts. Also, none of this text would have been written without his personal support and critical commentaries.

Borrowed Words

Introduction: The Controversial Literariness of the Misterios

> Our knowledge of literary history closely resembles the maps of Africa of a century and a half ago: the coastal strips are familiar but an entire continent is unknown.
> —Franco Moretti, *Signs Taken for Wonders*

> The nineteenth century, which we would like to expunge from our history, is the negation of the Spanish spirit.
> —Francisco Franco, 1950

THE MISTERIOS, NOVELS WRITTEN UNDER THE INFLUENCE OF EUGÈNE Sue's *Les Mystères de Paris* (1842–43) mostly during the years 1840–70, are usually included within the general label of folletín, a classification that needs some clarification. Folletín is generally meant to describe both a publishing process and a fictional mode. On the one hand, it refers to the market-induced fragmentation a novel underwent when published either in the folletín section of a newspaper or in serial form. On the other, it designates its inscription within the tradition of melodramatic writing and its association with a popular and mostly feminine readership. These general traits which frame the writing of folletín have become a kind of critical steamroller that cancels out all aesthetic differentiation among the texts that have had the misfortune to fall into this category. Thus, despite the increase in the number of studies dedicated to this type of text, we are still, as Romero Tobar was twenty years ago, struggling with the term—or terms—that better describe the diverse aesthetic and cultural nature of the so-called folletines. Indeed, the extensive and varied body of nineteenth-century Spanish novels written before 1870 is still a "confusing universe," and our knowledge of these works continues to be limited and muddled.[1] This is particularly true in the case of the misterios. The inclusion of the misterios—especially those written in the 1840s, but also those written until and during the 1860s—within this general category of folletín is often problematic. Although most of them were heavily influenced by melodrama and some (but not all) were published in serial form, other literary modes and cultural discourses found their way into these texts, and a readership larger than the feminine and the popular constituted its social audience.

As folletines, the misterios have usually been denied literary value. With few exceptions, scholars exhibit a widespread refusal to consider folletín-writing in general, and specifically the novelistic production before 1870, in literary terms.[2] The prevalent critical prejudices that support the supposedly nonliterariness of these novels center around the idea of progress applied to cultural processes. Based upon the application of nineteenth-century evolutionary theory to literature, the concept of literary progress throughout history—what Osip Mandelstam calls the "theory of betterment"— has conditioned our understanding of nineteenth-century Spanish literary history.[3] Accordingly, novel-writing in the last century is often perceived as a process from aesthetically deficient periods of preparation toward the mature literary movements that appear after 1870 (Realism and Naturalism). Hence, mid-nineteenth-century novelists are often referred to as "pre-Realists," and their works described as the "childhood" of the Spanish novel: "It certainly is a sort of infantile literature, but—given its themes and the interest it elicited among a wide audience freshly introduced not just to reading, but also to participation in national affairs—it deserves to be considered . . . as the 'juvenilia' of the realist novel."[4]

The notion of literature as a human activity subject to the laws of progress results in a specific critical practice: the imposition on the mid-nineteenth-century misterios of alien aesthetic considerations and cultural conceptions; in particular, those literary values embraced by late-nineteenth-century novels. It is in this context that Joaquín Marco tells us that "Ayguals is proposing what Benito Pérez Galdós will accomplish later." Thus, the critic often sets out to detect in these 1840 novels a few elements characteristic of the Realist writing, only to oppose them to other numerous traits of the misterios that openly betray that same Realist aesthetics.[5] Although the application of Realist parameters to the pre-1870 novel seeks on some occasions to vindicate the literary relevance of these works, the fact is that from this critical approach the misterios cannot avoid being perceived as the product of an underdeveloped aesthetic.[6] Catherine Jagoe has shown how gender differentiation is at the base of the strategies of cultural prestige that, since Menéndez Pelayo's time, have sustained the association between the supposed puerility of the mid-nineteenth-century novel and feminine authorship and readership. Accordingly, the Realist novel has been construed as mature masculine writing for a grown-up audience of men in opposition to—and at the expense of—the supposedly feminine and childlike folletín.[7]

The agreement of many contemporary critics with the aesthetic values expressed by Pérez Galdós and Ortega y Gasset highlights the epistemological dependence of many literary historians upon Realist and/or Modernist poetics. We easily recognize in their critical evaluation of these works Pérez Galdós's famous condemnation of the foreignness, narrative naivety, and excess of the pre-1870 novels, and Ortega y Gasset's contempt for popular forms of storytelling and their penchant for adventure and intrigue.[8] The consequences of such a dependence are important. First, with a few exceptions, we do not have studies that analyze the literary mode of these novels as the result of particular and differentiated writing practices. We know little about the system—or systems—of signification that constitute them, about the textuality that sustained the pleasure of their reading, or about the dominant forms of melodrama adopted in Spain.[9] Finally, the imposition of alien poetics to the pre-1870 Spanish novel prevents the proper enunciation of both the peculiarities and difficulties that characterize the emergence and development of the bourgeois novel in Spain.

The Realist/Modernist stand against the "orgiastic" nature of folletín inscribes itself within the established distinction of High and Low forms of culture. Accordingly, the supposed literary frenzy of the misterios and folletín in general has always been indiscriminately associated with market-oriented processes of publishing. The association of market and literary frenzy obliterates the fact that all nineteenth-century novels shared the same publishing infrastructure that supported the folletín.[10] There is in my understanding a misleading and indiscriminate identification of what Antonio Gramsci calls "the commercial aspect" of a work—"the fact that the 'interesting' element . . . is sought out from without, mechanically, and is doled out industrially, as a sure element of immediate 'success'"—with melodramatic writing."[11] This identification helps explain why the impact of capitalist publishing policies in the writing of late-nineteenth-century Realist novels is hardly ever analyzed. It is not my intention to deny the presence of radically different novelistic writings, or the existence of a folletín novel with its own ties to the market, but rather to point out that the traditional distinction between literary novel and folletín is erroneous and equivocal. Moreover, the indiscriminate association of folletín and market-oriented fiction has kept critics from considering the literary frenzy that characterizes these novels as a style in itself, or, more specifically, as the prevailing and all-encompassing mode of expression in the 1840–70 period.

The reductive association of the pre-1870 novel with market-oriented cultural products—and, consequently, the reiteration of its nonliterary character—finds one of its major expressions in the studies that approach this novelistic production from a sociological point of view. These studies do not subvert the traditional understanding of the nonliterary nature of these works, but rather confirm it. Books such as those by Juan Ignacio Ferreras—whose main, if not exclusive, focus is the social existence of these works—reduce the reading of the pre-1870 novels to sociological considerations and consequently deny them an aesthetic nature.

Expressions like "paraliterature"—"subliterature," "folletín," or "popular novel"—coined specially for them, define the existence of the pre-1870 novels in exclusively social terms, and sanction the substitution of schematic lists of contents for literary and cultural analysis.[12] In these studies we find that the pre-1870 novels lose all their singularity, and become mere examples of a statistical category, multiple and repetitive samples of an identical negation of poetics itself, works with no style, and examples of nonliterary texts. As Benítez puts it, "all serialized novels are alike—the formulas are repeated over and over again."[13]

These sociological studies sanction the supposition of knowledge and the application of generalities which has often characterized the critical evaluation of the pre-1870 novel, and allow the critic to forego literary analysis of those long, often unreadable, and boring works.[14] The absence of critical inquiry is blatantly exemplified in Joaquín Marco's comment on a fragment of Ayguals's *El tigre del Maestrazgo*: "The quotation," he says, "requires no commentary."[15] Therefore, what ultimately creates the impression of narrative uniformity associated with these works is not the texts themselves, but rather a critical discourse that, committed to strategies of cultural prestige based on class and gender exclusions, is reluctant to consider these novels analytically.[16] One can only wonder what could be said about the Realist novel—or, for that matter, any other kind of literary writing—if we were to apply the same critical indolence to them. Against this critical generalization, I contend that the misterios are a case in point of the morphological flexibility achieved by the melodramatic mode in the mid-nineteenth-century novel.

The authors of folletines are always described by their relation to the market, and consequently indiscriminately defined by production-oriented terms such as *intermediary authors* or *workers*.[17] These definitions deprive these novelists of their own individual names and, as Foucault has pointed out, an author's name is precisely the signifier for both the existence and status of a discourse within a society and culture: a discourse "that possesses an author's name is not to be immediately consumed and forgotten."[18] Indeed, and with the exception of Ayguals de Izco, the writers of the misterios are unknown to us; their names and works have been erased, and they are circulating under a collective pejorative denomination: *folletinistas*. In accordance with the alleged redundancy of their writing the name "folletinista" stands for the lack of individual originality, the reiterative nature of their common nonliterariness. The problematic character of authorship posed by collective writing practices—as in some folletines—or by imitative writing is hardly considered from the poststructuralist notion of a dispersed or dislocated authorship. On the contrary, collective names—either as authors (folletinistas) or as texts (*novela popular* or imitations)—continue to signify the depreciated, when not obliterated, mode of existence, circulation, and functioning of the misterios within literary histories. Yet the specific conditions of production that framed the writing of the mid-nineteenth-century Spanish novels question the degree to which these works were dependent upon market-oriented decisions. In fact, most of these novels were not exactly "popular," but rather were marginal enterprises. They were written on the fringes of the publishing circles, and their publication was often—as we will see—either a self-financed or institutional enterprise. Although they often had the support of the critics, they proved to be—with the exception again of Ayguals's novels—commercial fiascos as they failed either to captivate the imagination (and satisfy the expectations and tastes) of Spanish readers or, in many cases, even reach most of them.[19]

Moreover, these novels belong to a cultural period when the new market-oriented literary practices were in full swing, but the cultural denunciation of mass-produced popular culture—although in process of being conceptualized—was yet to be set in place. Only after *l'art pour l'art* emerged as the dominant aesthetic doctrine in Spain—as Jagoe has observed, during the revolutionary period initiated in 1868—was the question of the construction of national literature framed by the distinction between High and Low culture.[20] Consequently, the writing of the misterios is characterized by the conspicuous absence of strategies of cultural hierarchization so important in the later-nineteenth-century Spanish novel. In this sense, the misterios represent an interesting case of novelistic writing where the "commercial aspect" of the work—those commercially successful narrative formulas—is fused with, or hardly distinguishable from, what Gramsci calls the "naive" or "spontaneous" character of any true literary work. The misterios are both a commercially oriented narrative—as imitation of Sue's works they reproduce some commercially successful narrative formulas—and a literary enterprise undertaken by an educated elite interested in creating an autochthonous literature. They are commercial narratives driven by the desire to engage in the aesthetics of a foreign and popular genre. As such, they represent another form of those "novels in-between, hybrids of high and low" which Stephanie Sieburth calls attention to and identifies among modern Spanish novels. Their participation in both high and low forms of culture is related to the conflictive intersection of the different historical stages that characterized the modernization of Spain in those years.[21]

The identification of the misterios with the unsophisticated and childlike reading habits said to be found among the working classes and women also proves to be far from accurate. In this sense it is problematic to consider most misterios as unqualified "popular novels." Some twenty years ago Peter B. Goldman's analysis of the social and economic conditions supporting readership in mid-nineteenth-century Spain established the middle-class background of most readers of the early novel. His conclusions, openly contradicting the assumed working-class readership of pre-1870 novels, have been lately confirmed by studies on literacy in Spain. In particular, in the case of the misterios, the dense page composition, the use of footnotes, addendas, and small fonts—all distinctive traits of these novels to a greater or lesser degree—seem to point to an audience with more sophisticated reading skills than those of the literate working class. The proclaimed extraordinary luxury of the first editions of *María o La hija de un jornalero*, in addition to confirming the high cost of the book, seems also to be in agreement with the desire of an anxious middle class to acquire both social prestige and cultural capital.[22]

Also, and against the established idea of a mostly female readership, the intended audience of the misterios was the male reader. The male readership of the novels inspired by Sue's *Les Mystères de Paris* is consistent with nineteenth-century printed and written records. A male reader is depicted, for instance, in the caricature entitled "Lecture des *Mystères de Paris*" published in the magazine *Charivari* on November 22, 1843. Similarly, the small library owned by Dussadier (the representative of the committed revolutionary low middle class in Flaubert's *L'éducation sentimentale*) consists of three books and includes the novel by Sue. An intended male audience is also congruent with the novels' political nature. Rafael del Castillo, in the opening pages of his novel *Misterios catalanes o el obrero de Barcelona* (1862), not only identifies men as the appropriate readers of his text, but also warns off any possible female reader: "Our readers can take the trouble of interpreting it in their own way. We refrain from doing it in order not to offend the modesty of the few daughters of Eve who may have the fateful or delightful whim of reading us."[23] The social spectrum of the misterios readership in Spain is well exemplified by José María Álvarez—owner of a cake shop—who after his death in 1846 left a library consisting of, among other unspecified books, *Los misterios de París, Los misterios de Madrid, El judío errante, Nuestra Señora de París, Hans de Islandia*, and *La vida de Espartero*.[24] Despite their intended readership, however, different sources point also to a large feminine audience for the misterios and other mid-nineteenth-century political novels. Among these sources we can mention the numerous fictional and nonfictional stories about the figure of the "bluestocking" *("la marisabidilla")* during those years, or the numerous writing records left behind by politicians and social commentators warning about the dangers of intermixing political discourse and entertainment precisely because it was creating a politicized female readership.[25]

The middle-class, mostly male, and often politically progressive readership of the misterios is consistent with the social base of Sue's extensive readership. According to Gramsci, Sue was widely read by the middle-class democrats. The widespread use of the serial novel—in particular, of the misterios type of narratives—by politically minded liberals and, in some cases, by utopian socialists, questions also the preconception of illiterate readers seeking plain escapist entertainment.[26] Although it is accurate to affirm in general that the misterios belong to what Marx, and later, Umberto Eco, identified as the highly successful (as well as politically conservative) formula known as "literature of consolation"—works whose plots create the illusion of breaking with the monotony and prosaic rhythms of modernity, and satisfy both the reader's need for adventure and heroic deeds and his/her belief in a transcendental (and paternalistic) justice—the misterios are not alienating novels, nor are they all plainly conservative. On the contrary, the politically charged character of most of these novels, their intended portrait of contemporary social issues, and the public they addressed (often the progressive and democratic opposition to the conservative regimes), as well as their dense letter and page format, all point to both an educated and socially aware Spanish audience that enjoyed recognizing—or expected to find—their own social concerns, political anxieties, and aspirations in fictional narratives.[27] Moreover, the misterios locate themselves precisely at the center of the disparity between the rigid constitutional frame imposed by a system of representation based on strict property qualifications *(liberalismo censitario)* and the realities of a social opinion that was excluded from the system of representation and demanded its political access to the new constitutional system. Thus, and contrary to the perception of these novels as escapist and alienating literature, the emergence of the misterios in the 1840s is related to the will of political expression which gave rise to the daily press—a phenomenon inscribed in the process of consciousness-raising set in motion by the middle class outside the boundaries of the prevailing constitutional system. As an anonymous conservative critic—writing in 1850 from the pages of the reactionary paper *La Censura*—openly lamented, the unrestricted ideological field of public opinion duplicated itself in newspapers and novels as an echo against the restrictive organization of the state.[28] In accordance with Raymond Carr's assertion of the historical importance and political influence of the petite bourgeoisie sectors of Spanish society in the early 1850s, the misterios are located at the center of the formal abundance, cultural complexity, and ideological contradictions experienced by the Spanish mid-nineteenth-century middle classes.[29]

In this sense, and in contrast to Ríos-Font's statement about the irredeemable "reactionary spirit that always pervaded Spanish melodrama" in nineteenth-century theater, I contend that the misterios show the ideological width of melodramatic writing—that same "ambivalent blend of boldness and blindness" Peter Brooks has assigned to *Les mystères de Paris*.[30] Indeed, the misterios sanctioned basic forms of bourgeois authority and social order, but we have to remember that they also satisfied the symbolic needs of the political opposition to the moderado regime—progressive liberals, republicans, democrats, and utopian socialists. The ideological limitations of these political discourses (their ultimate alliance to bourgeois concepts of class and gender) should not prevent us from acknowledging the destabilizing role some of them had in mid-nineteenth-century Spain. As the misterios written by Ayguals or Ceferino Tressera show, mid-nineteenth-century writers, using melodrama to express their social concerns, questioned and pushed liberalism often to its limits before Marxist thought revealed the ideological shortcomings of their critical discourses. These misterios are, thus, addressed to those social groups that made possible the 1868 revolution and the First Republic, movements that stood for a social order that had little to do with the *Estatuto Real* or the Restoration.

The imagination found in the misterios is not detached from the historical conditions that gave rise to it, nor is it rigidly formulaic and meaningless. On the contrary, the particular type of imagination encompassed in the misterios is the aesthetic response—the form that confers meaning—to the historical processes transforming Spain in the mid nineteenth century. The misterios came into being in the years that witnessed both the dismantling of the absolutist state and the transition to new, liberal socioeconomic policies that found expression in the *Estatuto Real* (1833), the years that saw both the Carlist wars and the intense in-fighting among different liberal groups (their political struggle to impose a specific version of liberalism in Spain). These were years of profound economic transformations and intense social unrest, years that witnessed the first proletarianization of the working force, the first important migrations from rural areas to the cities, the introduction of the first steam machines, and the reconfiguration of the commercial relations with America after the Independence wars. One could say also that this was the period when different rhythms of economic development among the Spanish regions were definitively established; when diverse and multiple political interests were born, and with them mutually contradictory envisionings of Spain as a nation-state. As one of the first representations of Spanish society struggling with modernization, the misterios provide their own distinctive fictional response to the disruption caused by historical process in traditional forms of life, and reflect the anxieties and enthusiasm their readers themselves felt about the possibility of reinventing the country around a new modern state.

As *imitations* of foreign literary models, the misterios have been rejected as spurious literature and discarded as alien to Spanish processes of cultural and national formation. Since the misterios are said to perform a double shameful gesture—that of submission and that of cultural alienation—they have been aggressively obliterated in the study of literary history. The obliteration of the intellectual concerns and literary work of mid-nineteenth-century novelists hardly comes as a surprise when we consider both the Romantic foundation and the nationalistic purpose of most histories of literature. As is well known, the discipline of national literary history is a by-product of the notion of *Geist*, the belief in the unique spiritual configuration of a nation, the constant actualization of its *origin* in all its members. Imitations—lacking sincerity, idea associated with originality—are said to stand for the voluntary resignation of a supposedly authentic expression (both personal and national) and the acceptance of the mask as true identity. This presumed loss of identity is described by Montesinos as the despairing "confusion of the spirits," the "apathy," and "abdication of being" characteristic of the mid-nineteenth-century novel.[31]

Intrusions by foreign patterns of writing upon the sacred whole of native creativity—a self-sufficient and closed national monologue—are perceived as "severing the connections" (or as a "social fissure") between *"culture* (unrelated to its surroundings) and *production* (not springing from the depths of our life)." This is particularly true for the history of the nineteenth-century Spanish novel which, as Alda Blanco tells us, was written under the "obsessive fear of cultural invasion."[32] Critical awareness of the historical and ideological conditions that gave rise to the notion of *Volksgeist* has not been able to forestall the nationalistic project of most literary histories. It has not prevented the prevalent identification of national—that is, original—literature with the work of a few male authors, and the persistent engendering of imitation, to its discredit, as a feminine mode (that of female authors and readers).[33] On the contrary, many literary critics still approach a work of literature from the presupposition of its irreducible national originality, oblivious that literary life consists of both foreign and native literature.[34] Excluded from the prestige and authenticity associated with the notion of national uniqueness, the misterios are presented as aesthetically deficient, and their derivative writing (as a rewriting of a foreign text) is denied legitimacy. Since literary morphology is often seen as directly related to the originality of the work, statements relating the emergence of the nineteenth-century Spanish novel to a certain form of Spanishness—that of *casticismo*—are often taken for granted. Echoing this critical stand, the emergence of the nineteenth-century Spanish novel is identified with the 1849 publication of Fernán Caballero's *La Gaviota*. This identification disregards the numerous novels published before, and also that *La Gaviota* was originally written in French and translated by José Joaquín de Mora. Accordingly, for many literary historians the misterios constitute a sort of false heritage, or, as Romero Tobar says, the legacy of "false pioneers." Hence, no one has yet undertaken the analysis of what Romero Tobar himself called "the licentious adaptation, *more hispanico*, of the meaning of the *mystères*."[35]

Since in literature national uniqueness is constructed around the notion of originality (the genius of an artist resting on the ability to express anew the distinctive spirit of a community at a certain moment of its evolution throughout history), a critical evaluation of the nationalistic foundation in literary histories must encompass its revision. The concept of originality has been self-contradictory from the very first moment of its emergence. Its problematic nature is first revealed in its intimate association with the market-oriented process of printing and the subsequent emergence of authorship (and its derivative, plagiarism) as the legal guarantor of property rights. According to Thomas Mallon, "being in print would not be the vulgarization of authorship so much as its essence."[36] Originality and authorship, being concepts entangled with the legal sanctioning of copyrights, reveal themselves to be a by-product of capitalism. Consequently, as Roland Barthes has pointed out, their epistemological value depends on the ideological prestige conferred by capitalism to the idea of the individual, and on the identification effected by positivist thought of person (the psychological and ethnic location of originality) with author. This identification sustains the subjective foundations of originality as well as their direct transfer from the subject-creator to the object created, which is said, then, to be original. It also gives rise to a literary investigation that structures itself not as a history but rather as a chronicle, where a succession of biographies functions as the "final signified" for the texts and literary events of a nation.[37]

The construction of the individual *genius* as a self-sufficient talent reveals also the controversial nature of the notion of originality. Its precariousness is well described by Bate as the contradiction experienced by the eighteenth-century poets who, "exhorted to be 'original' at all cost," tried to distinguish themselves from their admired models without compromising sincerity. The paradoxical character of a creative act that, in order to be original, has to renounce its own acquired aesthetic convictions and pleasures without betraying any deceitfulness—"the fearful legacy to the great Romantics"—brought about a particular and successful notion of influence that supposedly canceled the contradiction.[38] I am referring to T. S. Eliot's, and later, Harold Bloom's concept of literary borrowing. This notion supposedly acknowledged the inescapable paradox in the idea of originality while preserving its central aesthetic value. But this idea of borrowing has tended to create further critical confusion. Instead of exploring the paradoxical nature of the creative act, Eliot's statement (based on the positivist understanding of the text as the expression of the author's inner truth) has generated the inconsistent, somewhat artificial, and often vague conceptual opposition between imitation (characteristic of "immature poets") and stealing (done supposedly by "mature poets").[39]

The widespread resort to evaluative terms close to ethical and psychological notions—such as mature/immature, strong/weak, good/bad, authentic/inauthentic—to examine complex processes of literary borrowing is well testified in Harold Bloom's analysis of literary influence. He relies upon concepts much like those used by Eliot to distinguish between original writing, as "misreading or misprision of poetic history" by "strong poets," and imitative writing—the result of the literary application of "weaker" talents, whose works are "an embarrassment to read." Ultimately, his notion of original writing as a "corrective swerve" is dependent on the notion of "betterment" characteristic, as I mentioned before, of Modernist theories.[40] The epistemological confusion and contradictions created by the notion of borrowing as a corrective swerve can be perceived in the lack of critical comments on close textual ties—in some cases, plagiarism— involving established authors. The same critics who disclaim or simply obliterate the misterios as imitations of foreign models disregard or play down many instances of imitation/plagiarism by canonized authors; for example, Mariano José de Larra's free use of contemporary foreign works (to which I refer later in this book). As Mallon reminds us, we are still living by the literary, psychological, and political ideals of the Romantic era. All we have done since then, one might say, is to play out their values in cynical awareness.[41]

The reduction of literary influence to a kind of "righteous" relation involving two "strong" poets has been denounced by Claudio Guillén as "the psychologizing of intertextuality." Opposing the traditional psychologizing of literary processes, Guillén's emphasis on intertextuality aligns itself with Barthes' assertion on "the truth of writing"—that "the writer can only imitate a gesture that is always anterior, never original."[42] Intertextuality, by posing new questions, points to new directions for the study of literary influence. The substitution of the interplay of textuality—as a network of what Barthes has called the "already written"—for the biographic notion of influence brings up most decidedly both the question of originality and that of authorship. If most nineteenth-century novels are "readerly texts"—a network of the "already written"—we should then ask, what is the particular literary nature of imitative writings? Does a poetics of imitation exist that is different from a poetics of originality? What kind of *authorship* is effected by intertextuality? I would argue that in order to begin answering these questions in relation to the case presented by the misterios we need to give full consideration to the modern conditions of cultural production.

Franco Moretti has documented the ruthless centralization of cultural processes initiated in the nineteenth century—processes that modified the creative conditions and cultural consciousness all over Europe. In the nineteenth century Paris and London dictated the forms of novel-writing and, supported by powerful publishing houses, actively exported them. Modern culture came to be identified with the events and artifacts produced by these two cities and a new hierarchical literary geography was created. Nations at different narrative stages became contiguous literary markets. The interference of the prestigious nineteenth-century English and French models of novel-writing in the literary life of other nations decisively modified the conditions of production of autochthonous novels within those countries and radically limited their aesthetic options. As Moretti explains, "Diffusion: the great conservative force. One form; and an imported one. . . . [I]n an integrated market—latecomers don't follow the same road of their predecessors, only later: they follow a different, a *narrower*, road."[43] To be a novelist in Spain at the time required framing one's work within the modes of writing dictated by the commercially successful French novel. For the first time, *to be a writer* meant to have or to aspire to have a socially wide readership, and *to write* involved *imitating*, to some degree, those foreign narratives whose commercial success revealed them to be the closest to the social imaginary. In this context, imitation is no longer an individual and sporadic phenomenon (the influence of an author A on an author B) or the sign of alleged discrepancies between civilization and those other belated cultures, but a literary practice circumscribed by the *narrowing* of morphological freedom imposed by nonsynchronic literary markets. As Roberto Schwarz pointed out, "Copying is not a false problem" if we free our critical discourse "from the mythical requirements of creation *ex nihilo*." Imitation is a discursive resolution to a crisis originated by the awareness of a provincial separation from modern cultural processes, and the driving force shaping the culture of new and peripheral countries such as Spain in the mid nineteenth century.[44]

I propose to reconsider the novelistic production of the 1840s by approaching imitation as a discursive practice which ranges from a simple act of reproduction to complex forms of parodic writing. More specifically, I would like to replace the irreconcilable opposition between original and imitative writing with the notion of appropriation. The term *appropriation*, as used in this book, acknowledges the processes of literary borrowings but analyzes cultural ascendancy as a "deep and productive" influence able to generate "a further creative development of another's (more precisely, half-other) discourse in a new context and under new conditions." In this sense, appropriation conforms with Bakhtin's understanding of the artistic work "as a rejoinder in a given dialogue, whose style is determined by its interrelationship with other rejoinders in the same dialogue."[45]

On the one hand, appropriation consists of the prolific ramifications of certain narrative strategies and plot traits among a group of texts constituting a specific and recognizable type of novel. In this sense, imitative writing is comparable to the writing within a genre: the circulation of "a certain number of resemblances and analogies" patterned on a particular work.[46] The Spanish novels written following the impact of Sue's works could be examined from the intertextual perspective determined by their genre, in this case, that of the misterios. On the other hand, the notion of appropriation acknowledges the active role played by the target culture in a context of cultural invasion. In this sense, it stands for strategies of absorption, adaptation, and replacement of the morphological constraints set by dominant foreign cultures. Appropriation is the conferring of meaning to another's word, that is, the hermeneutic "motion" that sustains all acts of interpretation and interlingual translation.[47] We can say that appropriation arises from a decentered literary consciousness, that is, from the acknowledgment of the aesthetic potential of an alien discourse to describe historical conditions shaping one's own nation. In this sense, appropriation resembles André Gide's understanding of *influence* as the artist's "eagerness for Being," a chosen influence which does not create but rather "awakens" a latent self: "It descended upon me so early that I cannot distinguish it from myself."[48]

Specifically, the imitative process involved in the writing of the misterios resembles the assimilative performance conjured up by two discursive practices discussed by Bakhtin: "the internally persuasive discourse" and "the bilingual literary consciousness." As internally persuasive discourse, the alien texts penetrate the autochthonous literary field not only as an "externally authoritative" discourse but also persuasively, stimulating their assimilation "tightly interwoven with one's own word." Accordingly, the internally persuasive word is caught in a creative struggle—in a "play of boundaries"—with other discourses existing within a linguistic and ideological consciousness which prepares the introduction and outcome of a new word (a word "half-ours and half–someone else's"). As bilingual literary consciousness, appropriation stands for the creative literary act of a subject that objectifies itself through someone else's word. It is precisely the persuasive interaction between literary languages—in our study, those of France and Spain—that brings out the peculiar nature of an autochthonous language. As Bakhtin put it, "In the process of literary creation, languages interanimate each other and objectify precisely that side of one's own (and of other's) language *that pertains to its world view*, its inner form, the axiologically accentuated system inherent in it."[49] Thus, appropriation does not imply the aesthetic and cultural abolition of the copy in and by their model, a superfluous literary writing, a blank—meaningless—aesthetics and a cultural betrayal. On the contrary, the appropriation effected by the imitative writing of the misterios supposes a consciously reified—objectified and intensified—style closely related to autochthonous conditions.

With regard to style, appropriation—the objectification of our own worldview by the half-other nature of one's own word—represents what Schwarz has referred to as "the experience of incongruity" that results from the juxtaposition of a foreign literary model and a local setting.[50] As an "incongruent" writing, appropriation realizes itself as a sort of "twist," a "maladjustment," the always improper affirmation of foreign ideas by the mechanics of the social structure of the host country.[51] In the displaced character of imitative writing lies what Schwarz refers to as the important problem of "composition" posed to historians by nineteenth-century cultural processes and literary practices. From a compositional point of view, the imitation of foreign modes involves two different writings. On the one hand, it may imply the acceptance and reproduction of the disparity. In this case, the work presents ideological incongruities and formal dislocations that "surface in an involuntary and undesired way, surreptitiously and as a defect." On the other, imitation presupposes, on the contrary, the display of incongruities and dislocations (often parodically or grotesquely) at the formal level. In this case imitation produces instances of master narratives where social processes are successfully transformed into autochthonous literary forms. The choice to accept or display the incongruity of provincial culture, however, was not so much a matter of personal judgment or skills, but rather a question of historical and cultural possibilities. The choices made were not—could not—be accidental. On the contrary, they were the result of the literary, political, social, and cultural relationships and functions that constitute an historical period.[52]

Schwarz's notion of "defective" literature and his understanding of the literary value of the incongruency shown by many imitations is most relevant for this study. For the Brazilian critic, the inconsistency between a foreign form and the local social scene should not be regarded as a "weakness," that is, "as a repetition of ideologies," but "as the imitation of an essential aspect of reality," as an instance of the mimetic force of the novel. Thus, a defective imitation is defined by its stylistic inappropriateness to the social conditions it is describing, not by comparison to a foreign model. Formal incongruency does not express a faulty actualization of a dominant form, but rather an imitative accomplishment relevant to the ongoing processes of literary creation. The inconsistency that characterizes some imitative novels "having constituted itself as form, becomes itself material, something to be turned into form in its turn."[53] The elucidation of what constitutes the incongruent writing of the misterios (the areas of unresolved stylistic conflict between foreign models and Spanish society and the excess of their literary language) reveals precisely the difficult and deviant character of the processes involving the creation of the nineteenth-century novel in peripheral countries such as Spain. The misterios show the complex processes that accompanied the introduction in Spain of the modern novel. In them we recognize the aesthetic hesitations, failures, and achievements of a new generation of literatos trying to make sense of the sociohistorical conditions of mid-nineteenth-century Spain by way of a foreign and newly hegemonic writing—the bourgeois novel.

The acknowledgment of the imitative practices brought by the integrated European literary market does not imply denying the specific conditions created by political borders in the constitution of a national literature, that is, the existence of national borders framing literary life. What it does is recognize *new* and *different* frontiers which destabilize the national confinement (as well as the nationalistic values) of literary histories.[54] As hybrid writing—both domestic and foreign—the misterios pose many and diverse questions which actively problematize the creation of a literary subject as the expression of a self-sufficient and self-contained national identity. In particular, it allows us to pose the question, how do these new conditions frame the construction of an autochthonous national subject and culture? The misterios defy both the restrictive ("frontiers within") strategies of national literary histories and the prestige associated in Western culture with the notion of *origin* and its attributes (originality, authorship, authority, authenticity, and truth). They represent a discourse that actively resists the setting of *transcendent* boundaries, either historical or cultural, between countries. In these novels, borders are experienced not as the demarcation of otherness, but rather as crossroads in one's own quest for identity. In appropriation, national literary distinctiveness is realized "in the light of" or "through the eyes of" *another*'s word—"a word with a sideways glance," "against the background" of another's language that is *"experienced* as indigenous."[55] It is in this sense that the notion of autochthonous literature will be used in this book. Thus, appropriation, as the literary practice of a decentered literary consciousness, does not represent the acceptance of one's own alienation, but a different understanding of what constitutes identity. Here the culture of a nation is not defined in relation to a demonized "other" but rather to an internalized one. It springs from the tension produced by a deep sense of affinity with the discourse of the other and the simultaneous need to assert one's own difference.

In relation to this it is important to point out that the considerable ascendance of German Romantic poetics and its notions of *Kultur* and *Geist* in Spanish literary circles during the 1840s—when the first misterios were published—with its understanding of nation as a transcendental *soul* (a set of unique, nontransferable, and transhistorical ethnic characteristics of a people), did not erase completely Neoclassical literary principles and practices or Enlightened political visions. Here I disagree with the approach to literary life in Spain during the 1840s that affirms the lack of alternatives to the conservative Schlegelian construction of national identity.[56] I also depart from Wlad Godzich's and Nicholas Spadaccini's notion that there is no aesthetic domain independent of the state in mid-nineteenth-century Spain.[57] In my opinion, our understanding of Spanish Romanticism as a homogeneous aesthetic movement and the question of the construction of national identity is shattered when we take into consideration the new and autonomous sphere of cultural production provided by the publishing industry in mid-nineteenth-century Spain. Also, I would contend, along with the New Historicists, that historical periods are discontinuous and contradictory entities, and that the emphasis placed on the impact of Schlegelianism in Spain during the 1840s helps to conceal the fluidity and openness characteristic of the processes of national consciousness formation in nineteenth-century Spain. The political philosophy of the Enlightenment sustained the Spanish Romanticism of progressive liberal tendencies, and the Neoclassical credo persisted as a pressing residue in a literary system dominated by Romantic Schlegelian notions of culture and nation. Thus, the practice of imitation as a literary strategy for the creation of the Spanish novel—the emergence of the apparently paradoxical (both foreign and domestic) writing embodied in the misterios—was sustained by the overlapping of two groups of conflicting aesthetic and cultural notions: the Neoclassical insistence on the universality, constancy, and timelessness of literary forms, and its belief in imitation as the foundation of all creative practices (together with the Enlightenment affirmation of the universal validity of its political principles on citizenship); and the Schlegelian contention of the irreducible cultural distinctiveness of a nation: the postulation of art as the highest expression of the aesthetic accomplishments and unique spiritual identity of a people *(Kunstgeist)*. The convergence of these disparate poetics made possible the emergence of a discourse where one's own identity is constructed through, and not against, the other.

A couple of last remarks. First, the idea of "appropriation" may resemble the traditional notion of "original writing" in its emphasis on local historical conditions and an autochthonous word, but it differs from it in at least one fundamental aspect: it denies national uniqueness and the transcendental relationship between culture and the people who produce it. In the notion of an autochthonous culture, "difference" is always relative. Second, in nineteenth-century Spain appropriation did not cancel the cultural politics that promoted the belief in the inevitable—and necessary—autochthonous character of literary creation. It did not exclude the synchronic axis of national literary rivalry.[58] On the contrary, it produced an acute awareness of the hierarchy of cultural prestige and political domination that organized and ruled the new integrated literary market. In this sense, as in the significant example of Larra (as we will see in chapter 2), the appropriation of French literary writings was, often enough, in open defiance of the subservient position of Spanish cultural productions. The struggle of mid-nineteenth-century literatos to emancipate Spanish literature from relations of cultural subordination was played out precisely in the intense quest for an autochthonous novel that appropriation made possible. The Spanish novel was envisioned and constructed through imitation. Consequently, and going a step further than Joaquín Marco, I contend that the "resurrection of Ayguals de Izco" and other 1840s novel writers should not be "sub conditione," but *a condition* for any history of the literary and cultural processes of nineteenth-century Spain.[59]

1
The Market Conditions in a Peripheral Literary Space

> The inevitability of cultural imitation is bound up with a specific set of historical imperatives over which abstract philosophical critiques can exercise no power.
> —Roberto Schwarz

THE TECHNOLOGICAL REVOLUTION IN PRINTING PROCESSES AND THE IMplementation of new capitalist policies in the traditionally restricted field of literary production brought about the emergence of the figure of the editor and the unprecedented expansion of the book market; the serial novel is the most representative and successful creation of this new printing era. The new conditions framing the production and consumption of literature radically modified the practices of cultural exchange among different countries. For the first time, European literary processes were subjected to a ruthless centralization which effectively established the artistic dominance of Paris and London. These two cities dictated the succession of literary movements and, specifically, the mode of the novel, while their powerful publishing houses actively exported them to foreign cultural markets. Paris and London became the hegemonic spaces of cultural creativity and their powerful publishing houses transformed most European book markets, whose functioning became progressively more dependent on French and English trends. As Moretti notes, this centralization established for the novel a literary market that was both unified and uneven.[1] It is this new structure for the production and consumption of cultural goods that we will explore in this chapter. In particular, we will try to answer two questions in regard to the central decades of the nineteenth century: How did this new literary market affect the constitution of the Spanish book industry? How did it condition the writing environment of the Spanish novelists? These questions are, in my view, of the utmost importance when approaching mid-nineteenth-century literary activity in Spain. In the context of modern cultural production, it is not enough to inquire into the forms of writing;

we also need to consider the conditions of the possibility of writing itself: "the question, 'how to write,' has been supplanted, or at any rate given a new complexity, by the question, 'how to be a writer.' "[2]

I would argue that in the mid nineteenth century the French novel was the center of Spanish publishing activity; all commercial publishing resources were invested in promoting and disseminating the French novel in Spain.[3] As a result, the French novel determined the habits and expectations of the Spanish readers and deprived the incipient Spanish novel of the domestic resources that could have supported it. Ultimately, it occupied and saturated the domestic literary market, denying the Spanish novel its own autochthonous space.

THE PROGENITORSHIP OF THE FRENCH NOVEL BY THE SPANISH PUBLISHERS

Our knowledge of the mid-nineteenth-century Spanish book market and, specifically, of the publishing procedures that sustained the massive penetration of French novels during those years is still limited and discontinuous.[4] We can note, however, some general features. Without question, the French novel held a practically exclusive centrality in the Spanish market. The dependence of the Spanish publishing houses on French literary production was not new. In fact, French translations already constituted an important segment of the Spanish literary offering in the 1800–1830 period. However, in the 1840s publishing practices in Spain underwent a profound change. The introduction of French best-sellers during those years marked the full participation of Spanish publishers in the cultural and commercial trends that gave rise to the European novel. In the 1840s Spain actively adopted the publishing practices that had already transformed the novel into a commodity in other European markets: the serial novel, the promotion of fashionable authors, and the simultaneous publication of their works in different literary markets. The numerous and continuous print runs of works written by fashionable French authors put a definitive end to the traditionally limited editions and the literary marginality of the novel. This change directly affected the volume of translated works and resulted in the central position the French novel came to occupy in the Spanish literary field. We can say that French best-sellers saturated the book market and that—with the exception of Ayguals de Izco's best-seller, *María o La hija de un jornalero*—only French novels were widely read in mid-nineteenth-century Spain.[5]

The commercial procedures that sustained the penetration of the French novel in Spain are ironically pointed out and bitterly commented on by the literato Modesto Lafuente in his 1846 article "Pleito ruidoso," in which he describes how the economic transactions involved in the acquisition of translation rights became in fact a process of adoption of the French novel by the Spanish publishers. According to Lafuente, their commercial diligence—their continuous and extensive investments in Paris—resulted in fact in the Spanish *prohijamiento* (progenitorship) of the contemporary French novel. Lafuente begins his article confessing to his reader that he had at first misapprehended the purpose of the fierce and frenetic commercial competition among Madrid publishing powers—"las potencias traductoras de Madrid." He had thought that all they wanted was to obtain the translation rights to the new French best-seller immediately *after* its publication; but now he realizes the competition was not about being the first publisher to obtain translation rights.[6] The intense activity of the Spanish delegates in Paris was aimed at facilitating the *simultaneous* release of originals in France and translations in Spain. The simultaneity, he says, was achieved by securing access to the French manuscript while it was being written. The access to the ongoing work made possible its translation chapter by chapter, even before the French had produced a first galley proof. This procedure made writing and translating simultaneous and transformed the release of a French novel into a coeval publishing event for both the French and the Spanish public.[7] On some occasions the Spanish publishers even managed to publish the Spanish translation of a French novel before it appeared in France:

> The plenipotentiary of the house in Paris found a way of negotiating an agreement with the publisher of the novel, so that from the very moment each original page reached the press he would be sent the first copy—not the proofs . . . but a manuscript copy; it did not matter if it contained errors, since it could be corrected here. And in this way the novel—or whatever it was—would arrive in Madrid day by day, page by page, and be translated and published page by page and day by day. If for any reason the printing was interrupted there in Paris, it necessarily had to be suspended also here. . . . It was a repeating clock which had its spring there—and as long as it was silent there, it would remain mute here, unable to run or rule.[8]

The image of a repetition clock provided by Lafuente summarizes the magnitude of the Spanish market's dependence on French literary production, and represents with accuracy the duplication of French publishing activity in Spain. The development of the Spanish publishing houses was based on a vicarious enterprise whose effect was the diverting of domestic productive energies and resources away from Spanish literary circles. Lafuente, both outraged and amused, tells us how the race to become the first Spanish publisher of a particular French novel even became a struggle to claim rights not only to the translation itself but also over the *intention* to translate.[9]

To secure the rights of mere intentions did not seem, however, to solve the many problems faced by Spanish publishers. The absence of international agreements regulating book imports and exports, as well as the inadequate Spanish copyright legislation, facilitated illicit competition among publishers and a proliferation of nonauthorized translations.[10] In this context of legal indefinition, the simultaneous publication of a French novel in Spain gave its publisher a precarious temporal advantage over his competitors, even though it could not, in any case, secure him exclusive rights. As Lafuente tells us, the presence of numerous Spanish literary agents in Paris frustrated and rendered all efforts to secure the coveted primacy of translation useless. This situation further stimulated the frantic activity of the Spanish publishers in France who, to protect their investments, sought then a new kind of contract that could better guarantee at least a significant temporal advantage over competitors. The new strategy started with the establishment of direct and personal negotiations with the author—this scheme is known as getting "directly at the source"—which often gave the Spanish publisher access to the novelist's work, not only before the French publisher had seen it, but, sometimes, even before the actual writing of the new novel had begun.[11] Thus, the Spanish publisher became, in fact, a promoter of the French novel. All the Spanish publishing activity that preceded the actual printing of a novel took place in Paris; all the productive energy that resulted in the release of a novel was diverted to France. Accordingly, and from this standpoint, we can say that the mid-nineteenth-century Spanish novel was written in France, or, in other words, that the French novel became Spanish through progenitorship:

> Printing the translation of a French novel in Spain almost as soon as in France, publishing it simultaneously, was not very honorable for Spanish literature. It was necessary to publish it in Spanish even earlier, to adopt and thus become progenitors of the French children before they were born in France, to naturalize in Spain a child that has not been born in his own land—and this is what *El Español* has accomplished by getting Mr. Eugène Sue to publish first his novel *Martín el Expósito* in Spanish rather than in French.[12]

The bibliographic data provided by Montesinos in the "Esbozo de una bibliografía española de traducciones de novelas (1800–1850)" confirms Modesto Lafuente's account of the Spanish promotion of the French novel.[13] Sure enough, French best-sellers were often released in Spain the same year (in some cases, a little before) they were published in France. At the same time, we find data clearly pointing to the frantic and illegal competition between printing houses described by Lafuente. For instance, *Los tres mosqueteros* was published by no less than four printing houses within the space of a few months: Oliveras (Barcelona), La Sociedad Literaria (Madrid), Cabrera y Laffore (Málaga), and La Revista Médica (Cádiz).

Similarly, *El judío errante* was published simultaneously in 1844 in Madrid (by three different printing houses), Barcelona, and Cádiz; Dumas's *Los cuarenta y cinco* had, in 1847, three different publishers in Madrid. Undoubtedly, the commercial strategies implemented by the Spanish printers in these years naturalized the French originals. The French novel, being at the center of any Spanish publishing effort, was likewise eagerly adopted by the Spanish readers, who immediately granted it Spanish citizenship. As the anonymous author of an 1844 literary article said, "On the one hand, as soon as a book is published in France, it is seized by Spanish translators and . . . on the other, the public usually prefers books coming from across the Pyrenees to those made in our country."[14]

Marginality and Orphanhood of the Autochthonous Novel in Spain

The success of the French novel, its literary reputation, and the intense practice of translation stimulated among the literatos a desire to write *original* novels that did not find support among publishers or readers.[15] The Spanish authors openly resented the publishers' lack of interest in their works and made them responsible for the precarious situation of the autochthonous novel. Complaints about the neglect of the incipient Spanish novel is a recurrent motif during the mid nineteenth century, and any occasion—but especially when a *novela original* happened to come out—seemed appropriate to lament it and to denounce the marginal role of the autochthonous novel in the publishers' investments. In his prologue to the novel *La casa de Pero-Hernández* (1848) by Miguel Agustín Príncipe, Ángel Fernández de los Ríos blames the Spanish publishers for the detrimental effect their indifference had on the new Spanish novel:

> Some newspapers have paid the French publisher a large amount in order to be able to print a novel here a few days before the rest of the competition, but we do not know of any that—taking upon themselves to protect our letters and setting an example of true patriotism that would certainly be appreciated—have decided not to publish a single novel that is not original.[16]

Spanish writers lamented not having an audience in their own country and, particularly, the hostility and lack of understanding with which both publishers and readers received their work. Used to the French novel and pleased with the diligence of publishers in providing the lastest Parisian novelties, the readers did not seem to miss an autochthonous novel. The Spanish readers were not much interested in the avowed cultural originality of the autochthonous novel or their social closeness to them; all they wanted was a Spanish novel that would conform to the foreign works they had been familiarized with. As Francisco J. Moya accurately pointed out in 1848, Spanish writers had to imitate the French novel if they wanted to "become popular."[17] The success of the French novel made the autochthonous writers redundant, when not superfluous, in the Spanish literary market.

The indifference of both publishers and readers to an autochthonous novel created an adverse environment for the Spanish novelists, who had to resort to small and economically precarious printing houses for the publication of their manuscripts. These smaller publishers either lacked the financial resources to compete for translation rights in Paris or had emerged as cultural, rather than profitable, enterprises with hardly any capital to sustain their activity. In these conditions, the actual publication of an autochthonous novel by any of those publishers was a rare and often unsatisfactory achievement. Even when they had enough money to complete the printing of the novel, no money was left for promotion or for the author's remuneration. The potential interruption of the printing process itself was especially frustrating for the writer because it interrupted the process of literary creation itself.

As most of the novels were published in serialized form, the number of copies printed depended on the number of subscribers, and the capital to print a work was often restricted to the money provided in advance by the readers. Writing adapted to this production process; novels were written chapter by chapter, making the author's work conform to the rhythm imposed by the needs of the printer and the demands of the reader. In this system, the discontinuation of printing often meant the interruption of writing. Consequently, the financial precariousness of the publishers that sustained the creation of the Spanish novel negatively affected the creative process of the Spanish authors as it made their work highly unstable. The vicissitudes and frustration that accompanied the writing and publication of a Spanish novel in the mid nineteenth century were related by Miguel Agustín Príncipe, one of the struggling and marginalized autochthonous writers of the period. As he recounts his own experience when writing *La casa de Pero-Hernández*, the writing of a Spanish novel appears tightly, and inevitably, linked to the financial well-being of its publisher; the constant interruptions of the printing of *La casa*, and the repetition of this fate with various publishers, determined the constant discontinuity of Príncipe's writing. Often he was interrupted for such long periods that Príncipe himself would lose track of his project and its purpose. For Príncipe, however, there was a rare happy ending: the difficult resumption of the writing and, finally, the complete publication of the novel were made possible by the effort and obstinacy of Fernández de los Ríos, who was at the time editor of the financially stable magazine *Semanario Pintoresco Español*:

This legend started publication twice in two different newspapers—one political, the other literary [*El Publicista* and *El Pensil del Bello Sexo*, respectively]—and both times it had to be canceled because those papers soon ceased publication, thus leaving in suspense the reading of such a marvelous story. The author, upset by these misfortunes, decided to forget about it, and more so as it was difficult to resume the thread of his ideas after being interrupted for such a long time that he did not even remember the original plan or his main goal in initiating his narrative. But the literary editor of *El Semanario Pintoresco* has insisted so convincingly in claiming it for its paper, that it has been necessary to please him and take up the pen again—not simply because this is what his kindness justly requires, but also because *El Semanario* is not in danger of disappearing before the conclusion of the legend in question, and therefore there is no longer an obstacle to the third appearance of *La casa de Pero-Hernández*.[18]

Given the generalized lack of support the Spanish writers received from financially sound publishing houses, they had no alternative but to take upon themselves the responsibilities of producing and promoting their work. The autochthonous novelist thus assumed the functions of author and publisher, and often those of bookseller as well.[19] Forced to be both artist and entrepreneur, the Spanish novelist was burdened by an overwhelming task. For Miguel Augustín Príncipe, getting his work published meant accepting numerous hardships and adversities, and a bit of good luck, but for most novelists getting a manuscript published was an impossible—and often destructive—financial project. The experience was often frustrating and futile.[20] Mariano Noriega relates in *La fisiología del poeta* (1843) the difficulties and trials undergone by those Spanish writers who were not discouraged when their works were rejected by the publishers because they were "original"; but were instead determined to publish their work without financial means or any kind of publishing know-how.[21]

The writers' involvement with the publishing and promotion processes took away all of their time and resources. First, Noriega tells us, he hesitated over whether he should serialize the novel or print it in one volume. After he decided it was easier to finance the cost of printing a serial novel, he realized that the promotion and distribution expenses were far greater than the income. To lower the costs, he decided to reduce the advertising and suppress the home delivery service. Relying on these cuts, and on the expected income brought by the sale of the installments, he went ahead and began printing. The sales, however, were low—far lower than expected—because the readers demanded from the author the same commercial facilities they received from professional publishers, and were not willing to make an extra effort to support the Spanish novel: "Forewarned against the original novel, very few readers go ahead and take out a subscription, and most of them regret doing it when they see that they have to go to the bookstore to get the pages."[22] But the writer, Noriega tells us, is not yet disappointed and decides to look for new subscribers in the provinces, beyond the boundaries of the capital. His novel, however, is no better received in the provinces, and after a short time the printing must be interrupted because the subscribers do not pick up the new installments, definitively stopping the flow of money. Having failed as a businessman, the novelist is left heavily in debt and full of skepticism:

> Without readers, even the most vibrant publication has to be discontinued. And our novelist is left with: twenty reams of printed paper, the work unfinished, his notebooks turned into odd pieces. On top of this, booksellers from the provinces return the previous installments, and since they send them by mail, the author has to pay huge shipment fees. He is hounded by the printer, who despite the abysmal success of the publication hands him an expensive bill which has to be paid without delay. The novelist thus repudiates his work and curses the day he decided to print it. In the end, however, not everything is lost: used-paper dealers buy anything at 22 *reales* the *arroba*, and the twenty reams will weigh one hundred pounds. So he gets paid 88 *reales* and now has enough to invite those parasites at the café, who benefit the same whether they give congratulations or condolences.[23]

It is hardly surprising, then, that Alfonso García Tejero, one of the few Spanish authors who published *original* work in Ayguals de Izco's publishing house, dedicated *El pilluelo de Madrid* (1844) to his editor, praising Ayguals's "españolismo" and denouncing the neglect of the autochthonous novel: "What a disgrace! . . . Our own people are loathed . . . [and] those coming from Paris have the greatest of times."[24]

The adverse conditions for the publication of Spanish novels contributed to the marginal role the writing of novels came to occupy in the artistic activity of the literatos. No author could afford to put the writing of novels at the center of his literary activity; on the contrary, it was always a sporadic occupation, and often a single experiment. There were no professional novelists in Spain in the 1840s and 1850s; not even, as we see later on, Ayguals de Izco (who managed to write a best-seller in the 1840s) or Fernán Caballero, who saw all of her novels published. Among the authors of novels written during those years we find literatos whose main work is in poetry or theater, or who are editors of newspapers and magazines, professors, doctors, and lawyers. The lack of interest shown by both publishers and readers actively contributed to making novel-writing a nonprofessional, secondary, and occasional occupation, often undertaken during the scarce and discontinuous leisure time left by other—more important—activities. Milá de la Roca, editor of the satiric newspaper *El Papagayo*, confesses in the prologue to his *Misterios de Barcelona* that he managed to write the novel taking advantage of the unexpected time of leisure—"aprovechando el accidental ocio."²⁵ Fernández de los Ríos thought that the financial difficulties faced by the Spanish novelists helped explain the diversion of literary energies away from the novel:

> The odd shortage of novels in Spain, despite the fact that Spanish history, traditions, and customs lend themselves exceedingly well to the genre, can in our view be clearly explained. While the novel is the area of literature that requires the greatest amount of work, it is not the most glorious for the writer, who can gain appreciation and admiration at a lower cost by dedicating himself to works of more importance and transcendence. This is the genre that gives the smallest compensation in this country, and thus writers who would otherwise eagerly devote themselves to cultivate it with determination, prefer instead to write for the theatre, where at least their efforts are rewarded.²⁶

Only in the late 1850s and the 1860s do we find a Spanish readership interested enough in the Spanish novel to promote the emergence of a new—although small—group of professional novelists. The popularity of folletinistas such as Fernández y González and Pérez Escrich, together with that of the new *novelas morales y recreativas* written by women authors such as María del Pilar Sinués, helped create the profitable market for Spanish novels that sustained, if somewhat precariously, the professional writing of diverse late-nineteenth-century novelists, from Pérez Galdós to Julio Nombela.

Given the lack of public interest and financial support afforded to the first *original* Spanish novels, it is not surprising to note that the only two mid-nineteenth-century novelists who appear in literary histories are Ayguals de Izco, owner of a prosperous publishing house, and Fernán Caballero, the writer who elicited the unconditional support of the cultural institutions of successive conservative governments. In the case of Ayguals de Izco, the functions of writer and publisher came together successfully thanks to the powerful printing house he owned and managed. All of his novels, and particularly *María o La hija de un jornalero* (1845–46)—the first Spanish novel to become a best-seller—owed a lot of their commercial success not only to the fact that they were imitations of Eugène Sue's works, but also to the intense promotional activity mounted around them. In any other regard, however, Ayguals is not different from the rest of Spanish publishers and writers. As chair of a powerful printing house, he hardly ever published Spanish novels, except, of course, for those written by him; as novelist, he was a sporadic writer who perceived his writing as an ancillary activity, secondary to his political, literary, and publishing interests.²⁷ Ayguals himself acknowledges his lack of dedication in the epilogue to *La marquesa de Bellaflor o El niño de la inclusa* (1847–48), where he apologizes to the reader for writing the novel, busy as he was, in "such an extraordinary rush."²⁸ The only significant difference between

Ayguals and most of the other Spanish writers who ventured into the new fashionable genre is the publishing support that subsidized his initiatives and got his manuscripts not only printed but, more important, marketed.

Fernán Caballero is another exception in mid-nineteenth-century Spanish literary life, but for different reasons. Although she did her writing in her spare time, as others did, she distinguished herself from her peers, first of all, by her resistance to allowing her novels to circulate as commodities. Her writing was confined to the private home, and her readership was originally intended to be that of her family and friends (financial problems forced her to actively seek a publisher for her works later on in her life). Thus, Fernán Caballero's writing was done not on the fringes of the market—as is the case of the authors of the *misterios*—but rather *outside* the constraints and possibilities dictated by publishing houses (and readers). Her manuscripts were conceived as a private exercise in moral entertainment, and until 1849 they stayed away from the public marketplace. In this sense, Fernán Caballero's works are alien to the market forces that sustained the emergence of the novel as fashionable and hegemonic genre during those years.

A second distinctive trait of Caballero's literary career is the fact that the eventual publication of almost all her works between 1849 and 1878 was due not so much to their commercial success, but to the political backing of her conservative supporters. The conservative literary establishment, at her own insistence, actively negotiated with—and sometimes pressured—publishers in order to get her work printed.[29] In this sense, the support she received from well-established literary figures was crucial in getting her works published, especially at the beginning of her public career (1849–56). Javier Herrero mentions both "the pressure" exerted by Juan Eugenio Hartzenbusch on José Joaquín Mora, editor of the newspaper *El Heraldo*, who ended up publishing *La Gaviota* in its folletín, and also the role of Fermín Puente in getting the publisher Francisco Mellado to print Fernán Caballero's complete works.[30] Similarly, Montesinos acknowledges the intervention of Hartzenbusch (as "mediator") in the negotiations between Fernán Caballero and her prospective publishers. His mediation made possible the publications of several of her short stories in the *Semanario Pintoresco Español,* in spite of the initial opposition of its editor, Ángel Fernández de los Ríos, as well as the publication of *Elia* in the journal *La España*.[31] Moreover, as Donald A. Randolph has pointed out, key figures of the conservative cultural apparatus in the Isabelian regime were instrumental in launching Fernán Caballero's literary career and reputation precisely "in those early years of her fame, when she was taking the first steps from obscurity and into the light of notoriety."[32] Indeed, this institutional support granted Fernán Caballero a literary reputation as a novelist that no publishing house or best-selling novel could ever bestow upon Ayguals de Izco.

The impact that peripheral market conditions had on the writing practices of the time cannot be ignored. The progenitorship of the French novel by mid-nineteenth-century Spanish publishers transformed the close economic and artistic collaboration between publisher and author—which sustained the emergence of the novel as a new hegemonic genre in nineteenth-century France and Britain—into a strictly economic transaction where the creative energy of the literatos was redirected toward translation. At the same time, the urgency to satisfy the demand of a readership whose literary taste had been formed by the French novel created a hostile environment for the writing of the Spanish novel and actively encouraged the writing of imitations. Translation and imitation were, thus, the forms of novel-writing brought forth by the peripheral position the Spanish literary market occupied in the new cultural order.

2
The Preoccupation with Autochthony

> Let us translate the masterworks of the greatest writers, and, if done with intelligence and discrimination, they will undoubtedly be extremely beneficial; but let us not have an exclusive predilection for foreign works.
>
> —Wenceslao Ayguals de Izco

The Foreign Discourse on Spain: The Other of Civilized Europe

THE QUESTION ASKED BY EUROPEAN PHILOSOPHERS ABOUT THE GEOgraphical and cultural borders of Europe was not limited to just Russia, as Denys Hay has suggested. It also implied many other countries whose geographic, political, and cultural eccentricity had been actively perceived and constructed by the bourgeois "northern Europe" since the seventeenth century.[1] The creation by the northern countries of the otherness of Europe in Europe, together with the clear demarcation of its borders, accompanies and complements the ideological process of differentiation "between the familiar (Europe, the West, 'us') and the strange (the Orient, the East, 'them')."[2] The scheme that separates Europeans from non-Europeans, although accurate for explaining the general dynamics of European presence in (and aggression against) non-European countries throughout the world, tends to obliterate the internal split and hierarchical reorganization that is at the base of the discourse on modern European hegemony. If the supposedly legitimate European superiority in the world—and, consequently, the assertion of its special mission in it—is ideologically constructed around its Christian identity, it is also true that it only crystallizes against the Catholic tradition, or, more specifically, the Latin countries.[3] European unity was forged around those new states and monarchies that more actively distanced themselves from the idea of the Roman Christian Empire, and where the new bourgeois notions of *virtù*—"the capacity for action, the creative energy of the individual"—evolved into Montesquieu's ideas of progress and liberty.⁴ Parallel to the orientalization of the world, northern European countries engaged themselves in the creation of inner borders that demarcated within Europe itself a space of otherness, equally identified—or constructed—as oriental. The critical disregard for what Said refers to as the "chameleonlike quality called (adjectivally) 'Oriental'" found in pre-Romantic and Romantic tropes has important consequences for understanding the cultural processes that took place in those countries identified with this "free-floating Orient."⁵ From the perspective of a peripheral European country such as Spain, the strategies of political and cultural hierarchization carried out mostly by France and England to legitimize their hegemony over the world (the orientalization of non-European cultures) are strikingly similar to those they effected to sanction the supremacy of the northern countries over non-Protestant Europe (the "Orient" in Europe).

Spain was one of those spaces of otherness identified by northern countries, and was, for that matter, a favorite one among the French. We could mention many well-known instances where the otherness of Spain within Europe is stated. Numerous literary references and most of the travel books written during that period by foreign visitors provide enough material to analyze the orientalization of Spain.⁶ For the purpose of this study, I will simply insist that this concept was ubiquitous in the ideological discourse about Spain found in French and English texts in the first half of the nineteenth century and limit my discussion of these references to two. The first reference comes from Jean-François Bourgoing's *Tableau de l'Espagne moderne* (1797). Bourgoing not only identified Spain with Asia, but made a point of emphasizing Spain's cultural strangeness and remoteness by locating it in the outer borders of the Asian otherness: "One would assume it to be," he says, referring to Spain, "at the tip of Asia rather than of Europe."⁷ The second reference comes from the last paragraph in George Sand's *Un hiver à Majorque* (1841). In this example we can appreciate not only the formulation of the *orientalization* of Spain, but, more important, its construction by an all-encompassing French discourse on civilization. Spain is *un-civilized* because it is *un-French*:

> When we entered Barcelona, we were so eager to be done once and for all with this inhuman race, that I could not wait for the boat to finish docking. . . . And as soon as we boarded the warship, which was maintained with the neatness and elegance of a salon, finding ourselves surrounded by intelligent and affable individuals, receiving the generous and assiduous attentions of the captain, the doctor, the officers, and the rest of the crew, and shaking hands with the excellent and witty French Consul, Mr. Gauthier d'Arc, we jumped for joy on the deck and cried with all our heart, "Long live France!" I felt like we had been around the globe and, leaving behind the savages of Polynesia, were returning to the civilized world.⁸

By mid nineteenth century, not only had Spain been constructed by the French as an exotic country, but its literature functioned as a repository for the fantastic imagination of the Orient.[9] As L.-F. Hoffman points out, the *crónicas*, the *romancero*, the *picaresca*, *El Quijote*, and so on had been and were "invaluable sources" for French authors, especially between 1800 and 1850: "Medieval Spain, renaissance Spain, decadent Spain—all the centuries have been plundered."[10] In fact, so many French Romantic productions had Spain as their subject, or its literary works and historical deeds as inspiration, that *Aben Humeya* by Martínez de la Rosa—whose première was in Paris in 1830—seems to be only another work in this Spanish-inspired wave of French literature, rather than the first Spanish Romantic play.[11] By 1845 the French creation of a fictional Spain had become real. Victor Hugo's *Hernani* (1830) and *Ruy Blas* (1838), Balzac's *El Verdugo* (1830), and Merimée's *Carmen* (1845) briefly exemplify the extent of "la mode espagnole" [the Spanish craze] and outline its meaning. The (mostly) French discourse on Spain's national character, either when romantically flattering (as the land of impossible heroes and passions, and of fabulous stories) or deprecating (as a backward state still dominated by feudal structures, an all-powerful clergy, and superstition), was definitively excluding Spain from the mid-nineteenth-century construction of Europeanness: "For the French imagination," says Hoffman, "Spain hardly belongs to the continent."[12]

The function of "la mode espagnole" in the constitution of the French modern consciousness is not unique. On the contrary, as Balzac says, it was rather an entrée, though an important one, among many others to be swallowed up by the Pantagruelian cultural hunger of the French: "We devour entire countries. Yesterday, it was the East; last month, Spain; tomorrow, it will be Italy."[13] As France (and Britain) culturally (and often politically and economically) consumed the world, the boundaries between Europeanness and its constitutive outside did not correspond neatly to geopolitical continental demarcations.[14] The concept of Europe—or, in Said's terms, "Occident"—appears to be more confined than the geographical space marked out by its Christian and feudal roots, while the "Orient" seems to exist well within the borders of Europe.[15] The specific function of this "European Orient" for the legitimation of the bourgeois societies of northern Europe—their processes of national and cultural formation—and its new international order has not yet been thoroughly studied.[16] Still, we can affirm that countries like Spain provided a place to experiment (and enjoy) the limits and extremes of European identity. Precisely because Spain shared and in many aspects acutely represented the European tradition, it provided, as Gothic literature did, a space where it was possible to approach and test the moral and political limits of the new European identity. The modern colonial powers needed to orientalize Spain as a process of self-definition, as a way of differentiating—and thus legitimizing—their new bourgeois rule from the old sacred order of Europe, and their new version of sovereignty based on commercial domination from Spain's crusading empire. In this sense it is significant that Henri Beyle (Stendhal) admonished his contemporaries about feudalism using Spain as a case in point: "Do you want to see the Middle Ages?" he asked, "Look at Spain."[17] Spain would then be the "us" we Europeans no longer are, or, better yet, the discarded identity hidden in our historical unconscious that haunts, threatens, and seduces us. It is in this context of legitimation of the new sociopolitical powers in Europe that we need to understand the fierce attacks on Spain by French Enlightenment authors.

The Spanish literatos were well aware that their country and its literary tradition were being constructed as one of the complementary imagined spaces against which the French and others were constructing their national and literary distinctiveness and greatness. The literatos openly resented the orientalization of Spain, and they blamed mostly the French for it. The words of the anonymous writer of the 1856 article "Algunas palabras sobre la obra que en francés y con título de *Estudios sobre España* ha dado a la luz el Sr. D. Antonio de Latour" express clearly both their awareness and resentment. The author refers ironically to those travelers who visit Spain, "in particular French and English," as missionaries whose mission was the civilizing of Spain: "They enter our country foolishly and maliciously hoping to *regenerate* and *modernize* us." He insists that preconceptions guide them and that they desire to feel outside familiar territory; they arrive in Spain determined, he says, not to feel "at home," not to find a "second fatherland." They come, he complains, to satisfy their own evasive drives, to fulfill their own created fantasies: "looking for adventure, . . . young girls with a dagger in the garter, . . . colorful thieves, . . . love affairs behind the wrought-iron grilles."[18] For his part, Ramón de Mesonero Romanos openly criticized the imposition on Spain of the civilization versus barbarism paradigm characteristic of the European discourse on the colonies—a paradigm that Spaniards had actively contributed to. Resisting the characterization of Spain as the "other" of civilized Europe, he humorously points out the absurdity of the attitude of the French traveler who visited Spain as if s/he were an explorer discovering an unknown and faraway territory: French writers know that "their purpose in life is to cross the Pyrenees . . . [and] uncover for France and the whole world this unknown and imaginary country which appears on maps as Spain." Similarly, using an irony that cannot be but bittersweet in a country that in 1839 still insists on affirming its colonial power, Mesonero refers to this same French traveler as "our trans-Pyrenean Columbus," stopping just short of bringing up references of conquistadors.[19]

The literatos knew also that the French and English characterizations of Spain as an uncivilized country did not spare the contemporaneous Spanish authors and their productions. On the contrary, it actively included them in the representation of Spain as a backward, barren, and foreign land. In the opinion of French and English, nothing of the political and cultural *grandeur* of the sixteenth and seventeenth centuries could be found in nineteenth-century Spanish writers: "If you search for a literary Spain," said Philarète Chasles in 1841, "you will only find imitations of Europe created by the most distinguished Spanish minds."[20] In fact, contemporary Spanish literary works were perceived as so remote from their own tradition that, as El Pobre Diablo (pseudonym of an unidentified critic) noted, *Don Quijote* was considered by foreign contemporary critics as a European rather than Spanish creation.[21] The literatos were aware of, and resented, the more or less open disdain shown by European literary circles toward their productions, especially at a time when, with the abolition of absolutism and the proclamation of the *Estatuto Real*, they hoped Spain's historical processes were finally those of the European liberal states. Larra clearly assessed the difference between the German (and, more generally speaking, the Romantic) enthusiasm for Calderón and other Spanish authors and works of the Golden Age, and the general indifference and contempt toward contemporary Spanish writers: "The Germans were the first to unearth our treasures, and Calderón became an object of veneration for them. However, what was still needed was a work that made them aware that Spaniards are both men and poets."[22] Larra's denunciation of the representation of Spain as a politically and culturally uncivilized country (Spain as lacking both *men* and *poets*), far from unique, is echoed by many Spanish writers of the time.[23] We see everywhere resistance to the (mostly) French declaration of the expendability of Spanish contemporary culture, and the urgent need to produce an autochthonous literary discourse from and on Spain that would reclaim both the representation of Spanishness and the literatos' rightful place within modern European culture.

The Uncertain Character of Modern Spain:
Literary Decadence and the Hope for Redemption

The literatos were deeply disturbed by the acknowledgment that the French had successfully replaced them in two important initiatives: first, in adapting and re-creating the Spanish literary tradition for contemporary audiences and within modern parameters (that of Romantic poetics); and, second, in creating for European and other foreign audiences the image—character and value—of Spain.[24] Spain had not produced a modern literature—and, more important, had no novel but a foreign one—and this fact was allowing others (especially, although not exclusively, the French) to create a fictional and highly successful discourse on Spain. The literatos wanted to create an autochthonous modern novel close to Spain's own historical conditions that could reclaim Spain's literary imaginary. But they knew also that the French interference in Spanish cultural processes was but a sign of the influence French culture had on a society that offered little resistance to, and had no alternative for, the seduction of its prestige.[25]

For the literatos modern Spanish identity was still in the making, undecided, trapped between an old, ineffectual social order and a new one too weak to overthrow the old. As Larra put it, "Our golden age is long gone, and our nineteenth century has not arrived yet."[26] Many literatos later on echoed Larra's perception of Spain's historical impasse and the painful contrast between the resolute socioeconomic transformations of advanced nations and the uncertain and vague character social unrest still had in Spain.[27] In this respect, the literatos themselves thought that Spain and Portugal were unlike other European nations, and more like the struggling former colonies. Like the colonies, Juan Eugenio Hartzenbusch said in 1847, Spain did not have a sense of historical destiny: "In their literature, lively and enterprising France proclaims her ambitions; England, her power and pride; Germany, her hopes; Italy, her wishes; Spain, Portugal, and South America hesitate over what path they should take."[28] The undetermined character of Spain's mid-nineteenth-century historical processes was perceived by the literatos as the immediate cause of the country's literary decadence and, more specifically, of the lack of an autochthonous novel. The intense translating and imitative activity dominating Spanish literary life was acknowledged to be a consequence of Spain's decadence: "In our delayed progress," said Bermúdez de Castro, "we hear belated and confusing echoes of those nations we are trying to imitate."[29]

The literatos thought that literature was the "thermometer" for the state of a civilization, and they were well aware that their own lack of originality was the result of Spain's having become an historically stale nation.[30] They had a clear notion of the intimate relationship between political and cultural hegemonies and knew that literary originality and recognition came with political power over the world. They were painfully aware that the modern bourgeois novel did not belong to countries whose political power had already faded, or to those taken by force from their own historical processes and violently incorporated into those of Europe.[31] They knew Spain's political supremacy was something of the past, as was its literary authority. As Larra vehemently put it, cultural productivity and prestige were a consequence of military might, and Spain could only dream of its old (and long gone) glory:

> A country that lives only for itself and does not overwhelm its neighbors with the surplus of its own life is condemned to obscurity. And where it does not

2: THE PREOCCUPATION WITH AUTOCHTHONY

reach with its arms, it will not do it with its letters; where the sword cannot leave a trace of blood, the pen will not print a single character, nor a phrase or a letter.

If it were possible for our flag to flutter again over the towers of Antwerp and the seven hills of the spiritual city, to dominate again the Gulf of Mexico and the mountains of Arauco, then the Spanish people would once more dictate laws, produce Popes, compose dramas, and find translators.[32]

While the conservative literatos relied on the stabilization of the moderado regime of Queen Isabel II to produce the emergence of the new Spanish literature, the progressive literatos were convinced that only by implementing the impending social transformations could they put an end to Spain's historical impasse and undecided identity. The progressive literatos thought that Spain had to put into effect deep political and economical transformations before it could envision a new civilization and create an autochthonous literature. Accordingly, they viewed their efforts to create a new literature—and a new Spanish novel—as closely related to their political struggle to bring forth the definitive triumph of liberalism in Spain. Spain had to complete its liberal revolution before it could claim literary originality:

> The supremacy of ignorance came to an end, and so did the monster of feudalism. From now on, we see with Lerminier two great things: the eternity of God and the eternity of the people—or rather, God and freedom, the freedom of nations. . . . Out of these two great elements a pure, majestic, and sublime national literature will be born—the literature of the people, the literature of freedom.[33]

The progressive literatos thought the triumph of the liberal revolution would put an end to the long period of cultural and political decadence brought about by the Counter-Reformation, and make possible the continuation of Spain's destiny. Some of them claimed the *Comunidades de Castilla* as the symbol of "national freedom" and the Spaniards' unrelenting desire for freedom as the true source of the glory of Spain.[34] Only with the triumph of the liberal revolution, and the subsequent incorporation of Spain in the historical processes shaping Europe, could the literatos envision the end of French influence and the rise of Spain's modern literature. Then they would no longer need the guidance offered by more advanced liberal nations. They would have no more need for "French baby walkers" to articulate what Spain latently was and what it wanted to become:

> If the literature of our golden age was brilliant rather than solid, died at the hands of religious intolerance and political tyranny, and could only be reborn with the help of French baby walkers, . . . let us hope that we will soon be able to lay the foundations of a new literature which will be the expression of our new society, . . . a young literature, like the Spain we now represent.[35]

In any case, both conservative and progressive literatos had high expectations in regard to the imminent renewal of Spanish literature and thought that the effective realization of Spain's and their own immanent potentiality was a matter of their collective volition.[36] The literatos were confident in Spain's literary renewal and often referred to it. They all felt that the time had come for them to fulfill the literary expectations that came with a new era and to accomplish the self-sufficiency Larra had wished for Spanish literature.[37] But liberalism came slowy and unevenly to Spain, as the sociohistorical roots of its decadence were hard to eradicate. The literatos' belief in the imminent redemption of Spanish literature turned soon into painful disappointment.

Some years before the writing of novels became a central preoccupation for the literatos, Larra had already written dramatic and very well known words about Spain's lack of a modern literary language, or, more specifically, about the impossibility of finding one own's voice when writing from outside the centers of cultural and political power:

> To write and create from the center of civilization and publicity, like Hugo and Lerminier, is truly to write. Because the written word needs to resound, and like the stone thrown in the middle of the pond, it wants to arrive repeated over the waves until the farthest corner of the surface, it needs to irradiate like light from the center to the circumference. To write in the capital of the world, like Chateaubriand and Lamartine, is to write for humankind. . . . To write like we do in Madrid is to make a note, to write a book of memoirs, to conduct a sad and desperate monologue with oneself. To write in Madrid is to cry, to search for a voice without finding it, as in an exhausting and violent nightmare—because one does not even write for his own people.[38]

Modern literature, he thought, was a product of a civilization that was in many aspects foreign to Spain. It was the expression of a progress—the natural outcome of the material and cultural accumulation observed in certain European countries—which seemed to elude Spanish society.[39] Like the universal language of science and technology, this new and foreign literature seemed able to speak to everyone (to write in Paris is "to write for humankind"), whereas the literature produced in the periphery, that written in and from Madrid, was condemned to lack design, to be a fragment ("a note"), to be an insular and obsolete utterance (to write a monologue or memoirs). It was the wordless howl of a sense of loss and waste, the expression of the nightmarish search for an individual and collective voice (to write "is to search for a voice without finding it"). Writers like himself could not be heard—"*no pueden tener eco*"—not only because they had hardly any diffusion, as Romero Tobar pointed out, but, more important, because no one in the periphery of the new civilization seemed to be able to find a voice with which to speak about oneself to the others and to one's own. As Fernán Caballero put it a few years later, "Only the French are endowed with such an admirable and flexible talent, an experience of the world and learned knowledge, a pen equally capable of writing a lovely poem or a work of science."[40]

The Decentered Literary Consciousness: Latecomers and the New Cultural Order

The position of the literatos with respect to the cultural hegemony of France over Spain and, specifically, the role French literature and other foreign influences should play in the creation of a modern Spanish novel was, thus, complex and often contradictory. On the one hand, the literatos would not accept the historical dependency and cultural marginality they seemed condemned to by Spain's slow process toward modernization.[41] They held a grudge against the French for their interference in Spanish literary practices and readership, and firmly opposed the intrusion by proclaiming the irreducibility of Spain's historical conditions to any foreign forms of the novel. The French novel seemed to them inadequate to represent Spanish society, to produce a foggy writing based on equivocal appearances.[42] The literatos insisted that to restore "a vigorous style" to the Spanish novel, which would enable it to represent new "sensations, concepts, and thoughts," the Spanish writers had to be able to produce autochthonous writing grounded in their own "ideas" and "imagination." After all, as El Pobre Diablo asked, "Do not we make our revolution differently from other nations and therefore see things in a different manner than their writers?"[43] The literatos strongly felt they had to be faithful to their own historical experience and keep close to the familiar and primal land and traditions if they were to free themselves from subordinating hierarchies.

On the other hand, the literatos also thought their claim to a place among those nations with political and cultural authority had to take into consideration the modern literary sensitivity and cultural order. In spite of their nationalistic praise of the narratives of the Golden Age, the literatos had an acute sense of their own alienation from Spain's novelistic tradition, which, they felt, was of little help to their artistic ambitions. In comparison to the new and foreign novel, the large, diverse, and prestigious Spanish tradition of fictional writing seemed to the literatos remote and useless in meeting the literary taste of mid-nineteenth-century Spanish writers and readers. As Leopoldo de Cueto pointed out in 1843, "the different species [of the novel] that satisfy contemporary society's taste do not exist among us except in the form of translations of foreign work."[44] The inability of the Spanish novelistic tradition to satisfy the narrative needs of the modern taste underlined the rustiness literary Spanish had acquired over the years. As Fernán Caballero put it, Spanish was "affected" and "tearjerking," appropriate for drama and poetry, but "awkward" and "inflexible" for the novel.[45]

The literatos also acknowledged the prestige the French novel had in Spanish letters and the inevitable influence it exerted over their writing. In 1843 Mariano Noriega was among those literatos who talked about the morphological constraints that limited all latecomers. For him, the influence of the French novel on Spanish writers who took upon themselves the task of writing a novel was as definitive as the unremovable stain left by wine on a new glass: "The taste for contemporary novels has impregnated our brains to such an extent, that—like the proverbial wineskin that retains the color of the first wine it held—everything that is coming out of the Spanish minds carries with it the foreign seal and the sign of imitation."[46] The literatos knew they were latecomers who had been forced onto a road that was not their own, a road they could not refuse, in part because Spaniards had come to perceive the alien novelistic imagination as their own. As Larra put it, a "strange phenomenon" characterized Spanish literary processes: "We find ourselves at the journey's end without having traveled at all."[47]

Furthermore, the literatos were well aware that the cultural influence of Paris and London over most of the world was sustained not only by the prestige they had, but also by the prestige they conferred. As Larra remarked when commenting on his contribution to *Un voyage pintoresque par l'Espagne*, to gain recognition a work had to be spotlighted in France.[48] The international success of Ayguals's imitation of *Les mystères de Paris*, *María o La hija de un jornalero*, confirmed that to gain recognition one had to acknowledge to some degree or another the hegemonic foreign discourses on culture.[49] To look beyond personal recognition, and to desire that one's own culture be embraced by the new European discourses on civilization, required the "de-centered literary consciousness" that Bakhtin assigns to the chivalric romance: the obligation "to deal with an alien discourse and alien world," the "translation," "reworking," and "re-conceptualization" of an "alien intention."[50]

Indeed, to succeed in Paris, as well as to succeed in one's own national territory, a Spanish author had—and very often sought—to negotiate his or her own alien and odd cultural position (that of a culturally peripheral subject) into the more *familiar* and *admired* grounds provided by the dominant cultural paradigms. Thus, on the one hand, the publication of a Spanish novel like *María* in the self-absorbed and self-sufficient cultural environment of French culture implied the bold and challenging affirmation of the existence of autochthonous literary processes in Spain—"Here we also know how to write," would say Antonio Ribot in the article that chronicled the European success of *María*. But, on the other, the publication of the novel also presupposed the acknowledgment, and sometimes the acceptance, of Spain's eccentric position within Europe.[51] Spanish literary and cultural creativity was to be acknowledged and to gain recognition only insofar as it was written in a language that was not fully theirs. This meant not only the trading of one's own local language for a more universal one (to publish in French), but, more important, a double commitment to, or a compromise between, one's own worldview and the hegemonic view (to publish in France). As Moretti has rightly pointed out, "Provincialism is not so much a matter of difference from the center, but of enforced *similarity*."[52] Thus, it should not come as a surprise that despite Ayguals's claim to authenticity, his work often conforms not only to foreign modes of writing—*María* is an imitation of *Les mystères de Paris*—but also to foreign cultural and literary discourses on Spain. *María*'s French title, *Marie l'Espagnole, ou La victime d'un moine*, as well as its representation of Spain as the struggle of a few heroes against the retrograde, conspiratory, lascivious, and all-powerful clergy, seems to belong with well-established Gothic and Romantic tropes found in French representations of Spain.[53] The same could be said of Fernán Caballero's idealist tendencies and, more particularly, of her description in *La Gaviota* of the desertlike landscape of Andalucia. Her "exact, true, and genuine idea of Spain"—made up of phantasmal monuments (turned into ruins), picturesque and backward ways of life (including the *corridas*, the *toreros* and their brutish social behavior), and a hot-tempered and highly sexual heroine—leads us directly back to the exotic Spain and its people as constructed by many European travelers.[54] Indeed, Ayguals's and Fernán Caballero's success both in Spain and in Europe was due largely to the familiar literary and cultural horizon their works provided. The prestige and effective authority held by Paris contributed to the conformity to French literary forms verified in Spain. How could it be any different?[55]

The literatos could not, and would not, ignore the prestige of the foreign models. On the contrary, they strived to incorporate the forms of modern culture into their writing practices.[56] As Larra had done before, the literatos recognized in the new literary forms, and specifically in the bourgeois novel, a language that spoke to everyone—the language of modern historical processes—to which they held a legitimate claim.[57] Accordingly, they willingly opened up their representation of Spain's particular historical processes—their own ideas and imagination—to the persuasive writing of the successful bourgeois novel. They insisted on what Larra had despaired of accomplishing; they wanted to find a voice that was their own but that spoke to everyone, as if uttered from the center of civilization. The other options were either silence or exoticism, and they rejected both.

The Rise of the Novel in Spain: The "Little Poor Speakers" and Their Conspicuous Thefts

Under the persuasion, and the pressure, of the skillful French novels, learning replaced creation, the literato inevitably became an apprentice, and translation and imitation (being a form of translation) took over as limited experimentation. Many literatos were eager to learn from the foreign masters. The willingness by Larra and other progressive literatos to learn from foreign authors has been recently analyzed by Jesús Torrecilla as a way to appropriate the "vitality and energy" of more advanced nations without submitting to them.[58] Pushing Torrecilla's argument to the limit, I would like to contend that the desire to *learn*, characteristic of so many literatos of the time, was a desire not only to *emulate*—that is, to do as well as, or better than, their masters—but also to arrogate to themselves the foreign writing. In my view, their ambitious emulation was based on the assimilation of what they experienced as the internally persuasive discourse of French literary and other cultural imports, and encompassed—beyond the nonsubmissive attitude toward learning pointed out by Torrecilla—a violent gesture against the masters driven by the aggressive desire to assert, against all odds, their own creativity. As Larra put it in his habitually shrewd words and bitter humor, they were not just learning, they were *stealing*. They knew, he wrote, that they were "poor little speakers who talk what was their own and what was someone else's," speakers who were forced to usurp from those foreign authors—those masters—who knew how to satisfy people's tastes:

> Our goal being to entertain by any means when our impoverished imagination does not produce anything sufficient or satisfactory, we openly declare our intention to steal materials wherever we can, publishing them in complete or mutilated form, because being poor speakers, we speak that which is ours and others', certain that what the public cares about in seeing something in print is not the name of the author, but rather the quality of what is written, and it is better to entertain with someone else's work than to pester with our own.... We will take our miserable talent and exchange it for the good one in others, and with different trimmings will appropriate it, like so many others do without admitting to it.... After we have stolen them, who is to say that such articles do not belong to us?[59]

In the caustic humor of Larra's words, as in the translating and imitative practices of his generation, we find a clear refusal to accept a world order in which their creativity was superfluous and their dependence inevitable. If, as Balzac said, France was "devouring" a country every month to satisfy its political and cultural hunger for domination, the literatos were "stealing" to fulfill their own frustrated creative energies. The emulative drive of the Spaniards matched and reversed the Pantagruelian cultural hunger of the French. It was a Heideggerian interpretative act where each act of comprehension (or reworking, Bakhtin would say) presupposed the "encirclement and ingestion" of another being, a translation "*into*."[60] Trapped between their country's historical lethargy and a new cultural order that condemned them to a peripheral position, the literatos refused to acknowledge the difference between original and imitative writing. This distinction—in fact, a creation of the centers of cultural production—was alien to their own peripheral literary systems: "Why shouldn't Figaro now and then steal from others?" asked Larra.[61] Invaded by a novel that behaved as just another imported commodity, the literatos reacted not unlike British and other European merchants when they were denied the right to trade with the Spanish colonies in America: they did not recognize the legitimacy of the order that excluded them and made stealing their own *de facto* activity. They became corsairs of the literary seas.

Stealing subverted the historical imperative of cultural dependency and empowered the literatos. In contradiction with Harold Bloom's scheme, in mid-nineteenth-century Spain stealing supported the creative effort of many weak, peripheral writers (not exclusively that of a few strong ones). Through imitation the literatos freely misread foreign writings and re-created them as if they were their own. Larra's defiant stand on his right to stolen property—someone else's texts—is clearly manifested in his refusal to defend himself against the accusation of plagiarism, in his bold admission of it, and, more important, in the assertion of his rights over someone else's material: "I will consider my play as my own and original, despite the scenes I needed and could steal from Scribe. And it should be noted that every time I write about a subject already treated by another writer I may consider superior to me, I intend to do the same, and will continue to call original anything that may result from that." Stealing was intended as a takeover; it was an act of cultural war against the order that condemned the literatos to the periphery of history: "I seized the idea [and appropriated it] by right of conquest." They knew that in order to be part of the political and cultural center, they had to show the same determination—the same unscrupulous desire—to dominate others than the French and British. Larra insisted: "They will be ours by right of conquest."[62]

Indeed, they tried. The literatos were determined to create, from an alien but all-pervading and persuasive literary language, an autochthonous novel that would represent the transformations that were shaping mid-nineteenth-century Spain. They wanted to reinvent a writing, to modify the foreign models of the novel and to adapt them to Spain's historical conditions and cultural traditions. In this unstable play of boundaries, they aimed at mastering the alien literary models—the languages of Europe's political and cultural domination—as a half-our and half–someone else's writing. They struggled to achieve a difficult balance between opening the country and themselves to foreign influence and holding to their own autochthonous processes of national formation. For a very short time, the popular and critical success of *María*, both in Spain and in Europe, and the critical praises dedicated to *La Gaviota* by French critics, seemed to confirm the strengh of their literary project and to announce that the moment of Spain's redemption from otherness had, finally, arrived. Antonio Ribot's enthusiastic article, published in *El Telégrafo* (1 February 1847), captures the literary and national significance that the popular and critical success achieved by *María* in Europe had among the Spanish cultural circles:

> All the periodicals in Paris, regardless of their political inclinations, pay great tribute to our friend and contributor Mr. Ayguals de Izco for his novel *María La Española*, which, written [i.e., translated] in French by the author, has achieved the most brilliant success in Paris.
>
> For fear of being biased, we would keep quiet if we were dealing only with an amazing triumph that places our friend among the leading European novelists. But we do not wish to remain silent before a literary event without precedents, because Mr. Ayguals's is not a purely individual achievement, but rather a vindication of Spain, a real Spanish triumph.
>
> At a time when many foreigners believe that we are no more than a horde of savages, a Spaniard who loves the glories of his homeland strives to vindicate our honor, and in a language other than his own dares to publish his novel in the enlightened capital of France, cradle of the most celebrated writers. At the same time when giants like DUMAS and SUE bring out their masterworks, the press declares that *María La Española* is the one that captivates the most attention and sympathy from the French public.
>
> The first, numerous edition has quickly sold out, and a second edition that will hardly suffice to satisfy the public's avidity and large orders from Belgium and Italy is now being published.
>
> This for Spain is of the utmost importance, since now not only are those foreigners aware of the fact that here we also know how to write, but, thanks to the work of our fellow countryman, they will also see the true state of our culture.[63]

A great triumph for the struggling literatos and their literary efforts. But Ribot's excessive celebration of the international reception of *María* betrays the literatos' deep sense of alienation from the new hegemonic cultural centers—an alienation that could not be redeemed by a few sporadic successes.

The truth was that, as in the case of the Brazilian novelists, the literatos had difficulties finding the means to appropriate the alien literary models.[64] The aesthetic accomplishments of the French novel hung intimidatingly over the Spanish novelists and forced them to admit the provisional and experimental character of their works. The skillfulness of the masters forced them to be modest: "Our writers do not dare to compete with such adversaries."[65] This generation was well aware of the personal and collective difficulties they had to face to master the most important paradigm of modern culture within their own local conditions, and, thus, to create an autochthonous literary writing where the historical experience that was shaping the new liberal Spain could be fully enunciated.[66] As Fernández de los Ríos commented, "undeniably, they [the Spanish writers] have recently been rather unfortunate in producing novels."[67] Prefaces and epilogues became a public warning on the literary deficiencies of the novel about to be read. They were apologetic frames used by the Spanish novelists to excuse what they perceived as the useless redundancy of their work. The authors, aware of the comparisons that would inevitably arise, acknowledged the precariousness of their novels hoping to exculpate themselves before experienced readers and harsh critics: "I do not present my work as a model," said Martínez Villergas, "because I know myself well and do not have the aptitude to produce masterworks."[68] Thus, the continuous attempts by the literatos to write a bourgeois novel in Spain resulted in a conscious recognition of the bold character of the project. As Francisco J. Moya put it in 1848, it took a lot of courage to publish a Spanish novel at the time since the literatos had no accumulated experience whatsoever in this genre. Not coincidentally, Milá de la Roca and Ayguals de Izco referred to their novel-writing as "a rash venture."[69]

Reclaiming the Image of Spain: The European Languages of Culture

The literatos would not give up the writing of novels, even though they often felt overwhelmed by their unfruitful efforts. True, Spain had fallen behind the more advanced European states, and the new novel had a foreign origin, but more important than any other consideration was their conviction that the novel was an integral part of Spain's literary tradition and one of Spain's major contributions to European culture. The literatos would not accept their apparent inability to successfully continue the writing tradition of the Golden Age, and the difficulties they were having with the contemporary form of the novel left them, in the end, quite at odds. As Fernández de los Ríos asked in 1848: "Do we by any chance lack in the present condition of our society, in our history, or in our beliefs the elements that are necessary for the novelist's work? Why, then, do not we write novels in Spain?"[70] They felt the continuation of their precarious and defective practice had legitimate political justifications: first, to master the literary paradigm of modern nations in order to reclaim the initiative in constructing Spain's image for both national and foreign audiences; and, second, to secure Spain's place at the heart of European cultural production. Thus, for Martínez Villergas as for many other literatos the writing of the modern Spanish novel became, regardless of their acute sense of aesthetic failure, a patriotic duty: "I can be proud," he says, "to have contributed to the cultivation of a national novel."[71]

This nationalistic enterprise took center stage and was to account for the first wave of nineteenth-century Spanish novels. The programmatic prefaces of the two most popular and critically successful novels in the 1840s, *María o La hija de un jornalero* and *La Gaviota*, openly articulate the preeminence of the political intention to produce an autochthonous literary discourse from and on Spain. Hence, despite the deep ideological and aesthetic differences that set their works apart, both Ayguals de Izco and Fernán Caballero coincided in introducing their novels as representations of Spain's new control over its own image and, therefore, as its regained national voice. As they themselves tell us, their inaugural novels were supposed to set straight the false, misleading, and illegitimate foreign constructions of Spain and to provide the authentic portrait of the nature and value of its civilization. These novels, their authors insisted, delivered the Spanish discourse on Spain. In Ayguals's words:

> In presenting the history of recent political events in Madrid, along with purely invented dramatic incidents, I also attempt to describe the customs of all popular groups, Spanish customs that, judging by your writings, are entirely unknown to you foreigners.[72]

Similarly, Fernán Caballero states in her prologue to *La Gaviota*:

> We would like for the European public to have a correct idea of what Spain is and what we Spaniards are, and to dispel those monstrous concerns, preserved and transmitted like Egyptian mummies by the populace, generation after generation. And to accomplish this it is imperative that, instead of judging the Spaniards according to pictures drawn by foreign hands, other nations see us as we paint ourselves.[73]

These novels, however, radically differed when it came to understanding Spain's character and its participation in the European heritage. In Fernán Caballero's works, as well as in other mid-nineteenth-century novels by conservative literatos, we find that the overwhelming display of Spain's local color is based on Schlegelian notions of culture and the affirmation of Europe's common Christian identity.[74] In *La Gaviota*, for instance, the spiritual brotherhood immediately felt by two strangers (a Spanish aristocrat and a poor German doctor) and their choice of Latin over other geopolitical languages as their means of communication when they first meet epitomizes the aesthetic purpose of the novel from its initial pages: the transcription in Spain's own terms of the sacred language of the Roman Christian Empire. For its part, *María*, as many other works by progressive literatos, reproduces those social discourses whose roots are the political philosophy of the Enlightenment and its republican understanding of the nation as a community of citizens. Schlegelian Catholicism and Enlightenment notions of the state constituted the two main European languages of reference for mid-nineteenth-century Spanish literatos. Between these two dominant discourses, a novel such as *Los misterios de Barcelona* constituted in its writing an equivocal alliance to both conservative and progressive forms of Romanticism.[75]

That Fernán Caballero's construction of Spanish identity differs radically from Ayguals de Izco's should not prevent us from observing their common purpose (shared by all novels of the period): to give Spain a voice of its own that would assert Spain's true identity and rightful place among European nations.[76] In both *María* and *La Gaviota*, as well as in most mid-nineteenth-century novels, we can recognize the purpose of redressing foreign misconceptions about Spain, the strong affirmation that Spain shared Europe's identity, and the desire to participate in the European languages of culture.[77] Furthermore, we perceive in these novels the unstable play of boundaries with foreign literary and cultural imports that supported the literatos' participation in European contemporary processes. In precisely the half-ours and half–someone else's word sought by the literatos, the European identity of Spain was to be achieved.[78]

3
The Critical Reception of the French Novel

> Why do the infernal [i.e., Madrid] newspapers pay so much attention to foreign writers and fail to mention the national ones, not even to make their works the object of the fiercest condemnation?
> —Juan Ariza

THROUGHOUT THE MID-CENTURY THE FRENCH NOVEL WAS WHAT Antonio Elorza—referring to the role of France in cultural and political processes of modernization in nineteenth-century Spain—calls a "privileged referent."[1] It provided the critical referential frame for both literary debates and novelistic experimentation. The French novels captured the interest of the literatos who read them with enthusiastic approval or irate dislike, and the criticisms or praises they could not bestow on a Spanish novel were addressed to those of the French. French works filled in the void left by the Spanish novel—a void created by the importation of these foreign texts—and functioned as a vicarious Spanish novel. They filled this role so well that the author of an 1844 literary review of the lastest novels published in Spain (among them, Spanish translations and imitations of *Les mystères de Paris*) could say, without feeling his statement was somehow paradoxical, that when he talked about the Spanish literary life of his time he was referring not so much to the books published by Spaniards as to those published in Spain: "The truth is that when we talk about our literature we do not use this designation to refer only to the very few national productions that occasionally come to light in Spain, but rather to all books published in our language, the majority of which come from the other side of the Pyrenees."[2] For the literatos, the French novel had a quasi-universal versatility, a potential adaptability to different national conditions, and a commonly acknowledged technical mastery.[3] Hence, Ramón de Navarrete would propose in 1847 to examine works by the most important French novelists of the time in order to determine what writing was the most suitable to Spanish tastes and the closest to Spain's own historical experience.[4] The literatos' critical fostering of the French novel accompanied, and sanctioned, the publishers' progenitorship of foreign narrative formulas. They tried to sort out the aesthetic and ideological principles found in the variety of forms present in the French novel and, disregarding the racket made by the constant publication of best-selling novels, tried to decide which of those writings could be the foundation of the Spanish novel.

Neither commercial success nor the saturation of the literary market is a sufficient reason to explain the persuasive power that the writing of French novelist Eugène Sue had over many literatos. To determine the different impact particular French authors and works had in the Spanish literary field we also have to take into account the literatos' critical views on the new hegemonic genre, and their own envisioning of an autochthonous novel. They are the ones who voiced the moral concerns and aesthetic preferences of diverse social groups and, ultimately, who turned their observations into the new Spanish novel. At the end of the article entitled "Pleito ruidoso"—commented on in the first chapter of this book—Modesto Lafuente described Spanish literature as a figure forgotten ("abandoned in a corner") by both publishers and readers, quietly observing the quarreling and lawsuits brought on by the Spanish progenitorship of the French novel. She stands there, forsaken by all, asking herself, "Whoever wins, what do I gain?"[5] The question, ignored in the hectic world of publishers, was taken very seriously by the literatos who rushed to answer it.

The Progenitorship of the French Novel:
The Exemplarity of *Les mystères de Paris*

The scrutiny of the French novel was a political act.[6] The central point of contention among the literatos was the social function the novel was expected to perform in the new liberal order established by the *Estatuto Real*. All foreign novels were analyzed and evaluated according to this criterion, and their originally alien nature actualized or neutralized in conformity with it.

The novels by George Sand, Honoré Balzac, and Alexandre Dumas, père (authors who, together with Eugène Sue, were the focus of most of the mid-nineteenth-century debates on the nature of novel-writing) did not meet the literatos' expectations. The literatos did not question their artistry, but believed that these authors' works fell quite short in regard to social responsibility. According to the progressive liberals, these works did not promote an active and outspoken citizenry, but rather seemed either to encourage the erosion of all foundations of society (including the liberal system they supported) or to engage in banal, apolitical entertainment. As Fernández de los Ríos denounced, most of the modern novels seemed to ridicule "the most revered and solemn things and institutions this society has established as unquestionable needs" and promote the "derision of any manifestation of virtue."⁷ This encapsulates how the literatos felt with regard to the novels by George Sand. With the significant exceptions of Carolina Coronado and Gertrudis Gómez de Avellaneda, Sand's works, as well as her life, were dismissed as "Baroness Dudevant's delirious derangement."⁸ More than the polemic around her hispanophobia and the political arguments between francophiles and francophobes, it was her use of the novel to criticize patriarchal rule and to defend women's rights that was deemed inappropriate in both artistic and moral terms. Sand's defense of the political rights of women directly challenged the patriarchal foundations of Spanish liberalism, even in its most progressive and democratic forms. The concept of family which dominated the thought of mid-nineteenth-century social reformers and utopian socialists excluded any possibility of a radical subversion of the sexual distribution of social and domestic labor.⁹ Thus, Ramón de Navarrete openly disapproved of Sand's use of the novel to convey what he perceived as the "exaggerated utopia of women's [social] rehabilitation":

> Her ideas, doctrines, philosophical principles—everything about her has become deplorably excessive, condemned by the accusatory finger of the world. *The rehabilitation of women* is George Sand's golden utopia. We have to confess we can hardly understand such an empty phrase. . . . Do women need this rehabilitation that is supposedly meant for them? They surely do not. And, if that was the case, is it appropriate to attempt it with the help of the novel? Such an enormous task is clearly out of its reach.¹⁰

The novels by Honoré de Balzac were also ultimately dismissed by most literatos. The praises they sang were always toned down by their disapproval of what they perceived as Balzac's lack of concern for moral teachings and political solutions. What fascinated Larra about Balzac's novels, what made Balzac in his judgment the first of all novelists, that is, his detached description of France ("the modern, dry society depicted in them, bare of any apprehensions but also of authentic illusions, and therefore dejected, harsh and despicable at times, and—unfortunately— how infrequently ridiculous!") was precisely what most of the literatos could not accept.¹¹ Balzac's writing represented the potential social dangers of a novel that took pleasure in moral ambiguity, or, in Fernández de los Ríos's words, in "eternal doubt."¹² Balzac, it was said, magnificently portrayed the social corruption and debauched desire (adultery, prostitution, greed) brought on by the new social power of money, but his view of society was materialistic and pessimistic.¹³ His novels denied the possibility of social reconciliation and reform, and did not encourage any individual or collective hope. He had a clinical eye, cold and pitiless:

Balzac usually simply draws a terrifying sketch, exhibits it before humanity's astonished eyes, and says: "That's the way you are!" He rarely tempers his bitterness with the consolation of religion by crying, "Have faith and do not despair." And almost never shows the remedy for such serious ills! Do we need to say how much we disapprove of his destructive results? The day men will live without hope, the day they will recognize that fate rules their destiny, that will be the day of their complete depravation, the day of dissipation and social anarchy![14]

In judging the novels by Alexandre Dumas, père, the literatos similarly denounced his lack of a moral stand and the conspicuous absence of social solutions that, according to the literatos, characterized Balzac's works. In Dumas's case, however, the problem was not his moral detachment, but rather his moral frivolity.[15] His novels were said to be shallow; his only interest, entertainment. They criticized him for writing plots just for plot's sake and for his disregard for moral propriety or social convention. He had a great imagination, they acknowledged, but his works were trivial, empty of all content. Ramón de Navarrete did not think Dumas worthy of literary discussion due to "the absence of a philosophical system and moral purpose" in his novels.[16] Thus, despite his appreciation of Dumas's literary qualities, he confined the French author to a footnote in the article he wrote on the appropriateness of different types of French novels for Spanish literature and character.

Most of the objections the literatos raised to the French novel—the threat to patriarchal rule, the moral detachment, and the socially irresponsible frivolity of entertaining novels—seemed to vanish before the writing of *Les mystères de Paris*.[17] The significance of Sue's novel was clearly expressed by Fernández de los Ríos: for him, Sue had accomplished the reformation of the novel; he had put an end to the "highly destructive" influence of Sand, Balzac, Dumas, and Soulié.[18] It is important to emphasize that the acclaim of Sue's novel, if not unanimous, came nevertheless from both progressive and moderado liberals. We can easily find high praises for *Les mystères de Paris* written by conservative critics, such as Guillén Buzarán who, after expressing his dissatisfaction with the dissolute morality of most foreign novels, includes Eugène Sue among those "outstanding" novelists of Christian inspiration such as Walter Scott, Arlincourt, Chateaubriand, and V. Hugo (for his *Notre-Dâme de Paris*).[19] Only the most conservative literary critics—those who rejected all melodramatic representation of social disorder and, embracing Schlegelian notions on national literature, opposed a novel that engaged in contemporary sociopolitical issues— rejected it. The rest recognized in *Les mystères* a writing that transformed the novel from a mere moral entertainment addressed to the supposedly apolitical domestic sphere into a space of political and moral argumentation where the new bourgeois society recognized itself. Indeed, Sue's novel satisfied the literatos' desire for a novel that would stimulate the creation of a national readership.

In *Les mystères de Paris* the literatos recognized their own liberal ideals and political engagement and, more important, the full realization of the novel's capacity as an arena for the construction of the new liberal sphere. Most critics agreed that the novel could not be mere entertainment or an exercise in aesthetic sensibility; it had to be a tool for creating a national readership, a space where citizens actively engaged in public debate. The novel should have "greater goals and higher aims—such as portraying the vices and unveiling the ills afflicting our society—and should propose appropriate and judicious remedies."[20] In the midst of the institutional crisis that accompanied the establishment of the liberal regime, the literatos (with the exception only of the most conservative ones) wanted the novel to give attention to problems and information previously restricted to a limited audience. Issues that had been discussed exclusively within the traditionally restricted audiences and domains of science, philosophy, and history had now to be incorporated in the novel. As it was celebrated by El Pobre Diablo, the novel provided access to "the sacred sanctuaries of knowledge" and to "the fundamental issues in science, ethics, philosophy, and politics" that sustained the ongoing activity in public opinion.[21] *Les mystères de Paris* transformed the novel into a site of political consciousness and public writing where fiction went hand in hand with social opinion and political dialogue. In it the novelist was above all a public writer whose language was permeated by the discourse of contention (*lexis*).

Just as the literatos had envisioned the novel, Sue's constant authorial digressions and use of footnotes that function as documental appendixes to the main text claimed for the novel, alongside journalism, the space for both public debate (political self-clarification) and the formation of a national consciousness in the middle classes.[22] In *Les mystères* literary language was expanded to incorporate all social discourses, making accessible a whole array of academic texts and commentaries to lay readers, who in turn do not hesitate to put them to work for the benefit of their own particular interests.[23] Thus, traditional disciplines lost their presumed independence from ideological concerns and openly became instruments of public opinion, sustaining the ongoing activity of national consciousness formation:

> In *The Mysteries of Paris* the gravest concerns of the people are presented, elucidated, and resolved. The depravity and corruption of certain classes are described and explained, being attributed in some to the lack of education and, in others, to the degradation to which they are condemned. The most difficult ideas are discussed by combining the appeal of the example with the rigor of

explanation. And even the most critical aspects of current social affairs are clarified and delineated with logical force, healthy reasoning, and admirable discernment.[24]

The narrative of *Les mystères de Paris*, merging with the space it came to occupy (the folletín as a section in the newspaper where fictional narratives, social talk, and journalistic miscellany of city news were published), embodied the folletín's interest in current affairs and city events, and the novelist became a social "chatterer."[25] The fusion of journalism and Sue's novel-writing effected in and by the same medium—the folletín within the newspaper—is clearly observed by the conservative writer Nicomedes Pastor Díaz, who stated that novels had become identical with the press: "The modern novel is not a literary work—it is journalism applied to the emotions, passions, and intrigues of life, using false or sometimes simply concealed names. The novelist is not a literary person, but rather a journalist. That is why the novel has become *folletín*."[26] The dependency of the novel upon the same laws that regulated the press testify to the common social space newspapers and politically minded novels came to share in mid-nineteenth-century Spain.[27] As Martínez Villergas noted in the epilogue to his work *Los misterios de Madrid*, "If the freedom of the press had not suffered so many attacks from those in power, I would have tried to develop my political and moral ideas [in the novel]."[28]

Opposed to the Schlegelian literary stand on the apolitical nature of the novel—as the nation's unique and transcendental expression of a catholic and monarchic soul (based on the notions of *Kultur* and *Geist*)—Sue's novel appeared to many literatos as a writing that, opening itself to the participation of the civil community, helped enunciate the collective experience. The transformation of the novelist into a public writer (as a voice of the nation) effected by Sue in *Les mystères de Paris* directly opposed the Schlegelian—and conservative—construction of literature as inspired by the people but produced by a restricted elite.[29] Following Donald E. Pease's distinction between "author" and "genius," which had been recently established, we can say that the writing initiated by Sue in *Les mystères de Paris* brought forward a writer who remained close to the original function of "author"; that is, Sue, and later on his Spanish imitators, maintained "a reciprocal workday relationship with the other cultural activities" of their societies and engaged themselves "in the emergence of an alternative culture."[30] In *Les mystères* a public author substituted for the genius, that is, for the genius's organic relation to the national collectivity and the inspirational, ahistorical, and intimate nature of his work. Opposed to the genius's individual and closed work, the novel-writing of Sue, the literatos realized, was constructed as an open and ongoing public text.

Of course, and as is well known, the literatos' praise for *Les mystères de*

Paris and its contribution to creating a national readership was dependent upon the fact that Sue inserted the representation of social conflicts within a liberal discourse of political reformation that was highly moralistic and unmistakably Christian—a writing that fiercely denounced abuses while securing wide social consent and bourgeois hegemony.[31] Although his novels described and denounced, sometimes bluntly, social illnesses (the social corruption and the individual suffering brought about by the new economic order of capitalism, industrialization, and urbanization), they also, most literatos agreed, positively articulated the fundamental moral values and political principles of the new liberal order. As Fernández de los Ríos put it, Sue's desire to "improve the condition of the human race by presenting a picture of its sufferings and miseries" opened up simultaneously "an immense horizon of bright expectations."[32] In this regard we should remember Umberto Eco's analysis of the novel's "consolatory" strategies and its message of social reconciliation under the aegis of the new bourgeoisie: "The reader finds consolation, either because hundreds of extraordinary events take place or because these things do not change the undulating flux of reality. . . . The book puts in action a series of gratifying mechanisms, the most perfect and comforting of which is the fact that nothing changes. . . . Within this mechanism, dreaming is free."[33]

In those mid-nineteenth-century years when widespread social insurgence (the continuous proclamation of local and general *Juntas*) and the threat of Carlism (due to the unsatisfactory conclusion of the first Carlist war, 1833–40) dominated Spanish politics, literatos with progressive or moderate political views (like Ayguals de Izco and Milá de la Roca, respectively) thought they had found in *Les mystères* the imaginary of social reconciliation that channeled and legitimized their own political expectations with regard to the highly unstable monarchy of Queen Isabel II. The need to promote social reconciliation in the turmoil of the mid nineteenth century helps explain the remarkably persuasive strength of *Les mystères de Paris* in Spanish literary practices, and the unique eruption of Spanish misterios that immediately followed its publication. Significantly, among the many French novels published during those years, only *Les mystères* received both the enthusiastic reception of the readers and the critical approval of a large number of ideologically varied literatos.[34]

The Radicalization of a Politics of Reformation: The Condemnation of Sue's Novel-Writing

The potential political radicalism of Sue's writing was, however, soon made apparent by the publication of his second major best-seller, *Le juif errant* (1844–45).[35] The radical nature of the social reforms proposed by this novel—the defense of the Fourierist commune as the basic social unit and anticlericalism—aroused many doubts about, and for some put a definitive end to, the politics of social consent identified with *Les mystères*.[36] Most of the progressive liberals, such as Fernández de los Ríos, however, frustrated by the increasingly conservative character of successive Isabelian governments, approved the highly melodramatic representation of social illness and, specifically, the harsher denunciation of the living conditions of the popular classes that characterized *Le juif errant*. They also praised *Le juif*'s magnification of desire and evil, and its insistence on the moral deceitfulness of social appearances. The progressive literatos applauded its clear stand in favor of utopian socialist and republican political reforms. The Fourierist Francisco Javier Moya commended Sue's interest in the people and *Le juif errant*'s unambiguous political commitment to profound social reform.[37] For them, *Le juif errant* did not renounce the politics of social reconciliation presented in *Les mystères de Paris*, or its Christian morality. On the contrary, the novel fought to preserve social harmony and morality in a society that was becoming increasingly materialistic and individualistic, as well as more unjust toward working classes and women.[38] Fernández de los Ríos praised the author's commitment in *Le juif errant* to "the welfare that the dispossessed legitimately deserve." The political solutions proposed by Sue, said this critic, did not promote social disorder; on the contrary, they were a call to the political authorities to take remedial action, a warning before the storm—"el preludio de una tormenta." In the opinion of progressive literatos, only selfish interests and short-sighted politics prevented their conservative counterparts from seeing Sue's contribution to social consent:

> The enemies of Sue have even condemned his works as immoral and dangerous. This clumsy slander is ludicrous, foolish, and does not deserve a refutation. Those who have read his books know that there are no other principles or ideas than those of the purest morality and the most religious emotions; every page by this era's popular novelist radiates with the spirit of reconciliation and peace.[39]

In Sue's highly politicized version of melodrama, the progressive literatos recognized a fruitful and particularly meaningful ground on which to express both the extreme vulnerability and violence that characterized the triumph of liberalism in Spain and their desire for profound political and social reforms. Hence, Fernández de los Ríos openly identified Sue's political and literary projects with his own and with those of his Spanish admirers.[40]

Less radical literatos, however, were not convinced. Ramón de Navarrete's comment on *Le juif errant* exemplifies the general disappointment felt by many right after its publication: "Very unfortunately, *The Wandering*

Jew to a large extent has come to eclipse the greatness [of Sue]."[41] Also, the literary reviewer of the moderado newspaper *El Fénix*, R. de Carvajal—who had before praised *Les mystères de Paris*—expressed his profound dissatisfaction with the new novel by Sue. In his view, the publication of *Le juif errant* had tarnished the well-deserved reputation Sue had achieved with *Les mystères de Paris* and had caused a real literary alarm.[42] They perceived in *Le juif errant* something deeply disturbing. In this novel there was no figure of order such as Prince Rodolphe in *Les mystères de Paris* to mediate in social conflicts and to secure social restitution and moral rightness. Society was now represented as permanently and inevitably corrupted by the economic interests of powerful groups. Against them, no one seemed able to do anything, not even the two supernatural figures of the *juif* and the *juive*. The powerlessness of these figures to protect the victims in the novel from their tragic and unfair destinies, or to give a satisfactory resolution to their suffering; the individual and collective affirmation of despair; and, more particularly, the fact that ultimately only a rural Fourierist-like farm can provide some consolation to the few, badly harmed survivors of selfish social interests, left many literatos with no doubt of both the pessimistic social message of the narrative and its defense of radical political measures.[43]

The reaction to *Le juif errant* from the most conservative literary quarters was, of course, less regretful and more belligerent. For these literatos, *Le juif errrant* dispelled any possible doubts one could have in regard to the real political purpose of Sue's writing; this novel, said Rubió y Ors, carried out "the disastrous logic of destruction." *Le juif errant*'s emphasis on the social injustice suffered by the popular classes and women meant for these critics a return to the topics and deviant morality of the novels by George Sand, and the beginning of an openly partisan narrative of socialist ideas:

> Has [Sue] ever considered that once it was established that the satisfaction of passions ought to be the supreme law of society, it was logical to deduce . . . that it should not recognize any limitations; if the respect for private property is a kind of violence, this right should be abolished; and that, if it is a deprivation not to desire another man's wife, it is necessary to put an end to the institution of marriage? Does not he see that such an attempt to refine society would take it back to a savage state?[44]

Le juif errant meant also, the conservative literatos claimed, a return to the moral detachment they had denounced in Balzac's novels. According to them, in this novel the representation of social evil had the quality of a forensic dissection. Sue's analysis of human feelings and moral attitudes was "very vague," and his approach to them was not psychological but rather anatomical: "He examines the soul and the nature of his characters as if he wished to dissect them. He analyzes instead of painting them. He forces readers to attend an anatomical exercise, and the result is that in the end they get upset and ignore the sections in which the author speaks as a doctor in order to follow him in the flight of his literary imagination." This "anatomical report" of society's illnesses reduced the world to mere matter and deprived human relationships of spirituality. Once human society had been deprived of its soul, Sue could make the social order and its moral foundations into the object of mere ideological experimentation. Nothing, then, was sacred for the novelist, and everything was political; Adriana—one of the female characters in *Le juif errant*—was simply, said Rubió, "the personification of the *Falansterio* woman dreamt of by Fourier."[45]

For those literatos who could not conceive of a literature independent of conservative morality, the unrelenting suffering of innocent characters signaled the spiritual emptiness depicted by *Le juif errant*, and the definitive displacement of Christian values and attitudes by a "natural religiosity" ruled by the law of desire and politics. Moreover, the substitution of the vague and conventional representation of evil in *Les mystères de Paris* (underworld criminals; often men driven to crime by poverty) with the unambiguous anticlerical accusation of *Le juif errant* (evil is identified with the socially powerful and morally influential Society of Jesus) seemed to the conservatives a natural development of the radical politics already implicit in *Les mystères*.[46] In their view, *Le juif errant* proved to be a lesson for those most moderate among both the conservative and the progressive literatos who had once praised Sue's writing. Those moderates agreed. In Sue's last novel they now discovered that no conciliatory writing could ever contain the moral and social dangers of radical liberalism. They joined, then, the ranks of those critics who had always insisted on the aesthetic and moral perversity of the French novel, and followed Eugenio de Ochoa's advice to stay away from it:

> Let us learn from the mistakes of our neighbor, France, which after playing too confidently with the respect that should be reserved for those sacred things that are the foundation of social order, has come to raze that same order to the ground and to question—who would have thought of this—even the most basic notions of natural law: property, family, and even authority itself in any form! . . . They start by ridiculing the institutions, and end up fighting them face to face. Alas, let us say it one more time: Let us learn from the example of our neighboring France! They start by throwing gibes in plays and serialized novels [and] end up firing shots in the streets.[47]

The rare agreement between critics, readers, and publishers that resulted in the publication of the first Spanish misterios soon vanished. From that moment on, the Spanish misterios were written mostly by progressive or socialist literatos (from the early novel by Ayguals de Izco, *María o La hija de un jornalero*, to the 1860 *Los misterios del Saladero* by Ceferino Tressera) and, consequently, shared to a greater or lesser degree *Le juif errant*'s radical politics. In fact, these Spanish misterios, with their emphasis on "the needy working classes," and their representation of the horrendous social corruption involving all social groups and institutions—"the disgusting caves," "the salons of the great world," and the general corruption sacrilegiously protected behind "the humble robe of the savior"—are often the result of the combination of the narrative strategies of *Le mystères de Paris* and *Le juif errant*.[48]

The artistic credo on the novel defended by the conservative literatos gained a greater hold on Spanish literary life, as did their denunciation of the French novel and its Spanish imitators. Their aesthetic disapproval of the melodramatic representation of social disorder and evil characteristic of the French novel was condemned regardless of its intent (either as mere frivolous entertainment or as the means of a political discussion on social illnesses). Their critique was, first, on aesthetic grounds. The French novel was the expression of "bad taste": "a frenzied and unbridled fantasy that has never respected the principles of good taste and poetic inspiration."[49] For them two erroneous aesthetic approaches to representation were the source of all the moral disorder depicted and promoted by the French novel: a lack of censorship in the presentation of reality, and/or its exaggeration. According to the conservative literatos, the novel had to renounce melodrama altogether as its mode of writing and embrace a kind of "realism" based upon Neoclassical aesthetic and moral constraints: "No doubt, the novel is of all creations the one that has to be closer to the truth, but that does not mean it is exempted from following the rules of good taste."[50] Second, and from an ideological point of view, the connection between Romantic poetics (its melodramatic mode), the penchant of the French novel for public writing, and the 1848 revolution, was clear to them. In 1851 Eugenio de Ochoa wrote:

> What could be the significance of those elegant follies of George Sand's novels and Dumas's plays? This absurd conviction allowed and even promoted the spread of literary disorder . . . as if it were a mere whim of fashion. And what happened? The supposedly innocent relief of the imagination . . . was no more than a bold attempt to subvert the social order, [which] twenty years later was on the brink of destruction.[51]

Conservative literatos argued that public opinion was not the result of a rational, political dialogue among intellectually competent citizens, but was instead the very symptom of social disorder. Fashionable French novels promoted the diffusion of ideas among the ignorant masses who, confused by issues they could not understand properly, vulgarized and degraded the bases of social order. Thus, for conservative critics, in the public writing of the French novel, ignorance masqueraded as wisdom and true rationality was mistaken for the ever-shifting rhythm of feverish states.[52]

The fact that the novel was being appropriated as an instrument of political awareness by those same groups that were excluded from the system of institutional representation was used as evidence of the supposedly natural ignorance ascribed to social opinion. The novel had been traditionally regarded as an educational tool precisely because of its ability to convey difficult truths to the uneducated minds of women and children.[53] The traditional depreciation of the genre as female and domestic and the conservative articulation of the public as ignorant and easily influenced offered a justification for the paternalism of censorship and political exclusion. The restrictive system of the *Estatuto Real* was thus presented not as the product of certain economic and political privileges, but as a transcendental moral requirement.[54] French novels such as those by Sue, with their unmistakable political purpose, were felt to pose a threat to the order established by the *Estatuto Real*, and to subvert most particularly what they perceived as the natural political dependence of the traditional social audience of the novel. In this context of conservative denunciation of the French novel as an immoral act, we can fully understand Catherine Jagoe's important statement about the significant role played by the apolitical writing of the first generation of Spanish women (specifically, the *novelas morales y recreativas*): they rid the novel of "the stigma of immorality."[55] The *novelas morales y recreativas* emerged in historical simultaneity with the popular French novel, and represented an alternative to both the moral seditiousness and the language of political contention that characterized the most popular forms of the French novel and its Spanish imitations.

Through the typically bourgeois displacement of morality onto women, mid-nineteenth-century conservative literatos engendered the novel as feminine.[56] The novel was depicted as a feminine genre precisely because it, like women, sprang from men; consequently, also like women, it was dependent on the male prerogative over creativity and action: "And since the novel was borne with man, and it is his inseparable partner . . . it will not die as long as he exists."[57] More important, and against those novelists for whom writing was an exercise in public contention, the conservative literatos prescribed a novel that was to be contained within the private home and read as a domestic affirmation of moral amenity and leisure (the novel as "housewife"). The critical recognition of Fernán Caballero as founder of the new Spanish novel—the "Spanish Walter Scott"—was based precisely on the strong feminine quality that, according to her conservative supporters, characterized her writing. Eugenio de Ochoa, wondering about the true identity hiding behind the male pseudonym of Fernán Caballero, was one of those conservative critics who insisted on the feminine character of the writing: "An exhausted imagination cannot conceive such *pure* and *beautiful* scenes, nor cast upon them this aura of delicate melancholy, which gives them such an *irresistible charm*."[58] More particularly, the conservative praise was based on the writer's active promotion of what Stephen Gilman has described as "the novelistic cultivation of what might be called the *antinews* of traditional folkways." As José Fernández Espino put it in 1857, the true Spanish novel "usually begins where history ends, in the bosom of private life. . . . While it can lack historical veracity, it nevertheless contains moral and poetic truth."[59] Thus, the mid-nineteenth-century Spanish literary establishment rejected the figuratively masculine—and French—handling of the pen as a "weapon" to create a national readership identified with the sphere of public opinion, and praised Fernán Caballero's feminine—and supposedly truly Spanish—use of the pen as "needle."[60]

On the other hand, the French novel's supposedly deviant public writing was identified with the figure of the stray and seductive prostitute—with immoral perversion: "If the novel gone astray prostitutes itself, it should be disciplined."[61] The conservative literatos completed their symbolic degradation of the French novel by focusing on its identification with folletín. Folletín, as commodity (a salable object with short-span enjoyment, affordable to many and often shared by many), was symbolically represented as a perverse female or prostitute. Thus, in 1846, José Godoy y Alcántara adopted the supposedly female voice of the novel-as-folletín to recount its—or better "her"—cruel birth as a low, pleasurable object and her control by a pimplike editor:

My birth was too cruel for me to remain silent about it. I came into the world broken into pieces, and as soon as my creator would give birth to one of them it would be placed in the basement of some newspaper, whose subscribers would every morning devour some of my delicate members while sipping their chocolate. It was the year 1835 when a Barcelona publisher decided to assemble my fragments in one single body in the hope that I would help alleviate his miserable fortunes.[62]

Through the degrading figure of the prostitute, conservative critics succeeded in describing the successful French novel as a prostituted literary form (as commodity, folletín) and as deviant writing (political writing or racy and light-hearted stories). Thus, sexually oriented notions of immorality such as corruption, perversity, or seduction were frequently used to denounce the immature instincts and the abuse of creative imagination supposedly sustaining the French novel and its Spanish imitators, and to forcibly associate the political danger of foreign writing with its proclaimed aesthetic banality and moral dubiousness.

According to conservative literatos, if the Spanish novel wanted to redeem itself from the literary corruption of the French novel, and overcome the creative impasse that frustrated so many attempts by Spanish writers, it had first of all to surrender its political ambitions, regain its domesticity, disavow its market origin, and return to the shelter of Spain's Catholic tradition. Moreover, it had to renounce its current imitation of French novels and engage in the copying of reality that characterized Fernán Caballero's work—"the innocent naturalism [she manages in portraying] our habits and customs."[63] Thus, a different form of imitation (that of reality) took center stage in mid-nineteenth-century Spain. This new form of imitation—of realism—defended by conservative literatos was perceived to be a quality of women's writing, the result of a woman's supposedly nonmediated experience of life, an imitation whose truth was attested to by a woman's nonintellectual approach to society. This feminine capacity to imitate (social) life—Fernán Caballero's "faithful and highly expressive picture of our nation's true customs"—was proclaimed to be the foundation of the authentic Spanish novel in opposition to the politically and morally perverse writing of the Spanish imitators of French novels—"extemporizers . . . literary hacks, despicable copyists who imitate those detestable models with which foreign publishers are flooding our market." A few years later, however, the same conservative establishment considered Fernán Caballero's feminine writing insufficient to bring about the new Spanish novel, and begun advocating a new male version of idealist realism.[64]

4
From Translation to Imitation

> What do we remember of those who translated Goethe and Scott, who were in fact the responsible agents of influence?
> —George Steiner

> The craze of translation has reached its limit.
> —Ramón de Mesonero Romanos

WE HAVE SEEN HOW THE URGENCY TO SATISFY THE DEMAND FOR FRENCH novels redirected the creative energy of the literatos toward translation, and how the close economic and artistic collaboration between publisher and writer—which sustained the emergence of the novel as a new hegemonic genre in nineteenth-century France and Britain—was replaced in Spain by a transaction between publisher and translator. This preeminence of translation has been traditionally considered detrimental to mid-century literary life and, especially, to the emergence of the novel in Spain. Romero Tobar's opinion is exemplary of the established critical position which asserts the negative impact of translation on the novel. As he put it, "The overflow of translations caused a notable decline in the use of the written language, and, more importantly in our case, a lethargy and inability to create original narratives." Translations are generally perceived as a castrating force transforming the supposedly fertile field of Spanish letters into a barren ground, and as the direct cause of the sluggishness and creative impotence of the mid-century novel. Thus, translation is opposed to *original* writing, and the originality of the novel is said to emerge against all forms of cultural invasion as the result of the sacred relation of the nation's language to the nation's history.[1]

Translation, however, played a fundamental role in the emergence of the nineteenth-century novel. A great part of the activity of the literatos consisted in translating foreign novels, and the relevance of this practice for Spanish letters was openly acknowledged.[2] So much so, that the literary prestige of a generation was closely related to the artistic quality of their translations, and the cultural standing of a city to the translations produced by its book industry. The literatos even believed, according to Juan Mañé y

Flaquer, that amateurs should stay away from literary translations since the task of translating a foreign literary work—the resolution of the aesthetic difficulties that arose from it—could only be satisfactorily taken in by literatos.³ In granting translation full recognition as literary practice, the literatos were concerned with more than just the need to benefit from one of the few lucrative jobs existing at the time for writers, or with the commercial success of their particular translations in a highly competitive market. For them translation was a genuine form of Spanish literature, a form of autochthonous writing. As a contemporary reviewer of Ayguals de Izco's translation of *Le juif errant* said, excellent translations of foreign works fully vindicated Spanish literature.⁴

In line with Reginald F. Brown's observation about the entanglement of *original* writing and translation in mid-nineteenth-century Spanish literary practices, I contend that the translation of foreign works provided an opportunity for literary experimentation (although a restricted one) that few literatos were willing or able to forego.⁵ Through translation, the literatos re-created the style of the bourgeois novel and, more often than not, tried out imaginary forms to account for both the foreignness and the familiarity of the new novel to the historical and cultural conditions of Spanish society. I contend that it was precisely through the hermeneutic motions—to use George Steiner's expression—which constitute the act of translation that the literatos performed some of the numerous aesthetic trials and ideological adjustments necessary for the adaptation of the bourgeois novel in Spain. Translation, located at the center of the process of appropriating foreign literary models by the literatos, was the site where many of the creative uncertainties and decisions that arose in the process of creating an autochthonous novel were tested out. There was no opposition between translation and *original* writing in mid-nineteenth-century Spain. As Larra put it in his anguished realization of Spain's cultural dependency, to translate was a "necessity" among them. As a subsidiary activity fueled by the importation of French works, translation was to be the first form of modern Spanish literature.⁶

In this chapter I analyze Juan Cortada's translation of *Les mystères de Paris* by Eugène Sue: *Los misterios de Paris* (Barcelona: Tomás Gorchs, 1845).⁷ I have chosen this translation for different reasons. In my view, it provides a fruitful ground to explore the half-our half–someone else's word that characterizes the literary production of mid-nineteenth-century Spain and, more particularly, the rise of the autochthonous novel. As a translation of what Steiner describes as a "close linguistic-cultural" novel—that is, the translation by a "European translator of a European 'foreign' work"— Cortada's version of *Les mystères de Paris* compellingly enacts both the resistance and the fluidity that binds one's own identity with otherness: that "state of recognition" where the "shock of difference is as strong as that of familiarity."⁸ Cortada's translation shows the conflictive movements toward and against recognition of self into and through otherness. The hermeneutic motions of his translation emphasize in some cases the closeness of the alien imagination to the sociocultural existence of his readers (the affinity with the alien text), while in other cases they highlight its foreignness (the resistance to the French novel).[9]

Also, my decision to analyze Cortada's translation has been determined by the fact that this text shares the spatial and temporal coordinates of production and reception of the imitation, which will occupy our attention in the next chapter: Milá de la Roca's *Los misterios de Barcelona* (1844). The historical context shared by both works bears relevance to the analysis of the strategies of appropriating foreign writing for a couple of reasons. The first is related to the characteristics of the publishing industry during those years. In mid-nineteenth-century Spain, the book industry was limited to provincial and regional markets; the production and circulation of foreign books was local and so was most of the autochthonous creation and reception of literature. Thus, Cortada's translation and Milá's imitation not only arose from the same sociocultural context, but also addressed the same regional readership—that of Barcelona and Catalonia in the 1840s. The second reason has to do with the reception of Sue's novels in Spain. Both the translation and the imitation were written before the impact of Sue's second best-selling novel, *Le juif errant* (1844–45), was fully felt by literatos and readers. Thus, Cortada's translation and Milá's imitation can be analyzed exclusively in relation to *Les mystères de Paris*. There is no trace in them of the influence of—or resistance to—the radical politics that characterizes *Le juif errant,* nor a reaction to Sue's abandonment of the consolatory formula (as in some misterios published after 1845).[10]

In my opinion, the common conditions of production and reception which bound translation and imitation are precisely what allows us to detect, from apparently random hermeneutic displacements, the emergence of autochthonous forms of novel-writing. What we perceive in embryonic form in the translation, we find fully developed in the imitation. My analysis will show that both texts share similar textual strategies of appropriation, and that their similarity resides in the fact that their literary imagination is rooted in the social existence of Catalonia at the time. I contend, thus, that the nineteenth-century novel emerged in Spain due to the pressure exerted by local conditions over the foreign imagination of the French novel.

The Naturalization of the Foreign Original: From Romance to History

The influence readers had in the actual writing of *Les mystères de Paris*, and Sue's willingness to incorporate in his ongoing text the readers' suggestions, reactions, and petitions regarding the plot and characters of his story, are well-known facts of literary history. The success of *Les mystères de Paris* as a political romance had a lot to do with the text's high awareness of its readers and the immediacy that existed between them and the fictional society depicted in the novel.[11] Juan Cortada, however, being a translator, was not concerned with the role of the reader as co-author, but rather with the reader as receptor of the creative act—that is, the implied reader addressed by the text and, specifically, the narrative grammar that inscribed him/her in the novel. The slightest change in the intended reader of a text such as *Les mystères de Paris*, where so many narrative strategies are invested in appealing to a specific sociocultural audience, was to have significant textual consequences. Indeed, the substitution of the Catalan reader for the French in the case of *Los misterios de París* brought about, as we will see, some of the translation's most significant hermeneutic motions toward or away from the French original, either stressing the affinity with Sue's text, or the difference that resisted it.

An analysis of *Los misterios de París* reveals Cortada's conception of his readers as both similar and different from Sue's. The translator's strong motion toward affinity with the foreign text is based on the class analogy predicated between both readerships; the translation posits the same bourgeois reader the French original addressed. Moreover, Cortada sets forth between the Spanish audience of the translation and the intended French readers of *Les mystères de Paris* the same class consciousness; his readers are similar to Sue's also in their bourgeois ignorance and fear of the proletariat. The close linguistic and cultural ties that exist between France and Spain—the similarity of the basic social structures of these countries where words often refer to comparable realities and discursive configurations—contributed to the class affinity set up by the translation. Cortada confers to his audience the same unfamiliarity Sue assigns to his with respect to the living conditions of the urban proletariat and the habits of criminals. He also presumes his readers to have the same average knowledge about the world, and a similar concern—which is, actually, that of the story—with the origins of social disorder and its possible political solutions. Both the French original and its Spanish version expect their supposedly ill-informed readers to learn about the misery and urgent needs of the urban underclasses, and to act upon their newly acquired knowledge with the same charitable determination shown by the novel's exemplary characters.[12] Thus, *Los misterios de París* strives to keep close to both the consolatory formula that organizes *Les mystères de Paris* at the level of the story—"if only the rich would know"—and the vocative structure that, at its narrative level, appeals to the readers' paternalistic concern and compassion for the proletariat—"if only the readers would know."

The literal translation of the foreign original often sustains the class analogy Cortada establishes between the French and the Catalan readerships of the novel. Hence, Cortada's translation of Sue's text often relies on a word-for-word transfer and closely reproduces those authorial digressions and footnotes whose function is to inform—and appeal to—the original French bourgeois audience about the specific living conditions of the low urban classes (such as the poor's frequent resort to contaminated meat to satisfy their hunger, or the functioning of the Mont-de-Piété), or about diverse social and political issues related to the control of these same social groups (references to the penal system, the city regulations regarding prostitution, or the treatment of poor people in public hospitals). Cortada reproduces also those authorial intrusions on the story containing a variety of information meant to compensate for the shortcomings of a middle-class lifestyle and education (as, for instance, when Sue explains the meaning of "libertinage") and those paragraphs and footnotes whose content, although theoretical and sometimes highly French, emphasizes Sue's moral message of social redemption (such as a fragment by Napoleon on the need to institute a "police of virtue" to promote reform and complement the fight against crime entrusted to the police force).[13]

The fundamental class analogy predicated in the translation between readerships is, however, counteracted by Cortada's keen notion of the peculiar historical conditions that characterized his own audience. Cortada inscribed in his translation the differences that set apart his readers from Sue's, and, in order not to compromise the basic class analogy that made the reading of Sue's novel significant for the Spanish audience, reworked *Les mystères de Paris* to accommodate the historical conditions of the Catalan readers. Otherwise, he would create a distance—nonexistent in Sue's text—between the translated story and its reader, and, consequently, would affect most dramatically the sociocultural immediacy the novel had with its bourgeois audience. Thus, in *Los misterios de París* foreignness is often displaced by a strong pull toward domestication; in those instances the word-for-word transfer of the French original is replaced by a decisive use of paraphrase and imitation. There are many different definitions of paraphrase and imitation, but for the purpose of the analysis of Cortada's translation, I find those by Friedrich Schleiermacher most appropriate. Schleiermacher describes paraphrase as the "accumulation of loosely defined details, vacillating between a cumbersome 'too much' and a tormented 'too little' . . . [that renders] the content with limited precision, but . . . completely abandons the impression made by the original." On the other hand, imitation is "a substantial transformation" of the foreign elements of the original that while "trying to maintain the sameness of reaction . . . sacrifices the identity of the work."[14]

The literal translation of the foreign text is, thus, abandoned whenever it problematizes the naturalization of Sue's novel, and continually interrupted when, becoming an agent of foreignness, it obstructs the immediate apprehension of the social threat communicated by the story. Hence, the translation often suppresses references too specifically French, such as the mention of Parisian figures, particular places or events, or learned quotations.[15] These references would be meaningful only, or mostly, to French readers, and probably foreign to the average knowledge and education of Cortada's readers. Cortada's purpose is to avoid communicative noise, and its main effect is the simplification of the message. The translator's determination to move away from literalness when it interferes with the direct conveyance of the story's message can be observed in the following lines spoken by the narrator:

> L'entretien suivant, éminemment *béotien* (s'il nous est permis d'emprunter cette expression au très spirituel écrivain qui l'a popularisée[(1)]) jettera quelques lumières sur cette importante question
> [(1)] Louis Desnoyers.
> La siguiente plática arrojará alguna luz a cuestión tan importante.[16]

Cortada's reliance on paraphrase and imitation to avoid communication noise is significantly strong in those instances that involve the depiction of the underclass characters and their dangerous and unlawful actions. The Spanish names Cortada assigns to Sue's characters provide an emblematic example of the translator's determination to re-create in distinctive Spanish terms (in order to bring them close to his readers) the social threat posed to the bourgeoisie by low-class criminality. Thus, while the names of the characters that supposedly represent the high and middle classes and the deserving poor are barely modified, preserving some of their foreignness— Fleur-de-Marie becomes Flor de María; Walter Murph, Gualterio Murph; and François-Germain, Francisco Germain—the underclass crooks and felons are given unambiguous Spanish names: la mère Ponisse becomes la tía Colasa; la Chouette, Mochuelo; le Chourineur, el Acuchillador; Pique-Vinaigre, Ajilimójili, and so on. The same can be observed in Cortada's translation of the language used by Sue's low-class criminals. In fact, Cortada's version of the highly distinctive language the criminals use in the French original is the most important instance of imitation in *Los misterios de París*. It is also Cortada's hardest literary challenge. Through imitation Cortada sought to erase the foreignness of the original and to achieve a complete domestic version of the social danger represented in *Les mystères de Paris*.

In his re-creation of the language of underclass criminals, Cortada had to account for both the sociohistorical conditions of his readers and the aesthetic requirements of romance. His readers had to be tricked to recognize in the language of the fictive criminals that of authentic urban felons while the exoticism of these characters and, thus, romance itself, was preserved. The results of Cortada's translation are mixed. He resorted first to an analogous Spanish argot to translate the distinctive speech the criminals use in *Les mystères de Paris*, but soon dropped it altogether to replace it with the language of the narrator (which he supplemented with the insertion of sporadic popular expressions). As we will see, Cortada's decisions regarding the translation of the argot of criminals are problematic. But before we continue the analysis of Cortada's translation of the language of criminals and reflect further on the consequences of his erasure of the social speech that marks low-class criminals in *Les mystères de Paris*, we need to understand the textual strategies that sustain the representation of social evil and the novel's politics of reconciliation in the French original.

Les mystères de Paris relies basically on two textual strategies to effectively convey Sue's message of class harmony: first, the sharp distinction between deserving poor and underclass felons; and, second, the reluctance to assign specific political affiliations to the urban poor (in Sue's novel, only the narrator and his social-conscious readers are politicized). In *Les mystères de Paris* low-class felons do not have a political ideology but rather a moral disposition—Christian or anti-Christian—toward their fellow men. The only significant moment when proletarian criminality is directly associated with radical politics is at the very end of the novel in the episode entitled "Le doight de Dieu." This chapter relates an orgiastic celebration by the Parisian underclass on the occasion of the public execution of Mme. Martial and her daughter, Calabasse. The diabolic popular party that threatens Prince Rodolphe's life and marks his departure from Paris is accompanied by the political slogan "Il n'y a plus de seigneurs.... Vive la Charte!" [There are no more lords now. *Vive la Charte!*].[17] However, the fact that the slogan is uttered exclusively by the young son of the well-known felon Le Maître d'école, Tortillard—no one else follows his lead—plays down the association of radical politics with the Parisian underclass. Furthermore, that the cry is uttered precisely at the moment when Prince Rodolphe is leaving France seems to convey more the possibility of a politicization of the proletariat if social reform is abandoned, than the desire to affirm the association of moral evil and radical politics.

As part of the inquiry on the causes of social evil, a great deal of *Les mystères de Paris* is dedicated to the socioeconomic conditions that often turn the deserving poor into criminals (as in the case of the story about the Martial family). But in Sue's novel the potential, indiscriminate association between urban poverty and criminality is counteracted by the highly marked and distinctive speech of the criminals. In the French original the low-class criminals have their own tongue, a French of their own creation used and understood only by them: *l'argot de la Cité*. The signs of proletarian criminality, as well as their exotic and romantic representation, are inscribed in the jargon spoken by those who live or hang out in that Parisian refuge of felons (la Cité), and the social isolation of these criminals from the rest of society—including the working classes—is indicated in the inability of all other social groups to understand their jargon. Thus, while at the level of the story Prince Rodolphe (the explorer who ventures to penetrate this fictional jungle located at the heart of Paris) is the only civilized character able to communicate with these urban *savages* and redeem those not totally corrupted, at the level of the narrative, Sue is the interpreter responsible for assuring the readability of the marginal and exotic language of criminals, and Prince Rodolphe's mission among them, for his bourgeois audience—162 footnotes contain Sue's translation of the jargon.

In contrast to this highly distinctive language of criminals, Sue lends the middle-class French he shares with his readers to those characters who represent the deserving poor (such as Rigolette or the Morels), even though, and for comic purposes, he resorts now and then to replicating a picturesque, more or less popular French (most notably in the case of Mr. and Mme. Pipelet). We can say, then, that in *Les mystères de Paris* the equivocal signs that, in an urban environment, tend to blend together deserving poor and felons are weakened and superseded by the unequivocal use of social speech. Moreover, the French spoken by the middle classes binds together the author, his readers, and all the characters of his story (with the exception of those from la Cité) to signify the possibility of understanding and reconciliation among social classes. In other words, the participation of the deserving poor in bourgeois morality (from sexual behavior and respect to property, to obedient acceptance of authority and Christian suffering), and their potential redemption from poverty, are signified in their linguistic communion with the middle classes.

As we have already mentioned, Cortada did not rely on a word-for-word translation of *l'argot de la Cité,* but rather on an analogous transference of meaning, that is, on imitation. In Spain there were no close equivalents to la Cité and, consequently, to the language of its criminals. Nevertheless, Cortada had to find a linguistic substitute that could translate accurately for his readers the social threat, immorality, and isolation represented by those speaking the jargon. He found the analogy, first, through a metonymic displacement: the identification of proletarian criminality with the social marginality of the gypsies.[18] Thus, at the beginning of his translation the jargon of la Cité is replaced by the language of the Spanish gypsies: *caló*. Cortada openly names the jargon he is using in chapter 6—"Tomás y Sara" (I: 52–57)—where he replaces the Chourineur's mention of *argot* with the Acuchillador's reference to *caló*:

> —Je vous ai dit que Bras-Rouge *pastiquait la maltouze*.
> Tom regarda le Chourineur avec surprise.
> —Qu'est-ce que ça veut dire, *pastiquer le mal*... Comment dites-vous cela?

—*Pastiquer la maltouze*, faire la contrabande, donc! Il paraît que vous ne *dévidez pas le jars*?
—Mon brave, je ne vous comprend plus.
—Je vous dis: Vous ne parlez donc pas argot comme monsieur Rodolphe?
—Argot? dit Tom en regardant Sarah d'un air surpris.

—Yo he dicho que el Tigre es *tomaor del dui*.—¿y qué significa *tomaor del dui*? ¿Qué diablos de lengua es esa?—¿*Tomaor del dui*? ¡toma! Hacer contrabando. Vos no sabeis el cristus del caló.—Amigo mío, yo no comprendo una palabra de lo que vais hablando.—Digo que no hablais caló como Mr. Rodolfo.—¡Caló! dijo Tomás mirando a Sara con la mayor sorpresa.[19]

The use of *caló* as a language of social danger analogous to the *l'argot de la Cité* is, however, abandoned very early in the story.[20] We cannot know why Cortada decided to discontinue his use of *caló*. He may very well have been motivated by his limited knowledge of the language of the gypsies, his unwillingness to put forth the effort required to use it consistently throughout the novel, or a combination of both. But we could also explain Cortada's decision to discontinue *caló* by pointing out the translation's decisive move against foreignness and exoticism. The resort to the language of the gypsies translates the exoticism of Sue's criminals and thus contributes to the replication of Sue's mode of writing, that is, that of romance. On the other hand, the language of the gypsies, although socially highly marked and exotic, did not carry the social threat posed to the bourgeoisie by the urban underclass the way the *argot* from la Cité represented it in the French original. Gypsies were too marginal to the social landscape of the city, their language too foreign, and their crimes often too petty to convey to Cortada's reader the danger the story was all about.

Once *caló* is abandoned, Cortada does not translate the *argot* of the criminals from la Cité by means of any analogous jargon. In a surprising move, he resorts to the middle-class language of the narrator: the 162 footnotes Sue adds to his story to translate the *argot* for his French readers become the source in the original of Cortada's translation. This decision effectively erases the sociolinguistic signs that both mark low-class criminals and distinguish them from the rest of the social groups. As we can see in the next example, la Chouette's socially distinctive tongue and criminal intentions disappear completely in the translation. In these lines, la Chouette is malevolently communicating to Fleur-de-Marie some information she has gathered on the young woman's unknown parents. In the original, the *argot* used by la Chouette is marked in italics and Sue's translation is given in the footnote that accompanies the character's speech. We could say that while in the French original criminality is overdetermined, in Cortada's version it is completely erased:

> Il lui a dit le nom de ta mère... C'est des *daims huppés*⁽³⁾, tes parents....
> ⁽³⁾ Des gens riches

> y este le dijo el nombre de tu madre: tus padres son señores ricos.[21]

In Cortada's text the substitution of the language of the narrator for the *argot* from la Cité is sometimes accompanied, and somehow compensated, by an inconsistent and sporadic use of popular expressions. Thus, the effect sought in the French original by means of the jargon spoken by low-class criminals sometimes comes to rely in the translation on an exaggerated use of popular Spanish. This is, for instance, Cortada's translation of the words spoken by the *ogresse*—the owner of the tavern where many of the criminals from la Cité meet—to one of her clients, in which she explains her unwillingness to collaborate with the police and her indifference to the criminal's fate:

> Le bonnet grec l'a demandé plusieurs fois pour des affaires qu'ils sont ensemble... Mais je ne *mangerai* jamais mes practiques. Qu'on les arrête, bon... chacun son métier... mais je ne les vends pas....

> El del casquete griego ha preguntado por él dos veces, diciendo que tenía algún negocio pendiente: pero seguro está que yo delate nunca a mis parroquianos; que los cojan, corriente: porque, como dice el refrán: Antón perolero, cada cual atienda a su juego; pero que yo los venda, eso ya es otra cosa.[22]

Whatever the reasons for these changes, the fact is that Cortada's translation supports a different reading of the story. In Cortada's version, Sue's fundamental distinction between criminals from la Cité and the deserving poor collapses. Criminals and proletariat are harder to distinguish, and no social group is securely isolated or its evil intentions signified—and, thus, contained—by linguistic barriers. Unlike Sue's original, where low-class criminality is marked and contained by a distinguishable *argot* of felons, in *Los misterios de París* the agents of social evil indiscriminately bear linguistic signs associated with both the middle and working classes. The decision to stop re-creating the distinctive social speech of underclass criminals failed to replicate the exoticism of criminality so important in Sue's romance (exoticism effectively translated, otherwise, in Cortada's decisive naturalization of the names of the felons). Furthermore, the erasure of the *argot* of felons directly affected the novel's comforting message of social reconciliation among classes by the redemption of those—and only those—who are the deserving poor.

Cortada's decision to erase the linguistic mark of criminality achieved quite effectively, however, his main purpose of naturalizing the foreign story. The omission of the *argot* of felons in the translation rephrases the social danger denounced in the French original in terms that relate more poignantly to the social existence and historical experience of Cortada's readers. In *Los misterios de París* the common language used by the narrator and all the characters of the story sustains Cortada's pressing determination to bring closer to his bourgeois readers—that is, to Barcelona's and Catalonia's own historical conditions—the threat of social disorder represented in *Les mystères de Paris*. Catalonia and Barcelona were at that time undergoing the painful social changes prompted by the Industrial Revolution, and had recently ended—with the severe repressive measures of the new conservative government—a long period of violent political strifes which had pitted, on the one hand, liberals against absolutists in the first Carlist war (1834–39), and, on the other, the commercial and industrial bourgeoisies against some sectors of the middle class, the proletariat [*el poble menut*], and the urban underclass [*la patuleia*] during the 1835–43 period. The absolutists, *el poble menut* and their radical middle-class allies, and *la patuleia* constituted Catalonia's own, real versions of the exotic agents of social disorder Sue's story depicted. The politically minded groups responsible for social uprising in Catalonia spoke, as in Cortada's translation of the *argot* from la Cité, like the narrator and readers of *Los misterios de París* did, sometimes with sharper popular terms. They spoke in a language familiar to the readers because between the agents of social disorder and those relatives, acquaintances, employees, and servants who had participated in Catalonia's political and class revolts there were no reassuring borders. Thus, in Cortada's decision to unmark the language of social evil we perceive the pressure of Catalonia's insurgence, the experience of class violence familiar to both the translator and his bourgeois readers, over the foreign imagination. In this sense, it is appropriate to say that in Cortada's translation, history displaces the exoticism of romance.

Cortada's textual erasure of the jargon of the French criminals most particularly affects Sue's reliance on the characters' speech to convey his message of social redemption for the deserving proletariat, and consequently seriously compromises the original message of social reconciliation. But it does express well Cortada's own political concerns and conservative alliances, as well as the social existence and views of many of his readers. Cortada's translation makes room for local contradictions and anxieties to convey accurately a meaning of social danger that his readers would understand better and fear more, but it does so at the expense of the novel's message and style. We can affirm that in *Los misterios de París* a *translator* is not needed since the "adventure" depicted in the foreign novel is told in terms that relate to the readers' recent social experience—the urban barbarians are rendered into more familiar foes and their exoticism highly diminished. At the same time, and due precisely to the preeminence of history over romance in Cortada's version of *Les mystères de Paris*, Prince Rodolphe's Christian message of social reconciliation and his crusade to redeem social evil become a more urgent need for Cortada's readers. We can say, to conclude, that by means of imitation, Cortada invades, extracts, and brings home not only the social imaginary of Sue's novel but also its literary forms.[23]

One last comment, however, is needed to understand the cultural and literary processes that shaped mid-nineteenth-century Spain and Catalonia. Although it is accurate to say that Cortada's translation moves away from the exoticism of romance (the alien *argot* of criminality) and toward the sociohistorical conditions of his readers (the mostly unmarked language of Catalan rioters), we need to take into consideration that Spanish was not the native language of Cortada, nor the language used by his readers or the insurgents they feared so much. Cortada, a Catalan speaker and an active supporter of the Catalan *Renaixença*, was addressing his Catalan-speaking readers not in Catalan but in Spanish, the language that, at the time Cortada wrote his translation, still functioned as the language of culture.[24] A century after the promulgation of the *Decreto de Nueva Planta*, Spanish was not an alien language to Cortada or his readers; it was the official language of culture and education. The Catalan middle classes were accustomed to reading about their society in newspapers written in Spanish, and to expressing their political discontent and hopes often in that same language. To read in Spanish about a collectivity that spoke Catalan was a usual activity among these classes. However, and despite the apparent naturalness of the cultural process just described, at the center of the previous observation is the not-so-natural fact that the Catalan reading community of the mid nineteenth century comprised in part a language that was not quite its own. Spanish, a language alien to the social existence of Catalonia, often functioned as the mediating language between the foreign and the familiar among the learned classes. The double act of translation that brought home the European languages of culture and their products cannot be obliterated when analyzing the processes of national formation in Catalonia. Moreover, we need to explore the role played by translation in the incompleteness that characterized all processes of national identity in Spain, an incompleteness that made possible the simultaneous and often contradictory emergence of the nationalism of the state and that of Catalonia and other regions. Finally, we need to analyze the impact of the linguistic dissociation between mother tongue and literary language, supported by centralist cultural policies, in the creation of the style and development of the nineteenth-century novel in Spain.

The Question of Authority over the Text: The Translator Against the Author

Against affinity and effacement of difference (the numerous adaptations and re-creations that characterize *Los misterios de París*) the translation sets up a series of resistant differences which highlight the foreignness of the text being translated. If affinity and naturalization are based on the common class consciousness, posited by the translation, between the French and Catalan readers of *Les mystères de Paris*, resistant difference is enacted to reveal the translator's own aesthetic preferences and political inclinations. The Spanish version of *Les mystères de Paris* achieves its own distinctive style by Cortada's free departure from literalness and resort to paraphrase. On the other hand, Cortada's own views are introduced into the foreign original as a conscious design to counteract some of the novel's political analyses and proposals (most particularly, Sue's utopian socialism). To impose his own style on the French original and to dispute the novel's politics, Cortada takes on the role of the author and fights Sue for authority over the text. As Steiner says, "Where power relations determinate the conditions of meeting, linguistic exchange becomes a duel."[25]

Cortada's stylistic preferences are manifested first in a greater reliance on the narrator's voice to tell the story. In the translation, narration is often preeminent over dialogue, makes up for omissions, and sustains creative drives. Cortada transforms the fragmented style and the predominance of dialogue characteristic of the original (and of most serial novels where the writer is paid by the line) into a text dominated by indirect speech and subordinate sentences. The narrator in *Los misterios de París* also summarizes events and information, avoids repetitions, or adds a brief remark. The different styles of the author and that of the translator are also observed in Cortada's frequent editing of *Les mystères de Paris*. Cortada freely suppresses fragments of the original text (sometimes it is just a few words or sentences; at other times, long or short paragraphs; and on one occasion, an entire chapter, "Une intimité forcée") or adds to it without warning his readers of the changes he is effecting in Sue's novel.[26] Cortada's additions tend to compensate for previous cuts; omissions create the narrative occasion for—as well as require—the intervention of the translator to bridge the gaps between the chapters and fill in the narrative void he himself has produced. It is important to note that, in a few instances which I discuss later, omissions are normally hermeneutically irrelevant.[27] A lot of this editing is probably related to the publishing requirements and conditions at the base of Cortada's task. The publisher's concern for the high production costs of Sue's extensive novel and the translator's usually small fee likely prompted Cortada to abbreviate and condense the original text.[28] Suppressions such as that of the comic and popular episodes about the tricks the artist Cabrion plays on the good-hearted and picturesque M. Pipelet are, however, hard to explain.[29] But we can affirm that the stylistic changes, and most suppressions and additions that characterize the Spanish version of *Les mystères de Paris*, all point to Cortada's dislike and editing of Sue's loose and often repetitive writing. Cortada's rendition of the final lines of the chapter entitled "Flor de María" ("Fleur-de-Marie") show the translation's distinctively concise style of narration against the French original's diffuseness of detail:

> Une demi-heure après, Mme. D'Harville, accompagnée de M. de Saint-Remy, emmenait chez elle la jeune orpheline, à qui elle avait caché la mort de sa mère.
> Le jour même, un homme de confiance de Mme d'Harville, après avoir été visiter, rue de la Barillerie, la misérable demeure de Jeanne Duport, et avoir recueilli sur cette digne femme les meilleurs renseignements, loua aussitôt, sur le quai de l'École, deux grandes chambres et un cabinet bien aéré, meubla en deux heures ce modeste mais salubre logis, et, grâce aux ressources instantanées du Temple, le soir même Jeanne Duport fut transportée dans cette demeure, où elle trouva ses enfants et une excellente garde-malade.
> Le même homme de confiance fut chargé de réclamer et de faire enterrer le corps de la Lorraine lorsqu'elle succomberait à sa maladie.
> Après avoir conduit et installé chez elle Mlle de Fermont, Mme d'Harville partit aussitôt por Asnières, accompagnée de M. de Saint-Remy, afin d'aller chercher Fleur-de-Marie et de la conduire chez Rodolphe.

> A la media hora la marquesa acompañada de Mr. de Saint-Remy trasladaba a su casa a la joven huérfana a quien había ocultado la muerte de su madre. En el mismo día por orden de la marquesa se alquiló y amuebló un modesto y salubre piso a donde fue trasladada Juana que encontró allí a sus hijos y una enfermera. Asimismo, reclamó para hacerla enterrar a su tiempo el cuerpo de la Lorena. Cuando Clemencia hubo colocado en su casa a Clara Fermont dirigióse al punto hacia Asnieres en compañía de Saint-Remy para llevar a Flor de María a casa de Rodolfo.[30]

Some of Cortada's additions to or omissions from the French original are directly related to the translator's political quarrel with Sue and, consequently, signal distinctive hermeneutic displacements away from, and often against, the author's text. In these occasions, the translation departs from the French original either to highlight the Christian doctrine already present in *Les mystères de Paris* but sometimes obscured by Sue's political radicalism, or to censor directly the novel's explicit association of the Church and the patriarchal system to social evil. The emphasis on the Christian meaning of social reconciliation over and against the novel's socialist notions of brotherhood is achieved mostly by the explication of connoted meanings which are implied, but not developed, in the French text. The Christian overinterpretation shown in *Los misterios de París* is based on an inflationary translation that actualizes certain readings of Sue's novel at the expense of a socially minded interpretation.[31] In the key chapter entitled "El castigo" ("Punition"), the employees of the evil Jacques Ferrand talk about a priest's charitable and honest qualities. The goodness of the priest, and, consequently, the sharp contrast between his actions and those of Ferrand's, is reinforced in the French text by the likening of his actions to those of a M. Champion, also known as "le Petit-Manteau-Bleu," a Parisian figure well known for his extraordinary generosity:

> Oh! ça, c'est vrai, et de celui-là faut parler sérieusement et avec respect! Il est aussi bon et aussi charitable que le Petit-Manteau-Bleu, et quand on dit ça d'un homme, il est jugé.[32]

The translation of the reference to a Parisian figure foreign to most, if not all, of Cortada's readers would have created several communicative noises that could affect the reading of these lines. First, since M. Champion was a layman, Cortada's reader could associate the generosity of this popular figure with the novel's utopian socialist ideas of social justice. In this possible interpretation, the political "charity" of M. Champion, being the measure of all goodwill, is not only comparable but also superior to the Christian charity of the priest. Against this dangerous reading, Cortada's translation moves, first, to eliminate the foreign reference that might carry the message he objects to. Then, it introduces a meaning absent from the original that stresses the reconciliatory function of religion in a class society:

> Eso es verdad, y del cura es menester hablar seriamente y con respeto, porque es muy bueno y muy caritativo, y ricos y pobres todos le elogian.[33]

In another example, Cortada's rendition of the words *la mère Ponisse* uses to address a police detective (Mr. Borel) emphasizes the Christian signification of the moral wickedness of *l'ogresse*:

> c'est bien à votre service..., dit gracieusement l'ogresse en s'inclinant avec déférence.
>
> Mr. Borel, soy muy servidora vuestra, dijo aquella grandísima culebra, adulándole con gracia y deferencia.[34]

Cortada, who in a clearly deficient transfer of meaning had previously translated *"ogresse"* as *"tabernera,"* expresses now the criminal connotations implied in *"ogresse"* and lost in *"tabernera"* by emphasizing her moral falseness and hypocritical behavior toward the police agent. To reinforce the *ogresse*'s hypocritical "deference," "s'inclinant" is substituted by "adulándole" and is complemented with "gracia," which is used in the original to modify the verb "to say." Furthermore, Cortada adds to the characterization of "la tía Colasa" the attribute of being a snake—nonexistent in the original—which not only overdetermines her falseness, but also frames the *ogresse*'s evil in explicit Christian symbology: she is the devil.

The actualization in *Los misterios de París* of the Christian worldview over the novel's social and political analysis of conflict and evil sometimes requires the decisive intervention of Cortada against the French original. These interventions, which amount to actual censorship of the novel to protect the authority of the Church, are a radical modification of *Les mystères de Paris*. In these intrusions Cortada makes Sue's text yield a meaning alien to it, a meaning that does not translate the foreign text but rather carries the translator's own notion of how the story should be told. There are just a few of these interventions, but they are all direct challenges against Sue's control over the story, moments when the translator becomes the true author of the text we read. One case of brief intervention that radically modifies the meaning of the original and transforms *Les mystères de Paris* into the translator's novel is Cortada's addition of a Christian epigraph to accompany (or, better, to oppose) Sue's quotation of the penal code at the beginning of chapter 5 (part VI) entitled "Les victimes d'un abus de confiance." The reproduction by Sue of the articles 406 and 408 of the French penal code aims at both showing the ineffective and insufficient legal regulation of criminal activity and encouraging the political revision of the law. The original intention of Sue's epigraph, however, is deeply transformed when the translator juxtaposes the following quotation: "La caridad del alma vale para los que sufren tanto como la mejor limosna" [For those who suffer, charity of the soul is as valuable as the most generous donation].[35] To Sue's political denunciation of the light punishment of crime (low fines and short-time prison terms), Cortada opposes the supposedly always comforting Christian charity; to Sue's call for action, the passive acceptance of suffering. Sue's epigraph inserts the story of the failure of the penal code to protect innocent victims from harm within a sociopolitical context of debate. In the translated version, Sue's original epigraph is an excuse to assert a higher notion of justice. In *Los misterios de París*, there is no need for social discussion—just a confirmation of faith.[36]

The emergence of the translator's own novel against Sue's can be better perceived in Cortada's rewriting of an episode of *Les mystères de Paris* in which Sue discusses the effect of bourgeois morality on sexual conduct. Cortada's intervention affects, in particular, Sue's digression on the unfair treatment and condemnation by society of unwed mothers, especially those who, due to economic hardship, have to abandon their newborn babies or, in extreme cases, are driven to kill them. Sue, influenced by utopian socialist readings, criticizes society's lack of assistance to women in this predicament and, more particularly, the moral hypocrisy that blames women for the illegitimate births while excusing the men. For the French author, society tolerates and even promotes men's irresponsible sexual behavior while injustly inflicting heavy punishments on those women seduced by them.

4: FROM TRANSLATION TO IMITATION 93

Sue carries out the accusation of moral hypocrisy by presenting the fictive trial of a young man—who has impregnated and abandoned a beautiful and poor young woman—who defends his irresponsible conduct before a jury of bourgeois *pro-hommes*. The young man's self-justification reproduces the male chauvinistic principles that rule *de facto* in a patriarchal society. The fragment modified by Cortada is part of the young man's sexist but socially prevalent reasoning on why women—and not men—should be blamed for the birth of illegitimate children and, on some occasions, their infanticide. Cortada's translation does include the sympathetic verdict of the jury in favor of exculpating the young man, but clearly signals his uneasiness with the whole digression, and his authorial disapproval of Sue's handling of the issue. In the following lines Sue explains the reaction of the jury to the young man's defense of his acts:

—J'ai quelque chose d'important à révéler à la justice.
—Parlez
—Messieurs les jurés.
"Cette malheureuse était vertueuse et pure, c'est vrai...
"Je l'ai séduite, c'est encore vrai...
"Je lui ai fait un enfant, c'est toujours vrai...
"Après quoi, comme elle était blonde, je l'ai complètement abandonnée pour une autre qui était brune, c'est de plus en plus vrai.
"Mais en cela j'ai usé d'un droit imprescriptible, d'un droit sacré que la société me reconnaît et m'accorde...
—Le fait est que ce garçon est complètement dans droit, se diront tout bas les jurés les uns aux autres. Il n'y a pas de loi qui defénde de faire un enfant à une jeune fille blonde et de l'abandonner ensuite pour une jeune fille brune. C'est tout bonnement un gaillard...
—Maintenant, messieurs, les jurés, cette malheureuse prétend avoir tué son enfant...je dirai même notre enfant...
"Parce que je l'ai abandonnée
"Parce que, se trouvant seule et dans la plus profonde misère, elle s'est épouvantée, elle a perdue la tête....
"Mais je trouve ces raisons-là pitoyables, permettez-moi de vous le dire, messieurs les jurés.
. . .
"Est-ce que mademoiselle ne pouvait pas, au moment critique, se rendre à temps chez le commissaire de son quartier, lui faire sa déclaration de... honte, afin d'être autorisée à déposer son enfant aux Enfants-Trouvés?
"Est-ce qu'enfin mademoiselle, pendant que je faisais la poule à l'estaminet, en attendant mon autre maîtresse, ne pouvait pas trouver moyen de se tirer d'affaire par un procédé moins sauvage?
. . .
"Que diable! Ce n'est pas tout, pour une jeune fille, que de perdre l'honneur, de braver le mépris, l'infamie, et de porter un enfant illégitime neuf moins dons son

sein... il lui faut encore l'élever, cet enfant! Le soigner, le nourrir, lui donner un état, en faire enfin un honnête homme comme son père, ou une honnête fille qui ne se débauche pas comme sa mère... Car enfin la maternité a des devoirs sacrés, que diable! Et les misérables qui les foulent aux pieds, ces devoirs sacrés, sont des mères dénaturées, qui méritent un châtiment exemplaire et terrible...

. . .

—Ce monsieur envisage la question sous un point de vue très moral, dira d'un air paterne quelque bonnetier enrichi ou quelque vieil usurier déguisé en chef du jury; il a fait, pardieu! Ce que nous aurions tous fait à sa place, car elle est fort gentille, cette petit blondinette, quoiqu' un peu palôtte... Ce gaillard-là, comme dit Joconde, 'a courtisé la brune et la blonde'; il n'y a pas de loi qui le défende. Quant à cette malheureuse, après tout, c'est sa faute! Pourquoi ne s'est-elle pas defendue? Elle n'aurait pas eu à commettre un crime...un...crime monstrueux qui fait...qui fait...rougir la société...jusque dans ses fondements."

Tengo que revelar cosas importantes a la justicia; esa desgraciada, señores jurados, es cierto que era virtuosa y pura, es cierto que yo la seduje, es cierto que la hice madre y es cierto que la dejé por otra; mas en todo eso no he hecho más que usar de un derecho imprescriptible que la sociedad me concede. El hecho es, se dirán en voz baja los jurados unos a otros, que ese joven está en su derecho, pues no hay ley que prohiba tratar amores con una joven y luego dejarla por otra. Al fin ese hombre no es más que un joven alegre de cascos. Ahora, señores jurados, puede continuar el joven, esa mujer supone que a muerto a su hijo porque yo la abandoné, porque viéndose sola y envuelta en la miseria se espantó y no supo lo que hacía. . . . Mas todas estas razones, señores jurados, me parecen, con vuestro perdón sea dicho, muy miserables. ¿Por qué no podía esa señorita irse a casa del comisario del cuartel y revelarle el secreto, a fin de que se la autorizara a colocar al hijo en la casa de los espósitos?

Todo esto y mucho más puede decir ante los jurados el joven en cuestión, y todos los individuos de ese tribunal exclamarán que ha hecho bien, que ni puede acriminársele, y castigársele mucho menos, porque no hay ley que prohíba lo que él ha hecho.[37]

In Cortada's version, the jury also exculpates the young man, but it does so for different reasons than those in Sue's text. First, the verdict is given by a socially undetermined jury, not by recognizable entrepreneurs whose dubious morality accompanies their economic success. The translator's decision to eliminate the traits that identify the jury as successful members of society softens the attack on the legitimacy and authority of the patriarchal system by protecting the integrity of its central institution: the bourgeois. Moreover, not only does Cortada's translation avoid an explicit articulation of the jury's motive for exculpating the young man (that is, the lascivious appetites and sexist views of the bourgeois), but also Sue's denunciation of the moral hypocrisy of the bourgeoisie, and his observation about the lust and greed at the root of the bourgeois existence, are effectively canceled. Cortada's omissions of the paragraphs that insist on the moral hypocrisy and libertinage of both the young man and the jurors also produces an ambiguous reading of the fact that the young man's irresponsible actions are not punishable by any law. In the French original the jurors and the law agree with the young man's defense of his innocence, and, consequently, the crime itself is denied; in *Los misterios de París*, the jury simply seems unable to punish the young man. The French reader is left perplexed and indignant over the denial of moral and criminal responsibility of philanderers and uneasy about the moral values that govern society; Cortada's reader exonerates the jury and, thus, patriarchal society, and blames a flawed legislation.

Cortada's determined application of authorial control over *Les mystères de Paris* culminates in the creation of a textual site where the translator addresses his readers on his own terms and, on some occasions, directly challenges Sue's authority over the story. Cortada creates this space in the paratext provided by the footnotes. In *Les mystères de Paris* the main purpose of the footnotes is to anticipate the reaction of polemical readers and their ideological resistance to the author's propositions. Aware of the controversial nature of the socioeconomic issues brought out by Prince Rodolphe's incursions in the Parisian underworld, Sue tries to answer some of the possible objections posed by the reader against the novel's political positionings by providing in the footnotes documentary and authoritative support for his claims. Following Sue's lead, Cortada adds his own "Translator's notes"—"Notas del Traductor"—and uses some of them to dispute the authenticity of Sue's depiction of social disorder, and to express his own notion of it. Cortada makes a point of distinguishing between the footnotes that belong to the French original and those he himself authors in order to exert his authority directly to his readers. The footnotes he translates are assigned an alphabetical notation—(a), (b), (c), etc.—while those added to the translation are given numbers. Cortada pens a total of thirty-nine of these translator's notes, and, in all of them, the translator becomes author, and the translated text becomes his own distinctive and manifest creation.

Some of the footnotes authored by Cortada contain information his readers need to understand the unfamiliar conventions and customs of French society—such as the habits of the Parisian washerwomen, French dinner habits, or a clarification of what the "Bons Pauvres" [Deserving Poor] are.[38] Others contain Cortada's comments on his rendition of a certain word.[39] But ten of these translator's notes are conceived exclusively as sites where Sue's authority over the text is overtly challenged and, on some occasions, revoked. In these translator's notes Cortada's fight over authorial control of *Les mystères de Paris* sometimes hides behind meek expressions such as "we believe" or "we cannot claim to be [experts like Sue]" to openly challenge the authenticity of Sue's depiction of French society.[40]

However, Cortada's pressure on the foreign text and his desire to overrule Sue's authority increases with Sue's progressive political radicalization of the story and culminates in the final chapter of the novel. In *Los misterios de París*, "El dedo de Dios" ("Le doight de Dieu")—the chapter that tells of the popular orgy that precedes the execution of Mme. Martial and her daughter, and frames Prince Rodolphe's departure from Paris—contains a lengthy translator's note where Cortada finally drops the pretension of humility and ignorance before the authority of Sue and openly arrogates for himself the right to give the reader his own version of the ills that afflict society. It is highly significant that Cortada's most aggressive attack against Sue's authority over the story comes right at the end of the novel (signaling the culmination of the progressive assault by the translator on the foreign original) and concerns an episode organized around the barriers of containment that in *Les mystères de Paris* distinguish between the deserving poor and low-class criminals. In the French original, the responsibility for the street riots and moral baseness depicted in the last chapter of the novel is exclusively assigned again to the group of criminals from la Cité.[41] Against Sue's exclusive association of social violence with the isolated group of felons, Cortada affirms that his own observation of contemporary French society allows him to contradict Sue's representation of social disorder. The translator, then, proceeds to give his alternative version of the story. In Cortada's representation of the moral viciousness of Parisian life, there is no mention of the criminals of la Cité; on the contrary, he depicts a wide participation of all classes in these licentious acts:

> Hallándonos en París, y casualmente en los Campos Elíseos, en la noche del 17 de septiembre del año 1843, entramos con cuatro o cinco compatricios nuestros en el *Salón Maville*. . . . [Allí] una buena orquesta . . . dirige los pasos de los que bailan entre otras cosas el *cancan*, danza . . . cuyos pormenores son un grotesco ridículo y salvaje; pero tan indecente, impúdico y repugnante que ofende la vista del hombre de costumbres más libres. . . . Autorizaban con su presencia esa triste escena de soez libertinage algunos empleados de policía y guardias municipales, y los concurrentes del baile pertenecían a clase muy mucho superior a la de Nicolás Martial y comparsa. Es un auténtico y lastimoso testimonio de la inconcebible desmoralización de París, y nos hizo concebir la consoladora idea de que nuestra patria dista aun infinitamente de ese estado de espantoso libertinage.[42]

> [Being in Paris and by chance in the Champs Elysées the night of the seventeenth of September of 1843, together with four or five fellow countrymen we went into the *Salon Maville*. . . . [There] a good orchestra . . . was leading the steps of those dancers doing, among other things, the cancan, a dance . . . the details of which are ludicrously grotesque and uncivilized, but so indecent, shameless, and repugnant that it offends the eye of the most tolerant man. . . . Such a disgraceful scene of crude dissipation was sanctioned by the presence of members of the

4: FROM TRANSLATION TO IMITATION 97

police, and the audience belonged to a class far superior to that of Nicolás Marcial and his friends. It is an authentic and shameful testimony to the inconceivable demoralization of Paris and made us consider the comforting idea that our nation is still infinitely distant from such state of dreadful dissipation.]

The major hermeneutic displacements that characterize Cortada's translation of *Les mystères de Paris* can be recognized in this view of Parisian life. In Cortada's representation of Paris, Les Champs Elysées (a popular gathering place where all social classes mingled and engaged in immoral actions) replaces la Cité (the gathering place of marginal criminals) as the site of social evil, and it does so for the same reason that the socially marked *argot* from la Cité is eliminated in the translation. For Cortada, Sue's confined space of crime—la Cité—is a misrepresentation of the social problems of Paris, because it creates reassuring barriers of containment against class conflict. As author of the footnote, Cortada's remark on the spread of social anarchy among members of all social classes in Paris is consistent with his and his readers' observations of the wide participation of all social groups in the revolutionary movements and social riots recently concluded with the bombardment of Barcelona by government troups. Similarly, Cortada's mention of the involvement of figures of authority in Parisian social disorder brings to mind the participation of the local police [*milicia urbana*] in Barcelona's uprisings. The hermeneutic displacements effected by Cortada to emphasize either affinity or resistant difference with the foreign text add up to point out the centrality of Catalonia's own form of social disorder in the literary imagination of the translation.

In Cortada's version of *Les mystères de Paris*, the foreign story is pressured by the familiar and recent revolutionary experience of Catalonia, and in the half-our and half–someone else's word of the translation we perceive the emergence of an autochthonous writing where Sue's representation is challenged and history constrains romance. Cortada's discontinuous assertion of his authority over the author's results in the embryonic emergence of the translator's own novel, or, rather, the insinuation of a novel authored by the translator about his readers' own society. The translator's fight for control of *Les mystères de Paris* creates the need of a separated fiction that could account for the peculiarities of Spanish society: the "infinite" distance that Cortada tells us still exists between social disorder in France and in Spain.[43] From Cortada's translation and, more particularly, from these translator's notes, arise the affirmation of difference (Spain is not quite like France) and, consequently, the need for an autochthonous fiction to give form to this otherness. Larra was right: with the exercise of authority came the realization of a different and autochthonous text.

Affinity or difference? Cortada's text is caught between the two poles unable to express fully its meaning. George Steiner has said that the dialectic of embodiment entails the possibility that we may be consumed: "Acts of translation add to our means; we come to incarnate alternative energies and resources of feeling, but we may be mastered and made lame by what we have imported."[44] It was in the hands of the Spanish imitators to defeat the masters, or, in other words, to bring home definitively the foreign novel.

Translation as Autochthonous Writing

The amount of autochthonous writing implied in most mid-nineteenth-century translations was openly acknowledged by the literatos who often added the expression *"traducida libremente"* [freely translated] after the title of a French novel. Larra's understanding of what it means to translate a foreign work clearly shows the blurred borderlines that separated translation from *original* writing in his own literary practice and that of his contemporaries: "To translate a comedy well is to adopt someone else's idea and plan that may have some connection to customs of the country for which it is being translated, and put them in words and dialogue as if it was being originally written. Consequently, and in general, to translate a comedy well it is necessary to be able to write original ones."[45] What may simply seem Larra's self-justification against those who accused him of plagiarism is, in fact, Larra's unambiguous formulation of the literary practice that dominated in Spain during those years. Itamar Even-Zohar has argued that, where a translated literature holds a central position—that is, when translations are a significant innovative force—"no clear cut distinction is maintained between 'original' and 'translated' writings, and often it is the leading writers . . . who produce the most conspicuous or appreciated translations."[46] Certainly, in mid-nineteenth-century Spain, under a translator's name appears an incipient novelist; and under a translated work we recognize the effort of a whole generation to create an autochthonous writing for the novel.[47]

The blurring of the distinction between a writing proclaimed to be *original* and the task of translating and imitating could be emblematically exemplified in Ayguals de Izco's and Fernán Caballero's literary practice. As we already know, Ayguals is the author of a Spanish imitation of *Les Mystères de Paris* (*María o La hija de un jornalero*), as well as of the French translation of that imitation (*Marie ou La victime d'un moine*). Now, we could rightly ask, when was Ayguals translating? When he translated *María* into French or, on the contrary, when he wrote the Spanish version of *Les mystères de Paris* (*María o La hija de un jornalero*)? A not-so-different case of the blurring of *original* and translating practices is also present in Fernán Caballero's work. As is well known but commonly disregarded, *La familia de Alvareda* was originally written in German, *Elia* and *La Gaviota* in French. Thus, the novels by Fernán Caballero, which are traditionally considered to be the first examples of the *novela original española* in the nineteenth century, are, in fact, translations into Spanish.[48]

There was no way out of translation and imitation in mid-nineteenth-century Spanish literary practices.[49] In 1840, Ramón de Mesonero Romanos expressed his generation's clear and painful understanding of the central role played by translation in the displaced nature of Spanish cultural life: "Our country, once so original, is now nothing more than a translated nation."[50] A translated and translating *nation*, indeed. However, it was precisely in the de-centered cultural consciousness of translation—in that voice both alien and indigenous—that cultural and historical processes managed to find a voice in Spain.

5
Imitation and the Autochthonous Novel:
Los misterios de Barcelona

> Barcelona was on top of a volcano.
> —Víctor Balaguer

IMITATIONS RESORT TO STRATEGIES OF TRANSFERENCE SIMILAR TO THOSE used in translations. They set up both affinities and resistance differences with respect to the original text being appropriated, but, more important, imitations take on the translator's desire to supersede the authority of the original author and set out to represent, against the original text, the differences that constitute peripheral societies. Imitation is a freer exercise than translation, one where the autochthonous elements of the story take precedence over the original; one where even the loosest notion of truthfulness to the model is replaced by the necessity to betray it—the inevitable twist of displaced ideas.[1] Nicasio Milá de la Roca's imitation, *Los misterios de Barcelona* (1844), was one of those texts that took up the task of narrating Spain both by means of, and against, the foreign imagination of *Les mystères de Paris*.[2]

From the beginning we observe the contradictory intentions that organized Milá's *Los misterios de Barcelona*. In the prologue to his novel, the author declares that he wants to write Barcelona's own mysteries: "quiero regalarte, Barcelona querida, tus misterios . . . escribir los misterios de una ciudad que tantos y tan raros los encierra" [I want to give to you, dear Barcelona, your mysteries . . . to write the mysteries of a city that contains so many and strange ones].[3] Milá's commitment, on the one hand, to Sue's form of narration—"mysteries"—and his determination, on the other, to represent Barcelona's society produce the incongruity between the form and the content of the imitation, that is, between the foreign morphology and the autochthonous object of representation that characterizes Milá's writing. Milá's intention to articulate and explain the not-quite-so-similar sociohistorical conditions of Barcelona puts constant pressure on his French model and results in the corrosion of Sue's narrative formula. Holding a full authorial position, Milá freely adapts the foreign writing to Barcelona's social existence and makes Sue's imagination yield to the expression of local aspirations. The pressure of local history on the foreign romance is, however, insufficient to produce full autochthonous forms of imagination, and the radical displacements *Les mystères de Paris* undergoes in Milá's hand add up to produce an unfinished and truncated writing. Sue's foreign plot and Milá's mimetic forces—or, in Roberto Schwarz's words, Barcelona's "different order of things"—resist and undermine each other, sustaining and, at the same time, limiting Milá's autochthonous writing.[4]

It is the compositional incongruity of Milá's imitation that we will analyze in this chapter. We will approach the unbalanced writing of *Los misterios de Barcelona* not as the faulty actualization of a dominant literary form, but, on the contrary, as the imitation's literary achievement.[5] I contend that the defective structure of *Los misterios de Barcelona* is the result of the strength of the mimetic forces that drive Milá's writing, and that its shortcomings are the product of Milá's ideological investment in a foreign literature of social consolation. There is no parodic writing of *Les mystères de Paris* in Milá's novel, nor the conscious design to subvert foreign literary worlds which characterizes late-nineteenth-century novels.[6] However, I believe that the literary incongruency of Milá's imitation reveals the processes of literary creation that are at the base of the half-ours and half–someone else's writing of the mid-nineteenth-century Spanish novel.

From Romance to History

The "sense des foules" [sense of the masses] that characterizes Sue's representation of the modern city in *Les mystères de Paris* is clearly the model for Milá's depiction of the social costs of industrialization and Barcelona's ongoing political revolution. As in its French model, the city is the imaginary center of the novel, and not a mere picturesque landscape or background for the plot.[7] The exploration of the collective existence of the city is the organizing principle of Milá's novel and, as in the case of Paris in *Les mystères de Paris*, Barcelona is the imaginary location of social disorder. The private and public spaces of Milá's Barcelona delineate a Parisian-like geography of evil, a space populated by the secrets (or mysteries) of individual and collective guilt—that "nocturnal castle" where space and vice mirror each other, and where "the depths of vice are, topographically speaking, the lowest part, the underworld."[8] Taverns, hospitals, brothels, miserable lodges, shops, private households, and so on make up the city as a network of interconnected places where individual and social evil, as well as the possibility of redemption, are inscribed.

5: IMITATION AND THE AUTOCHTHONOUS NOVEL

But Milá's desire to tell Barcelona's own secrets puts pressure on romance and on Sue's presentation of the city. The great contrast that exists between the first paragraph of Milá's novel and that of *Les mystères de Paris* exemplifies from the beginning the different conceptions that govern the construction of the fictive city in the French original and its imitation and, more generally, the different imaginations that dictate them. Sue's first paragraph sets his story of social evil and redemption as a tale of exotic criminals and alien social spaces. The Paris the reader is going to vicariously explore through the adventures of Prince Rodolphe is an unfamiliar and often threatening city and, consequently, the site of excitement and fear. In Sue's novel, the mysterious city is modeled on the haunted castle of gothic romance and the swamps and jungles of the adventure novels, and its criminals—the unknown urban barbarians—on the ghosts, wild beasts, and humanlike creatures that populate those fictions:

> Un *tapis-franc*, en argot de vol et de meurtre, signifie un estaminet ou un cabaret du plus bas étage.
> Un repris de justice, qui, dans cette langue immonde, s'apelle un *ogre*, ou une femme de même dégradation, qui s'apelle une *ogresse*, tiennent ordinairement ces tavernes, hantées par le rebut de la population parisienne; forçats libérés, escrocs, voleurs, assassins y abondent.
> Un crime a-t-il été commis, la police jette, si cela se peut dire, son filet dans cette fange; presque toujours elle y prend les coupables.
> Ce début annonce au lecteur qu'il doit assister à de sinistres scènes; s'il y consent, il pénétrera dans des régions horribles, inconnues; des types hideux, effrayantes, fourmilleront dans ces cloaques impurs commes des reptiles dans les marais.[9]
> [A *tapis-franc*, in the slang of the murderers and thieves of Paris, means a smoking-house or inn of the very lowest class. A discharged convict, who in this foul language is called Ogre, or a woman of the same class who is called an Ogresse, commonly keeps a tavern of this kind, resorted to by the refuse of the Parisian population: liberated galleys slaves, sharpers, robbers, and assassins congregate there. If a crime has been committed, the police casts its net in this receptacle of filth, and almost always the guilty one is caught. This beginning announces to the reader that he will witness sinister scenes; if he consents, he will enter horrible, unknown regions; hideous, dreadful types will swarm in these impures cesspits just like reptiles in the swamps.]

Following this model, in the initial paragraph of *Los misterios de Barcelona* Milá introduces the city that will be the focus of his and his readers' exploration, and places the main hero right at the center of the scene to reassure the reader with the presence of a benign and powerful authority even before the first sign of trouble appears in the story. But in Milá's fictional Barcelona there are no exotic social landscapes, lurid criminals, or out-of-bounds territory. The thrill of entering the den of criminality at night is replaced by the reassuring light of a summer morning, a popular and highly frequented site—the hill of Montjuïc—and the cheerfulness of a young man who is rushing to join some friends for a hunting day-trip:

> El sol describiendo un grandioso círculo rojo como una ascua ardiente levantábase ufano de las apacibles aguas del Mediterráneo, deslizándose majestuoso por un cielo puro cuyo azulado campo no empañaba el menor celaje; el astro radiante, a medida que se alejaba de las aguas, tornaba en refulgente amarillo su rojo color, dorando las hermosas torres y almenas de Barcelona, y matizando los verdes arbustos de la montaña de Monjuich, entre los cuales brillaban cual finas y castizas perlas los gotas del nocturno relente. El esplendente pabellón de Isabel 2ª ondulaba en las elevadas astas de Monjuich, de la Ciudadela y del fuerte de Atarazanas, mientras que las baterías de estas plazas saludaban por la 5ª vez los días de la Reina madre Dª María Cristina de Borbón.
>
> Un joven de 26 años . . . armado con una escopeta de dos tiros, y precedido de un hermoso podenco, trepaba con paso acelerado la cuesta de la cantera de S. Beltrán.[10]
>
> [Like a burning ember, the sun described a gorgeous red circle and was proudly coming up from the calm Mediterranean Sea, majestically gliding along a pure and blue sky with not a single cloud in sight. The radiant star was turning resplendently yellow as it rose from the waters, thus painting in gold the beautiful towers and battlements of Barcelona, and blending together the green bushes of Monjuich mountain, which were sparkling with the fine and pure pearls of the cold night air. The magnificent flag of Isabel II was flying over the high flagstaffs of Monjuich, the Citadel, and the Atarazanas fort, while the batteries in these fortifications were for the fifth time saluting the anniversary of the queen mother María Cristina de Borbón.
>
> A young man of 26 years of age . . . armed with a shotgun and preceded by a beautiful hound, was climbing up at a brisk pace the slope to St. Beltrán's quarry.]

Milá's fictive city has its privileged representation not in the arcane venues of low-class criminality (la Cité), but, on the contrary, in the popular Montjuïc mountain, an emblematic site of Barcelona's history frequented by all social classes. The exoticism of the gothic and wild landscapes characteristic of Sue's novel has been replaced in the imitation by a space of collective significance with old and recent history. Milá's Barcelona is both a familiar and an ideal space for Milá's readers: a highly rhetorical description of a well-known place and, at the same time, the peaceful setting of a dream world.

The initial focus of Milá's novel on Montjuïc is indicative, as the beginning of Sue's novel also is, of both the object of exploration of *Los misterios de Barcelona* and the literary project of its author. Montjuïc, with its military fortress on top, was at the time a space deeply marked by the city's recent political conflicts. It had been the site of riots and negotiations

5: IMITATION AND THE AUTOCHTHONOUS NOVEL

and, more important, a solid supporter in Catalonia of the conservative monarchy of the Regent Queen, María Cristina, against both the Carlist army and the city's radical liberals. Thus, as its beginning signifies, Milá's novel is not interested in exploring the alien and riveting urban refuge of Barcelona's low-class criminality, nor is Milá writing only a romance. His novel is not so much about exploring unknown territories, but rather about revisiting recent history; the city Milá's imitation is going to narrate is that of recent political conflicts, and the mysteries it will reveal are the causes of class struggle.

Accordingly, in Milá's romance, the main hero, Nemesio Torrellas—"the hunter" who appears in the initial description of the city—is not a mysterious foreigner, as Rodolphe is in Paris, but a top commanding officer of the warship "Isabel 2ª" with close ties to the city.[11] He is the fictional young officer of a real ship which, in the summer of 1836, was anchored (just as its fictional counterpart would be one year before) outside the port of Barcelona to show the support of the government for the city's conservative liberals, and to reinforce the government's military presence in a city agitated again by social turmoil.[12] In a narrative movement that takes the reader from the military fortresses (where the flags of the queen mother reassuringly flutter) to the hunter, the novel indicates its hero and its task: the young officer will be directly responsible for the safeguard of both the conservative order of María Cristina (and her daughter, Isabel II) and Milá's dream of conformist stability. In Milá's initial description of Barcelona, Montjuïc overlooks the entire city (from the Atarazanas to the Ciudadela) with gentle and protective authority signaling *Los misterios de Barcelona*'s commitment to both the history of the city and conservative liberalism.

The endeavor to write romance within the coordinates of history is at the base of one of the most important formal dislocations effected by Milá in *Los misterios de Barcelona*. Unlike *Les mystères de Paris*, where the plot of the novel and France's recent history of political unrest are dissociated (separation signified in Rodolphe being the sovereign prince of a German state visiting Paris), in Milá's novel, romance is inscribed within specific local and historical events. Milá demystifies evil and carries out his desire to write Barcelona's own mysteries by radically modifying Sue's strategy of framing romance within current social issues. Milá's imitation inserts social conflict within the particular network of socioeconomic interests that constitute Barcelona's and Catalonia's reality, and invests the miscellany of news characteristic of Sue's "social chatter" with the journalistic purpose of re-creating the present as both history and current events. Milá's novel appropriates the journalistic purpose of giving "each *event* its proper status in current affairs, history, and memory" and plunges its reader into the familiar landscape and time of Catalonia's social existence.[13] Therefore,

Los misterios de Barcelona depicts the collective existence of the city not only as the moral geography of evil or as a map of pending social issues, but also as a social space being shaped and unsettled by specific historical processes and political events. Ayguals de Izco had a name for the specific historical consciousness that characterized not only his and Milá's rewriting of *Les mystères de Paris* but also that of other mid-nineteenth-century Spanish imitators of Sue. He called it "historia-novela" [history-novel]: the journalistic relation of "the major events that took place . . . during the period of the Estatuto Real" and its transformation into "contemporary chronicles."[14]

The transformation of *Les mystères de Paris'* miscellany of social news into the historically based fiction of the imitation is both a literary achievement and a failure. On the one hand, and as Cortada would do within the particular constraints of a translation, the relation of recent social episodes characteristic of *Los misterios de Barcelona* succeeds in transforming Sue's exotic criminality into the household threats of the civil war, social insurgence, and political strife between conservative and progressive liberals of the 1835–39 period. Moreover, Milá's chronicle of events achieves a level of discourse integration unknown in *Les mystères de Paris*. Milá abandons Sue's resort to footnotes and digressions to connect the fiction to social issues and current events, and transforms the structural segregation of plot and society that characterizes his model into an historically based fiction.[15] The level of coordination achieved between plot and history by Milá can be observed from the first pages of the novel. From the beginning romance is unequivocally inserted within the history of political violence and generalized social unrest which accompanied the transformation of the Spanish state from an absolutist monarchy to a liberal one.

The story begins with the romantic situation of a hero rescuing a young woman in distress. The fullness of meaning and the uneventfulness that characterizes Barcelona at the dawn of both a new day and Milá's story under the regime of the queen mother is soon disrupted by a young woman's suicide attempt that melodramatically illustrates the deceptive nature of appearances and, precipitating the start of the narration, leads the reader back into history. The plot is immediately inscribed within recent history by the simple procedure of providing the exact day of the attempted suicide and successful rescue. The opening of Milá's romance is inserted within the highly recognizable calendric time and landscape of Barcelona in the summer of 1835. The suicide attempt is set in Montjuïc in the early hours of July 24, 1835, exactly one day after news of the violent clash in Reus— a city in southeast Catalonia—between liberals and Carlists arrived in Barcelona, and one day before Barcelona's frustration with the inability of the government to stop the Carlist forces and its slowness to implement

5: IMITATION AND THE AUTOCHTHONOUS NOVEL 107

liberal reforms was to be taken to the streets.[16] The violence of Carolina's suicide attempt—which disrupts Barcelona's pastoral morning—preludes the violence that one day later, on July 25th, will break out in the streets of the city and, as the novel will show, has the same causes. Characters and readers are suddenly roused out of their bucolic dreams and awaken to the turbulent times about to shake Barcelona. From the first pages the readers of Milá's novel (his readership being mostly local) would have known they were reading about the beginning of the revolutionary period that, at the time of the novel's publication, had concluded with the bombardment of Barcelona by government troops from the fortress on Montjuïc. Thus, *Los misterios de Barcelona* sets out the specific political question of to whom the city belongs and answers it by stating the legitimate authority of the moderado bourgeoisie over the city's economic and political destiny.

In *Los misterios de Barcelona* history frames the romance and also provides the obstructions the narrative needs to postpone its closure. Suicide attempts, seductions, love stories, plans of revenge, and misappropriations and restitutions of name and wealth are narratively linked to the recent constitution and political instability of the Spanish liberal state. And the narrative resolution of the story depends upon the key political event of the late 1830s, the *Paz de Vergara* (the peace agreement that ended the first Carlist war, signed on August 31, 1839).[17] The absolutist resistance to the liberal regime of Isabel II marks the beginning and ending of the story, while the political riots led by the progressive liberals that rocked Barcelona during those same years dictate the succession of events that obstructs the resolution of Carolina's romance and Barcelona's collective drama.[18] The obstacles that prevent the recovery of the documents that hold the key to Carolina's "mystery"—her family name—correspond to distinctive moments of social turmoil.[19] In *Los misterios de Barcelona* the war that finds absolutists opposing liberals frames the romantic plot of Carolina's and Barcelona's misfortunes just as the military conflict circumscribed the political plots that set liberal groups against each other during those same years. Milá's novel starts where Sue's ends. The potential politicization and historical contextualization of the plot of *Les mystères de Paris*—signaled, as commented on in the last chapter, by Tortillard's cry, "Il n'y a plus de seigneurs . . . Vive la Charte!" [There are no more lords now. *Vive la Charte!*]—is fully actualized in *Los misterios de Barcelona*.[20]

At the beginning of the novel Carolina's birth documents fall into the hands of a Carlist priest—Domingo Riudoms—as a result of the social confusion brought on by the first popular *bullanga* [riot]; at the end of the novel, the peace accord between liberals and Carlists makes possible the return to Barcelona of the Carlist priest—who is still in possession of the documents—creating, consequently, the opportunity for Carolina's friends to finally obtain them. The absolutist obstruction to the romance's happy conclusion, and, consequently, the dependence of the narrative's closure upon the end of the war, is emphasized by the convergence of interest that brings together at the end of the story a typical character of romance, José Bardisa (Milá's version of the evil usurer, Jacques Ferrand), and the Carlist priest, Domingo Riudoms (the character created by Milá to bring Catalonia's violent history of civil war into fiction). Back in Barcelona from the fighting fields, Riudoms wants to exchange Carolina's birth documents, coveted by Bardisa, for his passport which is in possession of the usurer. The priest's unbecoming violent behavior and political extremism (Milá's indictment of the faction of the Church that supported the Carlist cause) coincide with Bardisa's greed to threaten the romance's happy restoration of both Carolina's and Barcelona's peace. Moreover, Bardisa's greed, deprived during most of the story of ideological connotations, is unmasked at the last moment to reveal his absolutist sympathies. The excesses of the priest and those of Bardisa are, then, unmistakably identified with those of Carlism. Their alliance at the level of plot is shown as being far from accidental, and, on the contrary, is identified as the last threat posed by absolutism to the satisfactory resolution of both the romance and history. Only the constant alertness and decided efforts of the protectors of the orphan prevent the "seditious colonel" and the gluttonous "patriarch" from becoming instrumental in the triumph of Bardisa's plans and, consequently, make possible at the end the recovery of Carolina's birth documents.[21] In Milá's particular convergence of history and romance, the happy ending in Carolina's story is subordinated to the effective neutralization of the absolutist threat (the civil war) by Barcelona's *pro-hommes*.[22]

The violent political confrontations staged by the city's lower classes and the politically ambitious middle class give an historical basis to the arbitrariness of the plot's movement. The social episodes that marked the violent attempts by Barcelona's radicals to take over the city's government become in Milá's hands a distinctive and separate sequence of obstacles that also hold back the efforts by the orphan's friends to recover her birth documents. Milá records in his novel the events of the three uprisings that carried a higher historical and political significance in the period between the proclamation of the *Estatuto Real* and General Espartero's access to power in 1840. As I have already mentioned, the first riot is that of the festivity of St. Jacques, July 25th 1835, when the popular frustration with the tameness of the bulls—which prevented the spectacle of the *corrida*—ended up with the burning of convents. The second riot is the one that took place a few days later, on August 5th 1835, when the top military commander of Catalonia, Pedro Basa, was murdered by the rebellious mass and the Bonaplata factory (which had recently begun to use steam engines) was burned down.[23] The third and last one took place a few months later, on January 6th 1836, when the news of the Carlist execution of liberal prisoners in a nearby location triggered an assault on two military fortresses in the city—*la Ciudadela* and *las Atarazanas*—where Carlist war prisoners were being held. In this case, an archetypal evil character of romance—the selfish seducer of Carolina, Jorge Gollo—is dressed up in the plain clothes of a Barcelona laborer and given a role in the city's history: "Gollo, sin corbata ni chaleco, con el pantalón sujeto al cuerpo por un pañuelo de pita, gorra de cuartel, levita de paisano, con dos pistolas de arzón colgadas del pañuelo que le servía de cinto, y un gran sable en la mano, estaba capitaneando aquella horda de asesinos" [Gollo—wearing no vest or tie, his trousers strapped to his body with a twine cloth, a soldier's cap, a civilian frock coat, two saddle pistols hung to the cloth that served as a belt, and a big saber in his hand—was the leader of that horde of murderers].[24]

As a consequence of the first riot a trustworthy and good priest (father Tomás), who had come into the possession of Carolina's birth documents just the day before (at approximately the time Carolina is rescued by Torrellas from drowning), is forced to leave the papers behind when his convent is set in flames by the rioters. In the confusion of that night Domingo Riudoms—the Carlist priest—ends up with them. If the first riot sets off the plot, the second prevents its premature ending. The second *bullanga* hampers father Tomás's efforts to meet Riudoms and consequently prevents him from recovering Carolina's papers too soon for the story's sake. The street violence confines him to a friend's home and makes him unable to travel to Badalona where Riudoms has taken refuge. When he finally gets there, Riudoms has already fled to Genova and, from there, will join the absolutist army until the end of the war. Finally, the third civil insurgence, directed against Carlist prisoners, forces the evil seducer of Carolina and leader of the mob, Jorge Gollo, to hide among felons, out of reach of those friends of Carolina who want to drive him out of the city, further putting off the conclusion of the story.[25] In *Los misterios de Barcelona* historical events combine with romance to establish the novelistic imagination firmly in the memory of a collective experience (that of Barcelona's readers), and to provide the arbitrariness of romance with a sociopolitical causality.

Milá's reworking of Fleur-de Marie, Carolina, presents all the marks of such actualization and reveals, more particularly, the novel's obsession with the new processes of violent accumulation of capital, the loss of the colonies, and the political instability of the city's government. Milá's decision to make Carolina the daughter of a Catalan plantation owner and a slave allows both the play of the conventions of romance and its insertion within history: as the illegitimate daughter of a Catalan landowner and a slave, Carolina's character conveys the exoticism of romantic stories, while the plot around the usurpation of her inheritance neatly expresses the precariousness of the Catalan investments in America. Like Fleur-de-Marie, Carolina has been dispossessed of name and wealth, and, although not a prostitute, she is also a representation of a *vierge souillé* [soiled virgin].²⁶ Like Sue's character, Carolina is constructed as a series of antitheses, but her oxymoronic existence has little to do with the melodramatic figurations of social and moral extremes which constitute her French model: "the hereditary princess destined to a life of beggars and blows; the pure, blond child delivered to the hands of a putrid mob of convicts and degenerates; the singing bird in the urban jungle; the 'angelic and candid' girl of sixteen smeared with all the filth to be found in the underbelly of Paris."²⁷ Carolina's antitheses are determined mainly by Milá's understanding of the socioeconomical conflicts that undermine Barcelona's traditional oligarchy.

Carolina represents the basis of the power of the traditional Catalan bourgeoisie—that is, that constituted around the commercial and manufacturing opportunities that emerged since the promulgation of the 1778 *Ordenanza del Libre Comercio con América*. Both Catalan and Cuban, black and white, an officially recognized child of illegitimate birth, and dispossessed heir, Carolina embodies the cultural, economic, and juridic complications that threaten the profitable investments of the Catalan bourgeoisie in America.²⁸ She is all they can still lose: the remainder of the Spanish American empire—the markets, the raw materials, and, more important, a circulation of capital that has its last stop in Catalonia. The novel opens with the threat of Carolina drowning in the waters of the port of Barcelona and with her rescue by the young officer Torrellas, and ends— once her American wealth has been securely integrated within Catalonia's traditional bourgeoisie by way of her marriage to a Catalan landowner and lawyer—with that same young officer leaving for America "donde le llamaba su destino" [following destiny's call].²⁹ Once Carolina is safely anchored in Barcelona's society, Torrellas, the civil war just over, leaves the same port in a military mission to "save" what is left of the Spanish American colonies for that same bourgeoisie who have so much to lose if Carolina, and her fortune, is not integrated under their authority. The ending of the novel takes us back, then, to the beginning not only to mark the end of the narrative cycle, but also to signify the preeminence of history and political interests over romance. The tale about a damsel in distress, the intrigue around her origin, the efforts to recover her name and inheritance, and her happy marriage is, from the beginning to the last page, all about securing Cuba for the interests of the Catalan bourgeoisie.

For all these reasons, the death of Fleur-de-Marie at the end of *Les mystères de Paris* as "the only solution to the oxymorons of her existence" is overridden by Milá, who is less interested in the moral tale of Carolina's guilty fault than in her full integration in the society of Barcelona. It is true that Carolina's loss of virginity, unlike Fleur-de-Marie's, does not carry the unerasable mark of the sold body and "the mark de la Cité," but Milá's dismissal of Carolina's position as a *vierge souillé* is unconventional.[30] Carolina's death would problematize the highly symbolic rescue of Carolina by the officer of the Queen and, consequently, would make impossible the final image of Torrellas leaving Barcelona to "rescue" America. "¿Pero a dónde me llevas, mi salvador?" [But, my savior, where are you taking me?] asks Carolina abandoning herself completely to Torrellas's assistance; the answer cannot be "to die."[31] Carolina's death would signal the inability of Catalan society to protect her—and America—once under the ward of Barcelona's *pro-hommes*, a point especially important if we consider that Carolina's cruel and unscrupulous seducer is, and, in the context of the wars of independence and from the Spanish perspective, had to be, a Cuban *criollo*. Barcelona's benevolence and forgiveness toward Carolina's guilt is that of a tolerant *madre patria* protectively embracing her seditious colonies. In sharp contrast to the leniency shown toward Carolina, the cruel punishment endured by two other young and naïve women, Margarita Gili and Hortensia (whose sin is to fall in love with Jorge Gollo and an accomplice, and to agree to elope with them unaware of the true intentions of these two evildoers), leaves no doubt of Milá's commitment to patriarchal morality: Margarita is sent to a convent where she is to spend the rest of her life, and Hortensia falls sick "de una calentura pútrida y de una fiebre cerebral" [with putrid blisters and a brain fever].[32]

Similarly, the question of Carolina being of mixed race is completely bypassed in Milá's story. It is hard to imagine that the reader of *Los misterios de Barcelona* (who must have known *Les mystères de Paris*) would not, after finding out about Carolina's origins, recall Cécily, the liberated slave and adulterer who embodies, to the prejudiced eyes of the Europeans, the unrestrained lewdness of a mulatto woman, and the threat posed by female sexuality to patriarchy. However, Milá, going against all expectations, completely erases Carolina's Afro-Cuban heritage and briefly, obliquely describes her as a young and pretty woman with a slender figure and "beautiful black eyes."[33] In the novel she functions exclusively as the innocent daughter of the Catalan Pedro Palmas whose life and fortune have been, since her infancy, under the protection, or abuse, of Catalan entrepreneurs. She belongs to them. In this sense, she is truly a slave's daughter. But her identity is not, cannot be, an issue; otherwise, it would destabilize the novel's purpose of canceling Cuba's different and autonomous existence and right to independence. Carolina never talks or asks about, never misses, Cuba. Her world, if not her identity, is that of her Catalan father and future husband: Barcelona.

Milá's relation of the "mysteries" of Barcelona shows sometimes important narrative limitations which affect his representation of the city's life and reveal the shortcomings of his autochthonous writing. In this respect I should point out first that in his chronicle of the city, history and plot are coordinated rather than fused. Following Schwarz, we could say that *Los misterios de Barcelona* is organized by "two different reality-effects"— those of history and romance—which fail to create a unified narrative.[34] The concurrence, rather than the integration, of historical events and plot can be observed in Milá's characteristic juxtaposition of two different writing styles: a newspaper-like writing (to report historical episodes) and free direct discourse (to tell the fictional story). Chapters 3 ("Los toros") and 4 ("Es un viejo"), which narrate the violent events of July 25th, are good examples of Milá's reliance on the contiguity of styles to convey an historically motivated fiction. Although the two chapters form a unity where fiction (represented by reported speech) frames the narrator's account of the riot, in Milá's novel, history and romance alternate.

Chapter 3 starts with a brief description of a second-floor room of the restaurant "las Cuatro naciones" and then proceeds with a dialogue where the characters are introduced, as in a play script, by their names. Here I reproduce the initial fragment:

> *Guillén.* Está visto, camaradas, hoy se repite la misma función; ayer [Torrellas] nos encajó un solo de cuarenta y cinco minutos, hoy llevamos ya uno de treinta, soy pues de parecer que le esperemos a la vela, como él dice.
> —Sí, sí, exclamó la mayoría, le aguardaremos comiendo.
> *Beltrán.* Demonios, no pasa la hora, es la una y media y hasta las tres no empieza la corrida: podemos muy bien aguardar aun un cuarto de hora.[35]
>
> [*Guillén*—Apparently, comrades, we have the same routine today. Yesterday [Torrellas] kept us waiting for forty-five minutes, and now we have already been here for half an hour. I think we should get ready.
> —Yes, yes! cried most of them, we'll eat while we wait for him.
> *Beltrán*—What the devil, it has been no more than an hour. It's one-thirty and the bullfight starts at three. We can very well wait another fifteen minutes.]

After the opening scene that describes the lunch that the main hero, Nemesio Torrellas, has with his friends before they all go to the bullfighting ring (to attend what would become the famous *corrida* on the festivity of St. Jacques that initiated Barcelona's revolutionary period), Milá's text becomes newspaper to narrate the riot and, when the report is finished, adopts again the free direct discourse to return to fiction. As the following lines attest, the telling of the city's drama relies on newspaper-like reporting, and the return to plot, on its displacement, on dramatized writing:

> Los toros que se lidiaron en la corrida de que hablamos fueron mansos, o cobardes y malos como los calificó el público. Exasperados los espectadores después de los gritos, vociferaciones y confusión de que hemos hecho mérito, dieron principio a un barullo que más tarde fue un completo motín; arrojando a la plaza un sin número de abanicos, tras los cuales siguieron los bancos, luego las sillas y finalmente algunas columnas de los palcos.

5: IMITATION AND THE AUTOCHTHONOUS NOVEL 113

Algunos espectadores, los más atrevidos y audaces, cortaron la maroma que forma la contrabarrera, y atando con ella al toro que en la plaza había lo arrastraron con infernal algaraza fuera de ella y, engrosándose el grupo de alborotadores con chiquillos y mujeres de horrible aspecto, dirigiéronse a pasearlo por las calles de la ciudad.
. . .
Levántanse por sobre los terrados de Barcelona opacas bocanadas de humo que van ennegreciendo lo despejado de la atmósfera. . . . Seis vastos y ricos edificios . . . son presas de las llamas. Sus infelices moradores, perseguidos por la plebe desenfrenada cual animales dañinos, son horriblemente asesinados por las calles . . . ; y mientras . . . ningún otro edificio es víctima de aquellos voluntarios incendios; y entre tanta confusión reina en la ciudad un extraño orden; ni un robo, ni una riña, ni un insulto acontece entre el paisanaje y la tropa mientras las autoridades contemplan estupefactas y atónitas la representación de tan espantoso drama. . . . Crecidas brigadas de hombres, mujeres y niños cargados de faginas pasean en triunfo por la ciudad la tea abrasadora, y la cosa camina con tal ímpetu y presteza que arden a la vez las puertas de varios conventos. . . . Mientras [los conventos] . . . van siendo paulatinamente presa de las llamas, observemos . . . *la escena que pasa en la calle Fonollá.*[36]

[The bulls in the bullfight we are talking about were docile, or—as the audience put it—cowardly and bad. The spectators, exasperated after the shouting, yelling and confusion we have described, started a racket that turned into a riot— throwing into the bullring countless fans that were followed first by seats, then by chairs, and finally by some columns from the boxes.

Some spectators, the most daring and bold, cut the rope that forms the barrier and, tying up the bull in the ring, dragged it with infernal joy into the street, where they were joined by horrible-looking kids and women, and proceeded to drag it through the city.
. . .
Blasts of dark smoke rise over the roofs of Barcelona, blackening the air. . . . Six immense and sumptuous buildings . . . are in flames. Their unfortunate occupants, chased like pests by the violent populace, are horribly murdered in the streets. . . . In the meantime . . . no other building is damaged by these arson attacks, and in the confusion a strange order prevails in the city: not a single burglary, brawl, or insult takes place between citizens and troops, while the authorities contemplate in astonishment this horrifying drama. . . . Large gangs of men, women, and children loaded with kindling walk around the city triumphantly showing the burning torches, and such is the force of events that soon the doors of several convents burn at the same time. . . . While the fire takes hold of the convents, let us witness . . . *the scene taking place in Fonollá Street.*]

The contiguity of styles that characterizes Milá's insertion of fiction into history runs parallel to the dissociation we observe between history and romance at the level of signification. In *Los misterios de Barcelona* history frames the story, dictates the movement of the plot, and sustains the allegorical reading, but does not affect the way moral meaning is produced. Milá, who addressed his novel to the same Catalan readers (the same bourgeois fears and hopes) Cortada's translation was written for, and from a similar conservative position, kept close to *Les mystères de Paris*' politics of social reconciliation. Milá relied on romance to represent social violence and on Sue's consolatory formula to account for the evil that accompanied the consolidation of the new capitalist order in Catalonia. History and actuality give the plot a distinctive sense of collective time, but romance provides meaning to the violent episodes represented. Romance invests all social riots with irrational and malevolent motives and makes sense, or rather, makes a conservative sense, of the city's social turmoil. Within romance social violence is deprived of political content, and the politics of progressive liberalism and Carlism are identified as the cause of social illnesses. In line with this, Carolina's protectors function within the novel as agents of a Higher Justice or Providence, ensure the satisfactory resolution of conflicts (they vanquish evil), and restore a sense of purpose and Christian meaning to the distressing social conditions and suffering. They accomplish the escape from history, the cancellation of class struggle, and the return to the Promised Land of plenitude and uneventfulness disrupted at the beginning of the novel.

Moreover, the imitation of Sue's characteristic transformation of class struggle into the moral fight of good against evil significantly constrains the representation of Barcelona's own historical processes. The sociopolitical causality that sustains the plot in *Los misterios de Barcelona* is countered by Milá's reliance on the use of enigmas, characteristic of his model, to articulate the truth of both social relationships and romance. The hermeneutic code, that is, the identification of "secret," "origin," and "truth," dictates the representation and the possibility of meaning in Milá's novel. The search for origins, that is, the inquiry and discovery of Fleur-de Marie's unknown parents and the eventual association of her heavenly nature with her father's politics (she is an angel; her father, a savior), gives direction to and establishes the meaning of *Les mystères de Paris* just as the enigma of Carolina's birth and its deciphering organize and make possible the closure of *Los misterios de Barcelona*.[37] Thus, and in spite of the considerable dependence of the plot upon historical events, in Milá's own version of *historia-novela* the enigmatic code is the signifying system that formulates and discloses Barcelona's social existence. In Milá's novel romance ultimately imposes on history its form: the "mystery."[38] *Los misterios de Barcelona* depends upon romance to have meaning.

On a few occasions, however, Milá was able to turn mode variation into a more integrated narrative and to free representation and journalistic reporting from the signifying system of romance. The episode that relates the unfortunate life of the prostitute María Malat ("Miseria y prostitucion")

5: IMITATION AND THE AUTOCHTHONOUS NOVEL 115

is probably the best example. The nature of the topic he describes—the economic causes of prostitution, the functioning of brothels (with their particular mechanisms for exploiting poor women), and the somehow independent lives of street whores—probably contributed to overcome romance and to soften the fissures of narration. In fact, the narration on desire and abuse inscribed on and told by the decomposing body of a syphilitic prostitute does not quite fit in Milá's novel. Even though her story functions as a cautionary tale placed in direct opposition to Carolina's stained purity (to differentiate in social and moral terms the orphan's lack of virginity from prostitution, lust, and greed), María's first-person narration is not connected to the plot of *Los misterios de Barcelona*. The narrative of her life—her forced prostitution—constitutes its own novel, confined and separated from the rest of the story, in one chapter. In the following quotation, María, now on her deathbed (she has been raped and beaten by ruthless clients and made the object of the revenge of the *alcalde de barrio* [borough mayor] to whom she refuses her services) after a brief period of quiet content as an independent entrepreneur, tells first about her life in doña Mercedes' brothel and, later on, about her efforts to take control of her own body and life:

> Por último convino aquella mujer [doña Mercedes] en admitirme en su casa bajo las condiciones de que no saldría de ella sin su consentimiento; que le abonaría por la manutención, cama y limpieza de ropa, diez reales diarios; que debía admitir sin distinción las visitas que ella me mandara, y que las ropas que yo me quisiese hacer ella debía comprármelas con mi dinero. Acepté tan despóticas condiciones y desde aquel momento quedé esclava de doña Mercedes. Tres jóvenes más habitaban aquel lupanar con iguales condiciones que yo.
>
> No hay mortal que pueda explicar lo que una siente cuando se ve precisada a sufrir los voluptuosos halagos y tener que fingirlos y prodigarlos a un ser que nos repugna. . . .
>
> Aquel género de vida . . . se me hacía insufrible; una de mis compañeras me propuso un día separarnos y establecernos en un piso. . . . [M]e manifestó Julia que ella conocía una señora que nos fiaría vestidos pagándolos a plazos, y que a más nos alquilaría un cuarto amueblado. . . . [P]asamos a vernos con doña Catalina; era ésta una mujer linda que vivía en un cuarto principal de la Rambla, le dijimos nuestros deseos, nos miró con mucha atención y por el precio de 12 reales vellón diarios que debíamos pagar por adelantado todas las mañanas, nos alquiló unos entresuelos. . . . Y nos mandó hacer un par de vestidos a cada una, con la obligación de pagar dos duros semanalmente hasta quedar satisfecha de sus anticipos y los correspondientes intereses a razón de seis cuartos de duro la semana.
>
> Establecidas en nuestra casa tuvimos varias visitas de las que recibíamos en la de doña Mercedes, y estas fueron llevando otras; y como no admitíamos sino a quien nos acomodaba, entre el fango de mi prostitución era menos desdichada que en la casa de aquella que me tenía como esclava.[39]

[In the end that woman [doña Mercedes] agreed to take me in her house under the conditions that I would never go out without her consent; I would pay ten *reales* per day for food, bed, and laundry; I ought to admit without exception any visitors she may send to me; and that any clothes I would need she would buy with my own money. I accepted such tyrannical conditions, and from then on I became her slave. Three other girls lived in the brothel in those same conditions.

Nobody can explain what you feel when forced to endure lustful attention and in return to feign it for someone you find disgusting. . . .

That sort of life . . . was unbearable, and one day one of the other girls suggested that we leave the place and establish ourselves in a flat. . . . Julia told me she knew a lady who would rent us a furnished room and give us clothing for which we could pay in installments. . . . We went to see doña Catalina—a pretty woman living in a nice apartment in the Rambla—and told her our plan. She gave us careful attention and rented us a mezzanine for 12 *reales vellón* a day that we had to pay in advance every morning. . . . And she ordered a couple of dresses for each of us, which we would pay off on a weekly basis—two *duros* for the advance and six quarters in interest.

Once we were established in our own place we had some of the same clients we used to have at doña Mercedes', and they would draw others. And since we only admitted those whom we wanted, I was less miserable in the mire of my prostitution than in the house of a woman who treated me like a slave.]

In María's story of her decaying body we perceive not only the disintegration of melodramatic moral dualism and the relaxation of role playing, but also the emergence of a character striving to find her own plot—and meaning. In the narrative of the prostitute's life, the teller of Barcelona's recent history and contemporary life becomes the novelist that creates a plot—María's story—based upon the commodification of the female body, social exploitation, and a woman's suffering and guilt. At the end of her narration, María asks a charitable old acquaintance to warn her sister about the fatal consequences of a life of vice, to convince her to return to a virtuous existence, and to make sure she receives their American uncle's inheritance. We have here two familiar elements of romance—the loss of virtue and an unexpected fortune—but now the recovery of both is dependent not only upon the telling of a woman's social exploitation, but also upon the failure to find meaning in her suffering and weaknesses. Faced with the spoils of a body marked by social violence—virtue overcome by misery and fear—María's only explanation for her unlucky and undeserved destiny, God's punishment—"el Omnipotente castiga a la mujer liviana" [the Almighty punishes fickle women]—sounds like an empty and updated rhetorical reference. So does the consolatory plot of romance.[40]

We should not underestimate the pressure of history in Milá's use of the hermeneutic code. On the contrary, this pressure produces one of the most distinctive traits of Milá's autochthonous writing: the construction of the city as national community. The articulation of a collective identity is distinctively felt in the imitation's ambitious conception of the plot's genealogical quest. Differing sharply from the French original, in Milá's novel the search for origins is not only a hermeneutic inquiry about the social illnesses of the city, and its purpose is not exclusively the creation of a social consciousness rooted in notions of filiation and patriarchy. In *Los misterios de Barcelona* genealogy functions also as an investigation on the causes of Barcelona's loss of self.[41] The numerous misappropriation plots and usurpation schemes played out at the level of the plot to postpone the deciphering of the enigma of Carolina's lineage run parallel to a genealogical quest for the moral origins of Barcelona. The inquiry into the lost origin of the young woman in distress is also a quest for the forgotten edenic foundation of the city now in turmoil, and her protectors' efforts to regain her name and wealth are inserted within Barcelona's and Catalonia's struggle for identity. In this sense, the secrets that populate *Los misterios de Barcelona* have to do mainly with the false or absent fathers of the city; that is, with Barcelona's vanished moderado elite and its temporal removal from the city's government on the one hand, and, on the other, the want of a king-father, and his replacement by a false monarch, don Carlos, and a proxy queen-child, Isabel II. The false fathers violate the true origins of the city and thus Barcelona presents, and suffers from, all the symptoms of alienation. Barcelona is subjected to false authorities; as a consequence, the banner of Isabel II, flying high in the military fortresses that surround Barcelona, and which safeguards the bucolic order of the initial scene and oversees the city, is symbolically destabilized and put to the test. Barcelona's supporters of Isabel's moderado regime are not eliminated, only momentarily removed from power. *Los misterios de Barcelona* tells of their efforts to eradicate from the lives of both the city and Carolina the two forms of authority not recognized by the *Estatuto Real*: the absolutism of don Carlos and the liberal Constitution of 1812. Fighting both absolutism and progressive liberalism, the novel's heroes are able, at the end of the novel, to restore both Carolina's name and fortune and the conservative hold over the city against those old and new social groups that are threatening the economic resources and political hegemony of the city's oligarchy.

By way of the genealogical quest, Carolina's suicide attempt, which brings about the end of the pastoral and announces the civil strifes of the city, is set as the primal Fall—the sin against the Father—that started history. The initial plenitude of Barcelona becomes thus a violent present wanting legitimate authority, and the city, as the space of history, coincides with the space of sin and guilt. Carolina's loss of innocence (she has been seduced and abandoned) stands for the city's imminent rebellion against the authority of the queen, and the mystery of her birth (her lack of a father) for the absence of a king. Throughout the novel Barcelona (just like Carolina) is represented as an orphan forcefully alienated from the only legitimate authority and true spiritual roots that can secure its prosperity. If Carolina is under the violent and abusive guardianship of a supposed uncle, the evil usurer José Bardisa, Barcelona is at the hands of the city's ferocious underclass and the economically and politically ambitious middle classes, and threatened by a false monarch. Barcelona (like Carolina) is an abused and dispossessed body, thrown into confusion and misery, and reduced to exhaustion, by the illegitimate authorities that subjugate it. Against a present conceived as the infernal site of rebellious subjects, Milá opposes the immutable truth of origins, that is, a national character. In Milá's novel to possess the name of the true father means not only to regain name and fortune, but also to recover a common moral heritage. Genealogy becomes transcendental history and the search for origins implies the restoration of the collective existence of the city as a national community.

The forgetfulness of tradition—common moral herritage—that is causing the ills afflicting the city is evoked by the narrator in a nostalgic manner right after the violent episodes of the first riot, and is part of the inquiry into the causes of Barcelona's current conflicts. In chapter V Milá takes us back to the end of the eighteenth century to tell us about the moral degeneration of Francisco Piló (at that time, a young man from a good and industrious family). Milá presents Piló's progressive separation from the values that sustained the prosperity and the quiet life of his family as exemplary of the decomposition of the traditional order that has been affecting the city since those years. Piló's descent into vice marks a turning point in the history of the city, the moment when debauched spending—the new forces of greed and lust—started to corrode the city of merchants and artisans, the paternalistic order of the guilds. Milá idealizes the epoch of primitive capitalism in Catalan society and claims the familial organization of the old guilds as the true heritage of the city.[42] Moreover, he blames the new form of speculative capital, where money no longer has origin, for Barcelona's contemporary disorders. Against the historical processes uprooting Catalan people and wealth, as Milá reminds his readers, Barcelona's prosperity and peace have their foundation in the paternal order of the family, where name and money share a common, known origin and economic and moral heritages are one and the same:[43]

> En aquella época que llamamos ahora, bien que impúdicamente, de ignorancia y oscurantismo, existía en Barcelona una verdadera representación popular compuesta de todas las clases de la sociedad en los colegios y gremios.... Estas instituciones ... producían bienes inmensos así a la nación en general como a sus mismos componentes; eran un centinela avanzado del orden; una firme garantía al honrado operario y, por fin, una verdadera policía que alejaba de Barcelona esos inmensos enjambres de tunos y vagos que ahora la infestan....

5: IMITATION AND THE AUTOCHTHONOUS NOVEL 119

En aquellas admirables y pacíficas asambleas [del Consejo de Ciento] en que estaban completamente representadas todas las clases de la ciudad de Barcelona, no resonaban elocuentes ni fluidos discursos, pero sí resonaban por todas partes los sentimientos de paz, amor al trabajo, prosperidad del país, y sumisión y apoyo al gobierno.[44]

[In that era that we now rather brazenly call ignorant and obscurantist, there was in Barcelona a real system of popular representation for all social classes through associations and guilds. . . . These institutions . . . provided great benefits both to the nation in general and to their members, and were advanced guardians of order, firm guarantors for the honest worker, and finally, a veritable police force that kept Barcelona safe from these swarms of rogues and idlers that now plague our streets. . . . In those admirable and peaceful assemblies [of the *Consejo de Ciento*] in which each and every class in the city of Barcelona was completely represented, there were no eloquent and fluid speeches, but the love for peace and work, the concern for the country's prosperity, and the obedience and support for the government were everywhere.]

The search for origins functions in *Los misterios de Barcelona* as both the reconstruction of the past and the foundation of the future: the past holds the identity of the city and consequently is a true proposition for the future. But, more important, it establishes the continuity of tradition and heritage in conservative liberalism. The new monarchy of Isabel II represents, and secures, the return of the city to its roots. Milá signifies the association between the moral heritage of the old city and the political order of the new queen in the emotional bond that joins the orphan Carolina and Antonia Piló, and in the metonymic relation he establishes between the fictive orphan and the royal one. Antonia is the good-hearted and long-suffering wife of Francisco Piló, one of the villains. Like her husband, Antonia belongs to the old order of Barcelona, but unlike him, she has never forgotten or forsaken its values. Before the novel begins, Carolina has already chosen Antonia as her true and only family—she calls her "godmother" and, as the narrator tells us, the orphan loves her "as if she were her mother."[45] After her frustrated suicide attempt, Carolina places herself under the care of her surrogate mother who, finally a widow after years of helplessness under the selfish authority of her husband, now has some power to protect her. Their love bond is, then, a bond of suffering that reflects that of the city, and, as the novel progressively reveals, a recognition of true filiation: Carolina is the moral "daughter" of Antonia. She is the heiress to the values of the old city, just like Queen Isabel II is, under the vulnerable guardianship of regent queen, the heiress to her father's timid liberalism. They are the link between past and present and consequently represent the possibility of a future rooted in tradition.

The novel is, thus, fully invested in solving the mystery and establishing the rights of both their births. Carolina's irregular birth and plight for legitimacy parallels the anomalous origin of Isabel II's reign. The fictive orphan is an illegitimate daughter legally recognized by her father; the queen-child is a legitimate daughter whose crown is illegal under the *Ley Sálica* (which establishes the exclusive male successory line to the throne). Both orphans are caught between the implementation of the will of their respective fathers (in one case, the recognition of filiation, and in the other, the abolition of the *Ley Sálica*) and the requirements of legality (inheritance and succession are subjected to social and political regulation). Carolina's eventual recovery of name and fortune echoes the legal and military triumph of Queen Isabel II over don Carlos. The legitimacy avowed to the fictive orphan is metonymically conferred to that of the queen and the irregular birth of Spanish liberalism is, thus, redeemed.

Once their "mysterious" origins have been deciphered and the continuation of tradition in conservative liberalism stated, Carolina and Isabel II will be responsible for the restoration of order to both the fictional and the real Barcelona. It is Carolina who, acting with the sense of moderation and lack of greed that characterizes Antonia and, supposedly, the Barcelona of the godmother's youth, puts a definitive end to all pending monetary lawsuits and therefore to all plots of misappropriation of wealth, even against her future husband's will (he wants to continue fighting for her rights). As the narrator tells us, Carolina, determined to finish all relations with the usurer, "aprontó y entrególe [a Bardisa] una cantidad que por ningún concepto le correspondía" [got the money and gave [Bardisa] an amount he under no circumstances deserved]. Finally, Carolina's marriage to Beltrán (a benevolent and tolerant lawyer whose wealth comes mainly from landed money), and their extended and caring family of friends, mark the return of the city to the nation of the fathers right at the time when, according to the narrator, the army of the queen has killed Barcelona's last enemy—the usurer and Carlist José Bardisa: "Beltrán y Carolina . . . acababan de jurarse eterno amor y constancia al pie de los altares. . . . La señora Antonia abrazó llena de gozo a sus hijos adoptivos y . . . ya más se separó de ellos. . . . [Poco después] Bardisa acaudillando un grupo de rebeldes fue muerto por los defensores de la Reina y del orden" [Beltrán and Carolina . . . had just promised each other eternal love and fidelity at the altar. . . . Overjoyed, madame Antonia embraced her adopted children and . . . she remained with them forever. . . . Bardisa was later killed while leading a group of rebels by the defenders of the Queen and order].[46]

THE MYSTERIES OF THE CITY AND PROVINCIAL LIFE

One of the most important formal dislocations that Sue's imagination suffers as a result of the pressure of Milá's interest in local history affects

5: IMITATION AND THE AUTOCHTHONOUS NOVEL   121

the actual representation of the city and its inhabitants. The city undergoes a profound reconceptualization in Milá's hands and his narration of Barcelona as social space provides one of the most remarkable instances of autochthonous writing. At the time Barcelona was mainly a town run by commercial and manufacturing bourgeoisies whose paternalistic mode of operation was still closed to that of the old guilds. Milá could not, then, rely on the exceptionality of the city's social configuration or the strangeness of its urban scene to create his relation of mysteries and to explain Barcelona's continuous social violence. Besides, to imitate Sue's representation of the city as an exotic territory would have gone against Milá's ideal notion of Barcelona as a community led by paternalistic authorities and, more particularly, would have undermined his transformation of the city's continuous unrest into a family quarrel. In this sense, Milá's notion of Barcelona presents the same strong pull away from the exoticism of romance that we have already mentioned in relation to his narration of time (and also in relation to Cortada's translation).

In Milá's novel the alluring territories that shape Sue's Paris are highly downgraded to make room for Barcelona's local life. The "measure" of Barcelona, to use Schwarz's expression, is that of a provincial city and, as a consequence, the exotic spaces that constitute Paris—the palaces, blind alleys, rip-off joints, and underground caverns that Prince Rodolphe frequents and his friends and enemies inhabit—are absent from the imagination of *Los misterios de Barcelona*.[47] There are no urban sites of complete and adventurous otherness; no spaces of spectacular wealth, no grandiose scenarios, no swamps for the urban beasts. Milá's Barcelona lacks the fabulous dimension of Paris, the extraordinary spaces that in Sue's romance represent the power of Parisian old and new money, and the unprecedented slums of the new capitals of the world. Milá surely takes the reader to Barcelona's own exotic sites—an aristocratic house, a tavern, a gambling den, a brothel, etc.—but all these urban spaces and the social groups that inhabit them exude the moderate measure of the city's provincial middle classes. The domestic atmosphere that characterizes doña Mercedes' bordello is exemplary of the temperate mood that suits even Barcelona's hidden excitements. In the following quotation María Malalt describes the brothel while remembering her initiation into prostitution:

> Salí al fin de casa . . . fuimos con Mercedes [al mercado] de la Boquería y luego de haber bien provisto la cesta de las mejores viandas, me condujo aquella a su casa situada en la calle de S. Pablo. Allí encontré una señorita que estaba leyendo junto al brasero. . . . A poco rato entró un señor de unos 50 años muy bien puesto y muy amable, me preguntó si era de Barcelona, y después de algunas preguntas indiferentes, salióse y tras él la Mercedes cual me dijo que al momento vendría a darme labor.

Un cuarto de hora después volvió el mismo señor con un canastito en la mano en el que venían cortadas dos camisas y me dijo: amable niña, soy forastero y de paso en Barcelona: Dª Mercedes me ha dicho que es usted tan buena costurera y espero que tendrá usted la bondad de coserme cuanto más antes mejor este par de camisas. Me pareció aquel hombre tan bueno y tan franco que seguí conversando con él y concluí explicándole toda la desgracia de mi familia y nuestra triste situación.[48]

[I finally went out. . . . Mercedes and I went to the Boquería market and, once our basket was loaded with the best food, she took me to her house in San Pablo street. There was a young woman reading by the brazier. . . . A little bit later, a fifty-year-old man, well-dressed and kind, asked me if I was from Barcelona, and after some trivial questions he left—and with him left also Mercedes, who told me she would soon come back with some needlework for me.

Fifteen minutes later the same man returned with a little basket which contained two shirts and said, "Kind girl, I am not from Barcelona, I'm just visiting here, and doña Mercedes has informed me that you are such a good seamstress. Would you be so kind as to sew these shirts for me right now?" He seemed such a good and honest person that I continued talking to him and ended up telling the unfortunate story of my family and our present condition.]

The immediate marriage-like proposition of the "fifty-year-old man" to the virginal María fits well Milá's restrained and sober representation of illicit activity in a provincial city: "Si quiere V. seguir las relaciones que principiamos ayer y me asegura V. que no se entenderá con otro hombre que conmigo yo atenderé a la subsistencia de V. y de su familia" [If you wish to pursue the relationship we initiated yesterday and promise you will not be friends with another man, I will take care of you and your family].[49]

But Milá exhibits also a keen sense of the processes that were deeply changing the old town and undermining the city's traditional landscape and society. Industrialization was under way in Catalonia, as was rural migration to Barcelona; new financial and commercial opportunities appeared everywhere, and the constitution of a new Catalan bourgeoisie was well in progress, alongside the social and political influence of the middle classes. Sue's fictionalization of Paris was of little help in narrating the not-yet well-defined modernization of Barcelona and its volatile conditions, and Milá moved decidedly away from the foreign model in order to represent the sociopolitical processes of a city still in the making and to account for his vision of order. To capture Barcelona's ongoing modernization Milá relied on two narrative strategies. First, and in clear contrast to *Les mystères de Paris*, Milá substituted sites of public convergence for the geographical boundaries that mark and separate Parisian social groups. Milá set aside Sue's reassuring urban borders and transformed the city into a space of contention: the conflictive rendezvous for all social classes. In *Los misterios de Barcelona* the city is an open arena where the characters engage in a class struggle that parallels, not always figuratively, the political conflicts disrupting the daily existence of Milá's readers. Second, Milá unsettles his representation of Barcelona's provincial life by revealing the presumed acquaintance of the reader with the city as deceptive. Milá's Barcelona is a familiar place posited anew and made foreign to the reader. Common urban sites, such as a bullfighting ring, a boardinghouse, the customs building, the city's courts, or a neighborhood store fill Milá's novel not to provide a picturesque description of Barcelona, but to reveal the unexpected truth of the city: the annihilation of the old town and the emergence of the modern metropolis. This representation of the city as deceptively familiar corresponds not only with the melodramatic mode of the novel, but, more important, with the convergence of times that dictate Barcelona's existence—that is, its supposedly peaceful tradition and character and the current violent unrest. It supports and conveys the "mystery" that organizes the story at the level of the plot; in *Los misterios de Barcelona* the mysteries of the story are those of the uncanny doubleness of the city.

Milá's rendition of Sue's famous tenant building on *la rue du Temple*, "la casa de huéspedes de doña Rosa Lozano" [doña Rosa Lozano's boardinghouse], shows the autochthonous imagination that is at play in Milá's writing of Barcelona as a provincial town and a familial operation unsettled by new socioeconomic forces. While the tenant building of *Les mystères de Paris* is a *picturesque* representation of the social diversity of Paris and a mere locale where the characters of the romance conveniently happen to meet, doña Rosa's house is a "miniature" reproduction of the city as the politicized space where conflicting and contiguous classes meet.[50] The familiar site of a respectable boardinghouse mirrors the new social order of the *Estatuto Real* which regulates the life of the city, and its peaceful existence is threatened by those same enemies who are endangering the city's prosperity—the absolutists and the radicals.

After describing the class-based organization of the boardinghouse (each floor houses a different social group: from the lower to the main floors), Milá tells his reader of the "common table" which just like the restricted liberalism of the *Estatuto Real*, brings together all guests with the exception of those from "the lower floor" (poor students, shop assistants, low-rank clerical workers, and other hired hands). At this common table representatives of the Church, bourgeoisie, and middle classes meet and adopt different and conflicting political positions while they are "servidos por igual" [served as equals]. Doña Rosa's house is a bustling "national assembly" where her guests, just like the city's inhabitants, constantly engage in agitated debates, held together only by the presence of mind of the political center—the moderados—represented by don Cristóbal (an ally of the young navy officer, Torrellas). If don Cristóbal prevents the "house" from falling into open and violent civil war, doña Rosa oversees benignly the heated discussions as if she were Barcelona's own María Cristina, the regent queen of conservative liberalism:

> La mesa era común, y todos los pupilos de doña Rosa, exceptuando los del cuarto bajo, eran servidos por igual; aquella mesa era una especie de asamblea legislativa o llámese congreso, pues había derecha, izquierda y centro; ocupaban la derecha los cuatro señorones del piso primero, los que sin meter bullicio comían y lo poco que hablaban era entre ellos y por lo bajo: muy importantes debían ser las cuestiones que se agitaban en el extremo izquierdo, para que el otro tomara parte en la discusión; pero no sucedía así con el centro, representado y compuesto por la sola persona de D. Cristóbal, que a todas partes atendía y a todas interpelaba y contestaba.[51]
> [The dining table was common, and with the exception of those in the lower floor, all of doña Rosa's boarders were served as equals. The table was a sort of legislative assembly or so-called congress, since there were right, left, and central sections. The right was occupied by the four bigwigs of the first floor, who would eat without making a racket and speak among themselves seldom and very quietly. Only when extremely important issues were debated at the extreme left would the opposite side intervene in the discussion. That was not the case with the center, represented and composed by the only presence of don Cristóbal, who paid attention and would question and reply to all sides.]

In doña Rosa's boardinghouse, just like in Milá's fictive city, the intransigent silence of the "bigwigs" and their unwillingness to engage in political dialogue exist side by side, and join forces with the constant agitation of the "extreme left" to threaten and undermine the only authority that can prevent the city from becoming the site of imprudent politics and abuse of power: the moderado regime. In the imagination of *Los misterios de Barcelona* the structure of Spanish conservative liberalism provides both the form of the narrative and its sense of order.

The transformation suffered by the central figure of Sue's imagination, Prince Rodolphe, is directly related to Milá's particular writing of the city. The exceptional size and romantic character of Rodolphe, and his detachment from the political life of Paris, are at odds with both the provincial "measure" of Barcelona and the creation of the city as the space of political contention. In Milá's *historia-novela* the all-powerful prince and his mission of social salvation are distributed among three local figures who represent the city's traditional leading classes and their interests: the young officer, Nemesio Torrellas, who stands for the order of the *Estatuto Real*; the lawyer and landowner, Beltrán, who is a member of the local bourgeoisie; and *the indiano*, don Cristóbal, who represents the Catalan investments in Latin America and, most particularly, the dependence of Barcelona's economy on Cuba.[52] As mainstays of the socioeconomic system of the city, they are responsible for the restoration of both Carolina's name and fortune and Barcelona's order. But their actions are always within the scope of the power and social status they hold and their success is contingent upon the evolution of the political life of the city. Furthermore, and particularly interesting, is the autochthonous imagination that articulates the actions of these characters by means of both the plot and the city. Torrellas, Beltrán, and don Cristóbal do not behave narratively as figures of imported fictions. On the contrary, to resolve the conflicts entrusted to them, they act like true citizens of Barcelona. They combine efforts and operate just like one of those numerous committees of municipal authorities—*Junta d'Autoritats* or *Junta de Corporacions i Classes*—that would take over Barcelona's government after the city's rebellious riots. In Milá's displacement of Sue's foreign imagination, a political committee of Barcelona's *pro-hommes* takes over Prince Rodolphe's mission of social reconciliation, and a Catholic "trinity" substitutes for the Christian but foreign "savior."

To capture the transformation of the town into a modern city Milá also unsettles his representation of Barcelona's provincial life with constant indications of underlying and spreading corruption. In Milá's novel extensive moral and political perversion undermines the city's traditional order, and hardly anyone escapes the debauched desires that feed the new and ambitious classes. The moderate representation of Barcelona's mysteries is subverted by Milá's insistence on the city's social decomposition, and the reader is constantly made aware of its extent. Thus, and for instance, the temperate description of the brothel is counteracted with the affirmation that implicates "los caballeros de más tono y más valía de Barcelona" [the most distinguished and respectable gentlemen in Barcelona] with doña Mercedes' house, and the appalling revelation that "the fifty-year-old man" who corrupts María is don Cristóbal, one of Barcelona's *pro-hommes* and protector of Carolina.[53] Similarly, all the reasons given by Milá to explain Carolina's weakness—the psychological duress she endured for years, her loneliness and inexperience—fall short of justifying the orphan's illicit and continuous affair with the evil Jorge Gollo who agrees to seduce her for 300 *duros*. Following the lead of this last example, we can say that in *Los misterios de Barcelona* Carolina's loss of virginity (at the level of the plot) parallels the reader's figurative loss of innocence (at the level of the narration): the orphan's participation in the city's market economy corresponds to the reader's awareness of the new " 'free flow' of desire and money" that is starting to control the city.[54]

In Milá's novel social disorder brought by the emergence of the new economy contaminates the whole body of the city spreading like a devastating plague. The subplot around a good-hearted and well-meaning poor fisherman who becomes a successful shopkeeper exemplifies the corruptive power of money and political ambition, and acts out the disorder of progressive liberalism. At the very beginning, the poor fisherman, Gancho, seems to be Milá's benign version of le Chourineur, the redeemed murderer and former resident of la Cité who faithfully assists Rodolphe in *Les Mystères de Paris*. As in Sue's novel, Torrellas and Gancho meet in the opening episode when the fisherman helps the officer rescue Carolina from drowning; and as a consequence of this encounter he becomes Torrellas's assistant. But Milá's Gancho is not Chourineur, their opposing characterizations are signified in the fact that Gancho helps Torrellas to save Carolina while le Chourineur's aggression against Fleur-de-Marie forces the intervention of Prince Rodolphe. The narrative configuration of the character of Gancho is unusually complex if we compare it to other servantlike characters in romance. Its atypical complexity is related to its function in Milá's representation of the city's changing identity and the power struggle among its social groups.

Gancho has strong social roots with the city and its recent history. He belongs to that old social group of small entrepreneurs—his father used to own a cabotage ship that covered the cork commercial route connecting Barcelona and Palamós—that is rapidly disappearing from the city's social spectrum due to the transformation of its mercantilist economy into speculative capitalism.[55] A victim of such transformation (his father's business has fallen into Bardisa's hands), Gancho is now part of the rapidly growing new proletariat. His relationship with Barcelona's rioters is established precisely by means of his new class identity. He is an unemployed worker struggling, as are so many in Barcelona, to find work at a time when commercial and manufacturing companies, affected by both the civil war (which disrupts Catalonia's internal circulation of goods) and the loss of most of the Spanish American colonies, are constantly laying off laborers.[56] Gancho is an example of the downward social mobility threatening the class that sustained Barcelona's old socioeconomic order and, accordingly, the city's traditional political stability. He is a desperate man, unable to provide for his needs and those of his mother and sister, just like all those politically dangerous working men and women who, on the 25th of July, and later occasions, took over the city. We find Gancho among those "cincuenta personas del bajo pueblo" [fifty people of the lower class] who are rioting on Fonollà street.[57]

But Gancho—whose personality has been shaped by the strong sense of order and traditional moral values of the old artisans and merchant class—does not truly belong in the new proletariat and consequently does not share the mob's blind violence. In fact, and through the character of Gancho, Milá establishes the fundamental opposition between the impoverished class of small artisans and merchants (to which Gancho belongs) and the supposedly true figure of the city's new proletariat—an opposition that substitutes for Sue's distinction between deserving poor and underclass criminals. In the episode of Fonollà street, Gancho ends up saving the good father Tomás (who is fleeing the burning of his convent) from the violence of "un aborto de hombre" [a hideous man] whose brutality and physical deformity directly represent the social misery and moral infirmity of both his class origin and political intentions: "el hombre [era] contrahecho" [the man [was] deformed].[58] As one of the last—and endangered—representatives of the old Catalan social order, Gancho will be instrumental in the happy resolution of the plot and, in his role of assistant to Torrellas, an indispensable ally of Carolina's friends. Indeed, saving the good father Tomás from proletarian violence, that is, keeping the link to Carolina's birth documents from harm, this member of the old Catalan order (who does not truly belong with the city's new underclass) prevents the plot from concluding hastily and unsatisfactorily.

Gancho, who is not truly a proletarian by origin and temperament, becomes later on in the novel the owner of a prosperous store in the seafaring neighborhood of *la Barceloneta*. The restitution to Gancho of his late father's old social standing—necessary as part of the message of social reconciliation and hope for all classes conveyed by romance—is an act charged with political contradictions in the volatile Barcelona of the mid nineteenth century. On the one hand, Milá presents Gancho's restitution of fortune as the continuation of that family tradition of small merchants violently interrupted by the unbound greed of the new capitalists. The continuation of tradition is signaled both by the similarity of the son's trade to that of his late father (the store is a warehouse stocked with marine products) and by the continuation of social geography (the store is located in Barcelona's traditional marine neighborhood). It seems at first that the industriousness of Gancho's family and the success of his store takes us back to that other, model store in la Boria street and to those "peaceful and quiet" years around 1798—when "el torbellino del espíritu de partido y de la política no había envuelto a los españoles" [Spaniards had not been besieged by the turmoil of partisanship and politics]—that made prosperity possible. Indeed, Gancho's "neat and clean" family store in Santa Rosa street where his good-natured wife and sister pleasantly "served the patrons" reminds us first of those old times in Milá's idealized rendition of the city's primitive capitalism.[59]

But the implication of the continuity of a social order said both to protect the property and profits of small capitalist enterprises and the salary of workers and to prevent the threat of ruin and the dangers of proletarianization, is immediatedly destabilized in Milá's story by the fact that the restitution of Gancho's old social status is not accomplished by the parallel restoration of the old socioeconomic system of the city, but quite the contrary.[60] Gancho's success has nothing to do with the industriousness and sacrifices of an old artisan-like family, or with its slow but continuous saving. On the contrary, the restitution of Gancho's fortune is presented by Milá as a whimsical occurrence, emblematic of the speculation that sustains the new capitalist order of the city: he wins the lottery. Moreover, and in clear contrast to the hard-working and quiet owners of the store on la Boria street, whose social occupations were limited to attending church functions and participating in religious festivities, the reader soon discovers that Gancho's prosperity is intimately linked to the social ambitions of Barcelona's new middle class whose political aspirations are threatening the supposedly old democratic order of benevolent patricians.[61]

The gentle and humble Gancho, whom we are used to, becomes arrogant and presumptuous. Although the narrator, whose political interests favor class immobility, assures the reader that "Gancho" is still the character's true and appropriate name, given to him by his own peers—"fue bautizado [con este apodo] por sus vecinos y compañeros" [was thus nicknamed by his neighbors and friends]—he also tells the reader that Gancho now finds his nickname "repugnant" and expects everybody to address him as "don Miguel" or "señor Gili." Milá does not simply ridicule Gancho's pretentious claim, he also presents Gancho improperly displaying the signs of the bourgeois-citoyen: he takes care of his business while smoking a cigar and reading the newspaper. Moreover, Milá shows Gancho's transformation from a modest and apolitical shopkeeper into an inexperienced and pretentious politician taking on responsibilities of city government:

> Las vicisitudes de una nación gitada por las disensiones políticas y por el encarnizamiento de las opiniones, habían puesto en el poder a los hombres del progreso; y amigos estos de adquirirse popularidad, la buscaron halagando a las clases jornaleras y de pocos alcances. El Gancho, que se desvivía por figurar y hacer papel, se entregó en cuerpo y alma a las filas del progreso sin cuidarse de lo que quería aquel partido ni cuales eran las intenciones del bando político que abrazara. Algunos barriles de aguardiente que en ocasión oportuna supo distribuir, le valieron al fin la plaza de capitán en una de las compañías de la milicia y el honroso cargo de alcalde de barrio.
>
> Aquella época fue para el Gancho el apogeo de su dicha; ¡qué gloria y satisfacción para él verse al frente de su compañía, vestido de riguroso uniforme, con sus charretas y sable en mano, marchando tambor batiente por las calles de Barcelona![62]

[The vicissitudes of a nation shaken by political dissent and violent opinion had placed men of progress in power; and seeking to gain popularity, they found it in the ignorant working classes. Gancho, who did his utmost to be prominent and have a role in things, devoted himself completely to the ranks of the progressives without considering what they wanted or the intentions of the political party he joined. Some barrels of hard liquor he distributed at the right time were enough to make him captain of one of the companies in the militia and gain him the honorable office of borough mayor.

For Gancho, that time was the height of his fortune. What glory and satisfaction it was for him to be in command of his company, dressed in a severe uniform with epaulets, saber in hand, marching the streets of Barcelona to the roll of the drums!]

Milá tells us how his arrogance and inexperience prevents him from understanding that his newly acquired social eminence and political activism make him a target for other people's resentment and greed. He tells us also about Gancho's abuse of his political prerogatives and authority as *alcalde de barrio* when he mishandles complaints against a carpenter, and how his mistakes as a political officer create social conflict and even endanger his own prosperity.[63] Thus, either as a member of the *patuleia* or as a progressive liberal, Gancho embodies the illegitimate aspirations and political activity sustained by the new economy. In *Los misterios de Barcelona* the military uniform of the *milicia urbana* and the din of drums of the middle-class supporters of progressive liberalism join the war drums of the absolutist followers of don Carlos in preventing the success of Queen Isabel's conservative rule in Barcelona. Only Gancho's origin—that is, his "good heart," his "innate goodness and honesty," and his willingness to submit to Beltrán's moderate and well-meaning advice—will ultimately redeem him from political radicalism, and secure him, at the end of the novel, a prosperous, though subservient, position in Barcelona's newly restored conservative order.[64]

Milá's representation of the social decomposition of the old town clearly shows the extent of the displacements involved in his extensive reworking of Sue's city. In this sense the actualization of the narrative possibilities contained in the last scene of *Les mystères de Paris* is central to Milá's imagination. We have already pointed out how Milá's *historia-novela* realizes the potential political meaning of the riotous celebration of the Parisian underclasses in the occasion of the public execution of Mme. Martial and her daughter, Calabasse. I am going to comment now on Milá's transformation of the unruly revel into a metaphor for the social existence of the modern city.

Milá borrows from Sue the narrative motif of the excitement experienced by the urban underclass during the execution of the criminals in order to narrate the riot of July 25th, but transforms Sue's description of the brutish behavior of the criminals into a parable of the city Barcelona is becoming. The relevance of the episode of the bullfight and the other two riots in the development of Milá's novel contrasts with the marginal position the popular outburst caused by the public execution of the Martial women has in Sue's. This contraposition clearly points out the different imaginations that dictate their novels. To explain the political violence that began in a bullfighting ring, to make sense of the relation between the event that triggered the riot—the bullfight—and the riot itself, Milá substitutes the execution of the bull for that of the criminals, the senseless sacrifice of the animal for the act of social justice. In *Los misterios de Barcelona* the *fiesta* around the fury of the beast provides both the form and the content to describe and condemn the new social and power relations emerging in Barcelona. The *corrida* becomes the signifier of the *bullanga*, and the new sign, in turn, becomes the signifier of the new city.

The transfer of meaning from bullfighting ring to city is carried first by a metonymic displacement: the violence of the bull is assigned to the bullfighting fan; and second by a substitution: the fury of the mob substitutes—and compensates—for the tameness of the bulls that on July 25th enraged the citizens of Barcelona. In the narrator's eyes the city becomes the stage of irrational violence, the "grotesque madhouse" first observed as confined within the limits of the bullfighting ring:

> En el ancho y espacioso campo que forma el glasis de la Ciudadela fuera la puerta del mar con la punta Este de la Barceloneta y el fuerte de D. Carlos, elévase un soberbio Circo cuya inmensa gradería y dos pisos de palcos están atestados de todas clases de personas y categorías. Agítanse en convulsivo movimiento más de tres mil abanicos, y una confusa y desentonada gritería acompañada de silbidos y desorganizados sonidos de trompetillas, completan el cuadro de aquella monstruosa jaula de locos donde en breve van a luchar los hombres contra unos pacíficos animales útiles a la labranza, sacrificando a la irritada cólera de los toros otros seres [los caballos] tan útiles como estos no sólo para los trabajos agrícolas sino que también para los industriales. ¡Rarezas de la humana veleidad! Un pueblo pacífico y laborioso cual es el de Barcelona . . . se agita, se rebulle, se desmoraliza, en fin, puesto dentro de la plaza de toros. Allí desaparecen los sentimientos de humanidad y compasión; allí sólo impera el genio del mal. . . . [Si no hay caballos destripados, si los picadores no son derribados, etc.] ya no hay diversión, ya no se siente placer, ya la corrida es mala y los empresarios son unos galopines que le roban al pueblo el gustazo de presenciar desgracias.[65]
> [In the broad and spacious field forming the glacis of the Ciudadela outside the city wall, with the eastern end of the Barceloneta and Fort Don Carlos, there was a magnificent circus, its enormous stands and boxes crammed with people of all classes and ranks. The rustle of more than three thousand fans, together with a confusing and discordant shouting, whistling, and the disjointed sound of trumpets—it all completed the picture of such a grotesque madhouse where some men will soon fight against gentle farm animals, thus sacrificing to the bulls other creatures equally useful not only for agricultural labor but also for industrial work [the horses]. Peculiarities of human folly! A peaceful and diligent people like that of Barcelona . . . becomes disturbed, stirred—in a word, demoralized—inside a bullring. In there, the feelings of humanity and compassion disappear, and only the spirit of evil prevails. . . . [If the horses are

not ripped apart, if the picadors are not knocked over by the bulls, etc.] there isn't much fun or delight, the bullfight is bad, and the impresarios are rogues who deprive the masses of the great pleasure of witnessing a misfortune.]

While the town Barcelona once came together in the order of its institutions and the well-regulated forms of its public celebrations, the city Barcelona is manifesting itself in the sudden transformation of its "peace-loving and hard-working" inhabitants into an "infernal jaula de locos" [madhouse] carried away by a "ciego frenesí" [blind frenzy] and the "devoradora sed de sangre y matanza" [ravenous thirst for blood and vengeance]. The convulsion, the offensive and dissonant shouting that provokes the expectation of the animal sacrifice, moves from the ring to the streets. There is nothing exotic in the alienation of "the infernal orgía de salvajes" [infernal orgy of savages] that so often took to the streets. The monstrous cage of irrational beings becomes the mob that raises hellish joy while killing priests and burning convents.[66]

Most remarkable in Milá's conception of the city as the space of class confrontation and the site of hidden new economic forces is his willingness to incorporate into Barcelona's narrative those people ignored by the text of the *Estatuto Real* and romanticized by Sue: those tenants of doña Rosa who inhabit the lower floor of her house—the city's lower classes. The representation of the working classes of Barcelona differs most acutely from *Les mystères de Paris*, just as Cortada's translation did, precisely in the erasure of the barriers set up by Sue both to distinguish underclass criminals from deserving poor and to deprive their actions of political content or purpose. In *Los misterios de Barcelona* the city's lower classes are highly politicized and openly engage in class struggle against the hegemony of the bourgeoisie.

Milá's imitation of the *tapis franc*, "El Café de Levante," owes to its model, first of all, the discovery of a social space intimately linked both to the city's new urban development and to the increasingly social marginality of the *poble menut*. Already, in the brief introduction to his novel, Milá mentions the "borrascoso mar" [tempestuous crowd] that meets in "lupanares" [brothels] and "garitos" [gambling dens], and throughout the novel he repeatedly echoes Sue's notion of the *tapis franc* as the representation of the dark side of the new bourgeois city, a reminder to its affluent classes of the social ills and political instability which go hand in hand with the economic opportunities and social mobility the city affords its inhabitants: "Esas casas de desmoralización" [those houses of corruption], Milá warns his readers, are "sentinas del vicio y focos del crimen" [sewers of vice and centers of crime].[67] But Milá's "El Café de Levante" represents a social setting far more dangerous than Sue's *tapis franc*. The customers of the Café are not unspeakable murderers and criminals, but rather an undifferentiated combination of lower-class characters. In the Café petty criminals and prostitutes mingle with the working class, and social disorder is inextricable from political radicalism.[68] In Barcelona's *tapis franc*, where the day laborers spend "in a moment" their weekly salary, the signs and agents of "scandalous excesses" are also those of a radical politics that promotes—and feeds on—class struggle. We clearly hear the crowd shouting "vivas a la libertad" [long live liberty!] and Riego's anthem among provocative words, coarse shouting, and obscene laughter:[69]

> Los parroquianos del café del tío Curro eran contrabandistas, desertores, barateros, mujeres perdidas y relajadas. Acudían a sí mismo marineros de los buques anclados al puerto, y algunos viciosos operarios de la maestranza de los astilleros de la Barceloneta.
>
> Mientras que en el billar dos tahúres, haciendo rodar sobre el verde paño unos dados, alijaban los bolsillos de los jugadores arrancando de estos las más horribles blasfemias; en la sala del café tenían lugar las más obscenas conversaciones: en una mesa de la izquierda cinco hombres ebrios ya por el ron y el aguardiente, prorrumpen en vivas a la libertad y entonan con ronca voz el himno de Riego; en la mesa inmediata un marinero y un soldado de caballería toman entre sus brazos a dos muchachas, las besan y cometen los más escandalosos excesos.[70]
>
> [The patrons of Uncle Curro's café were smugglers, deserters, cheaters, lost and dissolute women. There were also sailors from the ships anchored in the harbor and some dockyard workers from the Barceloneta.
>
> Two sharpers were throwing some dice at the green table and unloading the players' pockets, extracting from them the most horrible blasphemies. In the main room the most obscene conversations were taking place: at one of the tables on the left, five men already filled with rum and hard liquor burst into cheers to freedom and hoarsely sing Riego's anthem; at the next table, a sailor and a cavalryman take two girls in their arms, kiss them, and commit the most disgraceful excesses.]

Finally, the contrast between the taverns depicted by Sue and Milá not only exemplifies the identification of social and political threats which characterizes the imitation, but also provides another miniature representation of the city's emerging order. The Café is the site of new economic encounters, where new social relations and radical politics are constituted; it is the locus where the cancellation of traditional morality unequivocally signifies class struggle and speculative capitalism. The Café located in the harbor area (right outside the medieval walls which cannot protect the city anymore) embodies the subversion of the rigid but precarious barriers set by bourgeois morality to conceal the true nature of its new economic order—its most "horrible blasphemies" and "obscene conversations." "El Café de Levante" is a crude but true replica of the modern Barcelona, the open display of its inner disorder. In Milá's rendition of Sue's *tapis*

5: IMITATION AND THE AUTOCHTHONOUS NOVEL 133

franc, the tavern mirrors the city: gambling replicates capitalist speculation; smuggling reflects the unrestrained capitalist's drive for maximum profit and free-market policies; and prostitution enacts the commodification of the world and the debauched impulses of greed and lust. So much so that the illegal activities of the Café closely parallel those of the new gambling dens—*rolinas*—located within the city and frequented by the wealthy classes. There the new entrepreneurs ("the bankers of gambling," their "private police" and "hirelings") "wipe out and destroy" also within moments "opulentas fortunas levantadas a costa de fatigas y penalidades quizá de toda una generación" [opulent fortunes made probably thanks to the suffering and hardship of a complete generation] by means of "a lucrative speculation."[71] Moreover, the Café de Levante reflects the illicit sexual activity we have already encountered in doña Mercedes' brothel, and points to the substitution of lust and illicit business for the sober habits and slow economic movements of the town. It is not a coincidence, then, that the office of a quack doctor, where all of the inhabitants of Barcelona, regardless of class, seek relief for their sexual diseases, is popularly known as "el café de los gemidos" [the moaning café].[72] The Café is the site of unregulated rendezvous and numerous possibilities where the increasingly unrelenting desires of the people of Barcelona are unmistakenly transformed into a financial transaction:

> Los que allí van a curarse están obligados a pagar de entrada cuatro duros, y otros cuatro cuando están restablecidos; suma total de 8 duros por enfermo, con los realitos de la pócimas y brevajes por añadidura; esto sí . . . allí se cura a lo vapor, aunque los enemigos de la casa murmuran que después de algunos días revienta el mal por otra parte y que se estropean los enfermos en lugar de curarse, pero esto es envidia, envidia no más.[73]
>
> [Those who go there to be cured are obliged to pay four *duros* to enter, and four more when they recover—a total of eight *duros* per patient, not counting the cost of potions and concoctions. . . . They do steam therapy, although the enemies of the establishment grumble that after a few days the illness reappears somewhere else in the body and the patients get worse instead of better—but that's just envious talk.]

In *Los misterios de Barcelona* the excesses and activities of the proletariat and those of the new capitalist classes are one and the same, and the sickness of the mind (gambling) and that of the body (syphillis) seem to best represent them. The city of the fathers is becoming a casino and a whorehouse where fortune is the sign of a wealth that rejects all circulatory codes based on land and family, of a socioeconomic order where money no longer has origin. The moderate accumulation of capital and the social regulation of salaries which characterize Milá's ideal Barcelona are rapidly being dismantled and replaced by a speculative movement of wealth where money signifies only itself—"the limitless process of equivalences . . . that nothing will ever stop, orient, fix, sanction."[74] The Café de Levante, the *rolina*, and the "café de los gemidos," contain all the unknown mysteries of Barcelona that haunt the peace of Milá's readers.

Milá's imitation represents yet another step in the effort to make the alien character of the bourgeois novel a little less foreign to the sociohistorical conditions of mid-nineteenth-century Spain. From the diffused borderlines between translation and *original* writing emerges *Los misterios de Barcelona* as a further blurring of edges, as another process of appropriation of the French novel by the literatos. Milá's imitative act represents a "traduction/trahison" and reveals some of the assimilative processes taking place during those years in the Spanish literary field. He struggles to transform "social questions into properly literary or compositional ones," but the formal incongruency of *Los misterios de Barcelona*—the difficulties he faces in creating literary forms that retain and reproduce the sociological conditions in which they are born and which they represent—does not signal Milá's faulty actualization of a dominant literary form by Milá.[75] On the contrary, the compositional problems observed constitute precisely, as Roberto Schwarz reminds us, the novel's imitative success. The defective composition and literary weakness of Milá's imitation are the result of its autochthonous imagination and represent the sociocultural limitations of the historical period that produced it.

Afterword

TRANSLATION, IMITATION, AND ORIGINAL WRITING WERE DIFFUSE PRACtices in the 1840s and 1850s, their boundaries blurred by a practice of loose translation and original writing that constituted itself as a free reworking and reformulation of foreign (particularly French) materials. We can only speculate how different the history of the novel in Spain might have been if it had emerged as the result of the same—and simultaneous—historical processes that gave rise to the novel in France and Great Britain; but we do know the literary form of those mid-nineteenth-century Spanish fictions whose authors claimed they were free from foreign influences. This is the case of Alfonso García Tejero's *El Pilluelo de Madrid* (1844).[1] In the prologue to the work the narrator—the little rascal himself—makes a point of both denying any influence in his narration of foreign novelists and asserting his exclusive indebtedness to the Classic and the Golden Age legacies. His work, he tells us, is just his own and "extremely" Spanish:

> Estoy sin libros, y esta desgracia me ha impedido conocer a los brillantes escritores como Chateaubriand, D'Arlincourt, Dumas, Balzac, Thiers, Jorge Sand, Irving y otros que son el esplendor de la Europa civilizada.
> Estos que aquí ves . . . son: los autores clásicos, el arte de Carrillo, la gramática castellana, Virgilio, Guevara, obras de medicina de Hurtado de Mendoza, el Derecho romano y otros por el mismo estilo. . . . Yo no incurriré jamás en esa petulante manía [de mostrar que se conocen bien la cultura y literatura de Europa], y mi obrilla será en extremo española y de mi propia cosecha.[2]
> [I am without books, and this misfortune has prevented me from knowing brilliant writers like Chateaubriand, D'Arlincourt, Dumas, Balzac, Thiers, George Sand, Irving, and others who represent the splendor of civilized Europe.
> The books you see here . . . are: classical authors, the art of Carrillo, the Spanish grammar, Virgil, Guevara, works of medicine by Hurtado de Mendoza, Roman Law, and others like these. . . . I will never fall prey to that self-satisfied obsession [of showing off how well one knows the culture and literature of Europe], and my humble work will be completely Spanish and of my own creation.]

Despite his claims of having been educated by the Roman and Spanish Classics, and the clear resonance of the picaresque genre produced by the title of his book, the fact is that, according to his own account, he had not been reading any Spanish novels from the Golden Age—apparently as uninterested in them as the rest of the Spanish readers. The dissociation of *El Pilluelo de Madrid* from the Spanish novelistic tradition is evident in the absence in this work of the compositional principles, ideological unity, and moral concerns that sustained the diverse types of narratives produced in the Golden Age. Alienated from a tradition acknowledged as his own, and, at the same time, rejecting contemporary narrative for being foreign, el Pilluelo—or García Tejero—ends up writing his own version of Larra's "apuntación" [note], a fragmented and incoherent narrative whose focus vacillates between the memory of the past and the issues of the present, and from one literary genre to another: his book, he says, "will contain legends, adventures, historical recollections of the glories of our ancestors and contemporaries, novellas, popular customs, poems, and this philosophical thought."[3] Deprived of literary strategies of both the old and the new novel, García Tejero is able to grasp only sporadically the historical processes that were radically changing Spanish society in the 1840s. Maybe without the interference of the narrative and ideological principles learned from the foreign bourgeois novel this self-proclaimed original narrative (or a different one) would have eventually given rise to a novel fully adjusted to the historical conditions of mid-nineteenth-century Spain. This is, however, hard to imagine. In any case, mid-nineteenth-century literatos could not— would not—wait. They were committed to making sense of the historical processes triggered by the proclamation of the *Estatuto Real*, and many of them felt the French novel was not so alien after all.[4]

The successful reception of *Les mystères de Paris* by both readers and literatos brings forth one final reflection about the relevance of melodrama (and popular literature) for the nineteenth-century novel in Spain. The extraordinary number of imitations of Sue's novel written throughout Europe and, more generally, the lasting influence of melodrama in the novels written from many peripheral countries (such as Spain) seems to confirm Moretti's understanding of the emergence of mass literature in nineteenth-century Europe as related to the representation of "the Other of Europe" and "the Other *in* Europe." We can understand the success of Sue's novel among both common readers and literatos as due to the appropriateness of its writing to the particularly "extreme situations"— the extreme vulnerability—that characterized the triumph of liberalism in Spain. The weakness of its industrialization process, the violence of the civil wars, the unfinished character of its political revolution (the constant *alzamientos*), the well-rooted centrifugal forces of regionalism (the *juntas* undermining the authority of the state), and the loss of the empire (when the most prosperous European nations were busy building them) did not find a vehicle of expression in the "solid and well-regulated world" that characterizes the "Realistic temper" of both the British novel of social manners and, after the revolution of 1848, the new generation of French novelists.[5] Thus, the narrative formula of melodrama—prone to unusual events and characters, to a clear-cut representation of conflicts and resolutions, and to the uncensored display of emotions—actively contributed to represent the *off-center* historical conditions of Spain with respect to the political and cultural hegemony of France and Britain.

In this sense, we can say that the history of the nineteenth-century novel in Spain has been, and often still is, a paradoxical enterprise, since it is prone to deny and ignore precisely the diversity and peculiarities that constitute the autochthonous production of the novel. Many literary historians choose not to explore the mid-nineteenth-century novel, and to disregard the influence of melodrama in the constitution of Spanish Realism. In fact, most of the literary histories and monographs covering the experience of those years, from Blanco García's *La literatura española en el siglo XIX* (1894–1904) to Romero Tobar's *Panorama crítico del Romanticismo español* (1996), adopt Gómez de Baquero's attitude toward the novelists who wrote before 1868; he refers to them as those "whom literary history will have no reason to remember."[6] Others choose to denounce any possible connections as deplorable instances of literary impurity and, as do Baquero Goyanes and Romero Tobar, lament the "filtrations," or "contamination," that compromises the literary quality of the late-nineteenth-century novel and, more particularly, Pérez Galdós's works.[7]

It is true that to acknowledge the deep influence of the folletín in the literary practices of the nineteenth century complicates the construction of cultural strategies of social distinction in the novel and, consequently, makes difficult the enunciation of the literary legitimacy of the Spanish novel within the frame of modern culture (as dictated by the prestigious French and English models). But, as Moretti has rightly observed, the popular novel does not represent a betrayal of literature, but "rather the coming to light of the limits of Realism," that is, its dependency on the historical and social conditions that produce it.[8] Within this epistemological context, the mid-nineteenth-century Spanish novel and, more particularly, its "filtrations" into Realism emerge not only as key elements in the history of the novel in Spain, but also as one source of its difference. We can easily argue that the effort of the mid-nineteenth-century literatos to create an autochthonous novelistic imaginary was not wasted, and that, on the contrary, their literary legacy is at the base—and not only as the object of parody—of the writing of the late-nineteenth-century writers. To describe the literary processes involved in creating an autochthonous fiction, we just need to pay more attention to the numerous translations, imitations, and folletines that, so often, we take for granted.

Appendix: Plot Summary of *Los misterios de Barcelona*

THE NOVEL BEGINS IN BARCELONA IN THE EARLY HOURS OF 24TH JULY 1835, with a young man (Nemesio Torrellas) rushing to join his friends for a hunting trip. He is on the nearby hill of Montjuïc giving chase to his pals when he happens to see a young woman (Carolina) jumping into the sea. Torrellas acts immediately to save her from drowning and, with the help of a poor fisherman (Gancho) who is passing by with his boat, manages to rescue her. While she regains consciousness, Torrellas, who is examining the garments left by Carolina on shore, finds a suicidal letter in which Carolina has written the reasons for her desperate action: she has been seduced and abandoned by a young man (Jorge Gollo) and can no longer face the cruel treatment her relatives subject her to. Torrellas, who is a commanding officer of the warship "Isabel 2^a," takes pity on her and decides to protect her. With the assistance of the poor fisherman, he takes her to the warship while he arranges her transferral to the house of the only relative who has ever shown love and pity for Carolina: her godmother, Antonia Piló. While Torrellas instructs the fisherman how to proceed to help Carolina, he finds out about Gancho's harsh situation: he is a good and hard-working man struggling to support his mother and sister after his father's tragic death at sea, and the unscrupulous schemes of his father's former partner (José Bardisa) have left him with nothing but debts (his father used to own a cabotage ship that covered the cork commercial route that connected Barcelona and Palamós).

That same morning, and while Torrellas and Gancho are busy rescuing Carolina, Francisco Piló (Antonia's husband) is lying on his deathbed confessing to the good father Tomás that years ago he had stolen from an innocent orphan both her name and fortune, and that recently he had arranged for her illicit seduction in order to increase her desperation and cause her death. Before dying, Francisco gives the documents that prove his allegations to the priest. The death of Francisco allows the good and long-suffering Antonia to open her house and give protection to the distressed Carolina.

The next day, July 25th, the first political riot that would shake Barcelona breaks out. Gancho, who is in the streets with the rest of the city while convents and churches are burned down, happens to see an attack on the good father Tomás, whom he knows very well, by a group of lower-class rioters, and intervenes to save him. The badly shaken priest is upset because he was forced to leave behind the documents confided to him by Piló when his convent was set on fire by the city mob. Fortunately, he soon finds out that Domingo Riudoms, a priest who lived in his convent and to whom he had confided the importance of the documents entrusted to him, was able to rescue the papers before abandoning the burning building. In the following days Gancho, Torrellas, and the priest try to recover the documents which they suspect explain Carolina's origin. The confusion and fear that dictate the life of the city during those violent days and the break-out of a second riot in early August further hinder all efforts to retrieve the documents from Riudoms. Carolina's friends find out the priest has fled the city, and, after a short stay in Badalona, is on his way to Italy. Later Riudoms joins the Carlist army and will not return to Barcelona (with the documents) until the end of the civil war—and the end of the novel.

While all these events take place, the narrator resorts to a flashback to tell the story of Francisco Piló and his evil associate, José Bardisa. He narrates the corruption of the once good and naive young Piló by his friend Bardisa who awakens his lust and greed, the eventual ruin of his family business, the abandonment of his wife, and his hasty departure from Barcelona to Cuba. Once in Cuba, Piló continues to pursue his illicit desires and, under false pretense, befriends Juan Bardisa, the good-natured brother of the evil José, who owns a successful business in Havana and is the legal custodian of an orphan, Carolina. It is now that the reader finds out about the orphan's origin: she is the illegitimate daughter of a Catalan plantation owner, Pedro Palmas, and a slave, the mulatto Encarnación. Palmas, who loves Carolina dearly, recognizes her as his daughter, bequeaths part of his fortune to her, and, faced with an untimely death, places the child in the custody of his friend Juan Bardisa. Another untimely death, this time that of Juan, puts the child and her fortune in the hands of the unscrupulous Piló, who wastes no time in usurping the orphan's wealth and hiding her name. When he finally returns to Barcelona a rich man, Piló hands the orphan to José Bardisa telling him that she is the daughter of his brother, Juan. Carolina is left under the guardianship of her "uncle" who does not love her and often mistreats her. In Barcelona Piló leads a hypocritical existence hiding his sins under a facade of religious devotion and charity. The narrator also tells the reader about the fraudulent origin of José Bardisa's fortune. The narrator tells about his unscrupulous abuse of the goodness and trust of his former employer, the merchant Basny, and his evil and successful scheme to marry one of his daughters: Bardisa tells Mr. Basny that his daughter is pregnant and that the man responsible, an army officer and aristocrat, has forsaken her, and offers to marry her.

The story goes back, then, to the contemporary Barcelona of the 1830s and to Torrellas's and Gancho's quest for the truth. In order to help Carolina, Torrellas requests the assistance of his good friend Beltrán, a Catalan landowner and lawyer who belongs to the city's bourgoisie. In their efforts to locate the documents and to find out the truth of the orphan's birth, the protectors of Carolina have to counter the social and economic power the usurer José Bardisa holds in the city. Bardisa is connected to all kinds of illegal economic activity, from prostitution and gambling to theft, and, even at the end, when Carolina has recovered her name and heritage, the power of the usurer is left unchallenged. Only his death in the battlefield fighting for the Carlist cause puts an end to his domination. Later in the story the *indiano*, don Cristóbal (a Catalan who, after making his fortune in Cuba, has returned to Barcelona), joins Torrellas and Beltrán in their efforts to restore Carolina's name and heritage. The *indiano*, who has wide connections in Cuba, plays a fundamental role in both getting information about Carolina's origin and opposing the evildoings of Carolina's seducer, Jorge Gollo, the son of a very wealthy Cuban *criollo*, who supposedly is in Barcelona to complete his education. Gollo instigates social violence (he is one of the leaders of the third city riot), and when his father (having been informed of his son's misconduct) limits the amount of money assigned to him, he resorts to seducing old and vain rich women.

Meanwhile, Beltrán and Carolina fall in love. Beltrán's forgiveness of Carolina's affair with Gollo is countered by the opposition to their affection declared by the orphan's supposed uncle and guardian, Bardisa. At the same time the poor fisherman wins the lottery and marries the good-natured Luisa. We follow Gancho's social rise, the emergence of his political ambitions, and the serious trouble he gets into due to his active participation in city politics as a progressive liberal—his inexperience has harmful consequences for a poor artisan, and his new wealth attracts envious and greedy enemies (such as Bardisa). It is also during this time that Beltrán assists a dying prostitute, María Malalt (whom he knew as a young girl before the death of her father brought ruin to the family and forced her into prostitution), to take care of her last will: to seek forgiveness and the redemption of her young sister (who is also a prostitute), to inform her of their recent inheritance from an American relative, and to distribute some of her newly acquired fortune among the needy. María's sister, after a stay in Madrid as a high-class courtesan, returns impoverished to Barcelona and joins the criminal activity that Gollo and other evil characters carry out in the novel. Following all these characters, we scour the whole city and its emblematic places: the courthouse, the bullfighting ring, a tavern, the customs building, a brothel, a neighborhood store, a boardinghouse, a hospital, and so on.

At the end all comes together. Forsaken by all respectable society, Jorge Gollo has come to live among low-life criminals and is caught by Carolina's friends trying to trick the young sister of Gancho into a phony marriage. Following instructions given by the senior Gollo, he is expediently placed in a ship that is about to set sail for Cuba. Gancho is rescued from his legal problems by the wise legal advice of Beltrán and, having learned his lesson, goes back to managing his store leaving the government of the city to the traditional oligarchy of Barcelona. The Carlist priest Riudoms returns to Barcelona at the end of the civil war and is caught also by the orphan's friends trying to illegally exchange the documents he has kept all this time for a passport Bardisa is holding. Once the documents are in the hands of the orphan's protectors, Bardisa has to give up all pretension of authority over the girl. The documents confirm all we already know about the orphan's origin. The fortune misappropriated by Francisco Piló is returned to Carolina who, then, gives some of it back to her good and dear godmother, Antonia. Carolina, a free and rich woman, marries Beltrán. Bardisa dies fighting in the battlefield, and Torrellas, his mission done in Barcelona, leaves his friends happily ever after in a pacified city and sails toward America where unspecified trouble has arisen.

Notes

PREFACE

1. By *literato* I mean the writers, critics, professors, and publishers who participated in Spanish literary life in mid-nineteenth-century Spain.
2. The distinction between *moderado* [conservative] and progressive literatos is indeed a broad one. Many and often important differences in cultural and aesthetic preferences are found among literatos sharing similar political agendas. However, the distinction, although general, is pertinent in that it highlights the basic positions involved in the issues discussed in this book. The most relevant trait that distinguishes one group from the other is their commitment or resistance to the highly restricted form of liberalism imposed by the *Estatuto Real* upon Spanish society.

INTRODUCTION. THE CONTROVERSIAL LITERARINESS OF THE *MISTERIOS*

1. Leonardo Romero Tobar, *La novela popular española del siglo XIX* (Madrid and Barcelona: Fundación Juan March/Ariel, 1975), 35.
2. For a more detailed analysis see Elisa Martí-López, "Historiografía literaria y folletín: Notas para un debate crítico sobre el siglo XIX español," *Siglo XIX (Literatura Hispánica)* 4 (1998): 109–30.
3. See Osip Mandelstam, "About the Nature of the Word," in *Osip Mandelstam: Selected Essays* (Austin: University of Texas Press, 1977), 65–79. Ortega y Gasset insists on the idea of the progressive evolution of literature in his 1925 essay "Ideas sobre la novela": "Each work, more perfect than the previous one, cancels it and all those at its level" (in *Teoría de la novela: Aproximaciones hispánicas*, ed. Germán Gullón and Agnes Gullón [Madrid: Taurus, 1974], 32).
4. Reginald F. Brown, *La novela española 1700–1850* (Madrid: Dirección General de Archivos y Bibliotecas, 1953), 35. These notions have been repeated extensively throughout the years. See, for example, Juan Ignacio Ferreras, *La novela española en el siglo XIX (h. 1868)* (Madrid: Taurus, 1987), 53; Peter B. Goldman, "Toward a Sociology of the Modern Spanish Novel: The Early Years. Part I," *MLN* 89 (January–April 1974): 180; Eduardo Gómez de Baquero, *El renacimiento de la novela española en el siglo XIX* (Madrid: Mundo Latino, 1924), 35; José F. Montesinos, *Introducción a una historia de la novela en España en el siglo XIX; Seguida del esbozo de una bibliografía española de traducciones de novelas (1800–1850)* (Madrid: Castalia, 1980), 79, 129–30; Isabel Román Gutiérrrez, *Persona y forma: Una historia interna de la novela española del siglo XIX: Hacia el realismo* (Sevilla: Alfar, 1988), 127.
5. Joaquín Marco, "Prólogo" to *La Bruja de Madrid*, by Wenceslao Ayguals de Izco (Barcelona: Taber, 1969), 18. Verisimilitude, the key aesthetic construction of Realist writing, is used by Marco as a pattern of literariness in his analysis of works by Ayguals

(10). See also Pilar Aparici and Isabel Gimeno, eds., *La literatura menor del siglo XIX: Una antología de la novela de folletín (1840–1870)* (Barcelona: Anthropos, 1996), 1:10; Rubén Benítez, *La ideología del folletín español: Wenceslao Ayguals de Izco (1801–1873)* (Madrid: José Porrúa Turanzas, 1979), 47; and Román Gutiérrez, *Persona y forma*, 69. Marco also assigns value to Ayguals's works as precedent for Valle Inclán's *esperpento* (11).

6. See Carlos Blanco Aguinaga, Julio Rodríguez Puértolas, and Iris M. Zavala, *Historia social de la literatura española (en lengua castellana)* (Madrid: Castalia, 1978–79), 2:105–10.

7. See Catherine Jagoe, "Disinheriting the Feminine: Galdós and the Rise of the Realist Novel in Spain," *Revista de Estudios Hispánicos* 27 (1993): 225. For a critical examination of the values that sustain the formation of the canon for nineteenth-century Spanish novels see Hazel Gold, "Back to the Future: Criticism, the Canon, and the Nineteenth-Century Spanish Novel," *Hispanic Review* 58.2 (spring 1990): 179–204.

8. See Benito Pérez Galdós, "Observaciones sobre la novela contemporánea en España," in *Ensayos de crítica literaria*, ed. Laureano Bonet (Barcelona: Península, 1972), 115–32; and Ortega y Gasset, "Ideas sobre la novela." See also Juan Armada Losada, "Fernán Caballero y la novela de su tiempo," in *La España del siglo XIX: Colección de conferencias históricas (curso de 1885–86)* (Madrid: Ateneo de Madrid, 1887), 2:303; Benítez, *La ideología del folletín español*, 44–45; Miguel Galindo, "Breves notas sobre el periodismo y el folletín en la prensa castellonense del XIX," *Boletín de la Sociedad Castellonense de Cultura* 46.2 (1970): 175; and Marco, "Prólogo," 10–11. For a critical commentary of the "Observaciones" by Galdós see Alda Blanco, "Gender and National Identity: The Novel in Nineteenth-Century Spanish Literary History," in *Culture and Gender in Nineteenth-Century Spain*, ed. Lou Charnon-Deutsch and Jo Labanyi (Oxford: Clarendon Press, 1995), 120–36; Jagoe, "Disinheriting the Feminine"; and Mario Santana, "The Conflict of Narratives in Pérez Galdós' *Doña Perfecta*," *MLN* 113 (1998): 283–304.

9. A few studies approach the pre-1870 novel by trying to answer some of these questions. See, for example, Alda Blanco, "The Moral Imperative for Women Writers," *Indiana Journal of Hispanic Literatures* 2.1 (fall 1993): 91–110; Alicia Andreu, "Maternal Discourse in *La Cruz del Olivar* by Faustina Sáez de Melgar," *Revista Canadiense de Estudios Hispánicos* 19.2 (winter 1995): 229–40; Jean-François Botrel, "Nationalisme et consolation dans la littérature populaire espagnole des années 1898," in *Nationalisme et littérature en Espagne et en Amérique Latine aux XIXè siècle*, ed. Claude Dumas (Lille: Presses Universitaires de Lille III, 1982), 63–98; Marina Mayoral, "*La hija del mar*: Biografía, confesión lírica y folletín," in *Romanticismo 3–4, Atti del IV Congresso sul romanticismo spagnolo e ispanoamericano (Bordighera, 9–11 aprile 1987)*, ed. Ermanno Caldera (Génova: Biblioteca di Lettere, 1988), 80–89; and Noël Valis, "The Language of Treasure: Carolina Coronado, Casta Esteban, and Marina Romero," in *In the Feminine Mode: Essays on Hispanic Woman Writers*, ed. Noël Valis and Carol Maier (London and Toronto: Associated University Presses, 1990), 246–72.

10. As Romero Tobar reminds us, "popular literature of the traditional sort relies on the same means of propagation as highbrow literature, and is therefore subjected to the same commercial and ideological mediations" (*La novela popular*, 14). On the publishing production of the 1840 novels see—besides the numerous studies by Botrel—Victor Carrillo, "Marketing et édition au XIXe siècle: La Sociedad Literaria de Madrid (Etude d'approche)," in *L'infra-littérature en Espagne au XIXe et XXe siècles: Du roman feuilleton au romancero de la guerre d'Espagne* (Saint Martin d'Heres: Presses Universitaires de Grenoble, 1977), 7–101, and "Radiografía de una colección de novelas a mediados del siglo XIX," in *Movimiento obrero, política y literatura en la España contemporánea*, ed. M. Tuñón de Lara and Jean-François Botrel (Madrid: Cuadernos para el Diálogo, 1973),

159–77; and Agustí Duran i Sampere, *Contribució a la història de la imprenta a Barcelona* (Barcelona, 1936), and *Editores y libreros de Barcelona: Estivill, Piferrer, Brusi Bastinas* (Barcelona: Bosch, 1952). About the commercial aspects of the Realist novel of the last third of the century see, for example, Botrel, "Producción literaria y rentabilidad: El caso de Clarín," in *Hommage des hispanistes français à Noel Salomon*, ed. Henry Bonneville (Barcelona: Laia, 1979), 123–33; Botrel and Josette Blanquat, eds., *Clarín y sus editores: 65 cartas inéditas de Leopoldo Alas a Fernando Fe y Manuel Fernández Lasanta, 1884–1893* (Rennes: Université de Haute-Bretagne, 1981); Geoffrey Ribbans, "*La Desheredada*, novela por entregas: Apuntes sobre su primera publicación," *Anales Galdosianos* 27–28 (1992–93): 69–75, and "*Doña Perfecta*: Yet Another Ending," *MLN* 105.2 (March 1990): 203–25; Romero Tobar, "*Pepita Jiménez* en folletín: La historia interminable de publicaciones efímeras," *Insula* 562 (October 1993): 4; and Ana Navarro, "Historia editorial de *Pepita Jiménez*," *Cuadernos de Investigación de Literatura Hispánica* 10 (1988): 81–103.

11. Antonio Gramsci, *Selections from Cultural Writings*, ed. David Frogacs and Geoffrey Nowell-Smith (Cambridge: Harvard University Press, 1985), 348.

12. "The study of serialized novels," says Ferreras, "requires from the start a set of criteria that are to a certain extent extraliterary; we thus move into the domain . . . of sociology. But only in social and economic terms is it possible to unravel a novel that was dictated by publishers and inspired by readers" (*La novela por entregas, 1840–1900: Concentración obrera y economía editorial* [Madrid: Taurus, 1972], 12). The notion of "paraliterature" is already present in Gómez de Baquero's 1924 critical work on the Spanish novel (*El renacimiento de la novela española*, 44). I disagree with Aparici and Gimeno's opinion about the nonderogatory connotations of critical terms such as "subliterature," "paraliterature," and "infraliterature" (*La literatura menor del siglo XIX*, ix). For a semantic analysis of these terms see María Cruz García de Enterría, *Literaturas marginadas* (Madrid: Playor, 1983), 12–13.

13. Benítez, *La ideología del folletín español*, 155. For the creation of the folletín as a narrative stereotype see Romero Tobar, *La novela popular*, 61–71. The habit observed in certain scholars of resorting to dictionaries in order to give a precise definition of folletín can serve as an example of the tendency to neglect the novels themselves and the a priori approach which often characterizes their analysis. See, for example, Román Gutiérrez, *Persona y forma*, 152–53; and Blanco Aguinaga et al., *Historia social de la literatura española*, 2:107. The identification of market-oriented novels with narrative uniformity is so powerful that it influences even those studies, such as Iris M. Zavala's *Ideología y política en la novela española del siglo XIX* (Madrid: Anaya, 1971) (hereafter cited as Zavala), that view the pre-1870 novel, and in particular the *Misterios*, as the result of complex mediations between publishing policies and utopian socialism; and those, such as Romero Tobar's *La novela popular*, that insist on analyzing them as an integral part of nineteenth-century literature.

14. Franco Moretti says that the historian must seek out the "unbearable 'uncontemporarity' " of these novels; see *Signs Taken for Wonders: Essays in the Sociology of Literary Forms* (London and New York: Verso, 1988), 14.

15. Marco, "Prólogo," 10.

16. See Stephanie Sieburth, *Inventing High and Low: Literature, Mass Culture, and Uneven Modernity in Spain* (Durham, NC: Duke University Press, 1994), 10. I side here with Sieburth's statement that misleading generalizations "are routinely made about cultural products with no consideration of time period, political context, actual readership, format, or circuits of production" (9).

17. Ferreras, *La novela por entregas*, 12; Botrel, "La novela por entregas: Unidad de creación y público," in *Creación y público en la literatura española*, ed. J.-F. Botrel and S. Salaün (Madrid: Castalia, 1974), 125–29.

18. Michel Foucault, "What Is an Author?" in *Language, Counter-Memory, Practice: Selected Essays and Interviews* (Ithaca: Cornell University Press, 1977), 123.

19. The case of Ayguals's *María, o La hija de un jornalero* is entirely exceptional: it was a best-seller with eight prints during the years 1845–49 and with an estimated print run of between 13,000 and 27,000 copies. See Carrillo, "Marketing et édition au XIXe siècle," 36, 46.

20. See Jagoe, "Disinheriting the Feminine," 225.

21. Sieburth, *Inventing High and Low*, 11. See also Néstor García Canclini's analysis of the blurred distinction between mass-produced and artistic culture in Latin American modernity, in *Culturas híbridas: Estrategias para entrar y salir de la modernidad* (Mexico: Grijalbo, 1989), 65–93.

22. See Peter B. Goldman, "Toward a Sociology of the Modern Spanish Novel: The Early Years. Part I," and Part II in *MLN* 90 (January–April 1975): 183–211. On literacy rates and readership in nineteenth-century Spain see Carrillo, "Marketing et édition au XIXe siècle"; Agustín Escolano, ed., *Leer y escribir en España: Doscientos años de alfabetización* (Madrid: Fundación Germán Sánchez Ruipérez, 1992); Ferreras, *La novela por entregas*; Robert Marrast, "Libro y lectura en la España del siglo XIX," in *Movimiento obrero, política y literatura en la España contemporánea*, ed. M. Tuñón de Lara and Jean-François Botrel (Madrid: Cuadernos para el Diálogo, 1974), 145–59; and Jesús Martínez Martín, *Lectura y lectores en el Madrid del siglo XIX* (Madrid: CSIC, 1991). For editions of *María* see Carrillo, "Marketing et édition au XIXe siècle," 28–32. Ayguals de Izco, appealing to a middle-class and well-off readership, promoted his novel *María o La hija de un jornalero* with a reminder to the prospective reader that "the text will be interspersed with beautiful engravings and elegant lithographs" (Carrillo, "Marketing et édition au XIX siècle, 28).

23. Rafael del Castillo, *Misterios catalanes o el obrero de Barcelona* (Barcelona: Font, 1862), 169.

24. For illustrations and records of *Les Mystères de Paris*' reader see Martyn Lyons, *Le triomphe du livre: Une histoire sociologique de la lecture dans la France du XIXe siècle* (Mayenne: Promodis, 1987), 243; and Botrel, "Narrativa y lecturas del pueblo en la España del siglo XIX," *Cuadernos Hispanoamericanos* 516 (June 1993): 73.

25. The Duke of Rivas was one of those voices: "Who can doubt—he asks—that the novel penetrates into spaces where neither political disputes nor the controversies of the press arrive?" ("Discurso de contestación a Don Cándido Nocedal, del Excmo Sr. Duque de Rivas," rpt. in Zavala, 310). See also the anonymous articles "Folletines: Literatura" (1850) and "Folletines de los periódicos" (1844), rpt. in Zavala, 268–69 and 266–68, respectively. For a fictionalized account of a politicized *marisabidilla* see Manuel Bretón de los Herreros, *El editor responsable* (Madrid: Repullés, 1842). On female readership in the nineteenth century see Jagoe, "Disinheriting the Feminine"; and Susan Kirkpatrick, *Las Románticas: Women Writers and Subjectivity in Spain, 1835–1850* (Berkeley: University of California Press, 1989).

26. Gramsci, *Selections from Cultural Writings*, 370. Armand Lanoux reminds us of *Les mystères de Paris*' connection to mid-nineteenth-century utopian socialism: "*Les mystères* is published—it is a success. Then, it happens: people recognize themselves in the work and the socialists endorse it. The dandy is assailed by other forces that set up and anticipate not just 1848, but the subsequent foundation of the International. Victor Considérant, socialist and editor of *La Democratie pacifique*, said, 'I see what the author is trying to do: he aims to depict the suffering and needs of the working classes.' . . . He is a prisoner of his own myths and characters, of the opinion of Socialists and Republicans! . . . Eugène Sue has become, in spite of himself, a socialist writer" ("Introduction" to *Les mystères de Paris*, by Eugène Sue [Paris: Robert Laffont, 1989], 12–13). For Sue's role in the revolution of 1848 and his commitment to a democratic republic against Napoleon III; and on the different possible

readings of the political message of *Les Mystères de Paris*, see Umberto Eco, "Socialismo y consolación," in *Socialismo y consolación: Reflexiones en torno a "Los misterios de París" de Eugène Sue* (Barcelona: Tusquets, 1970), 18–22, 36–37.

27. As Victor Carrillo has shown in the case of Ayguals de Izco's novel *María o La hija de un jornalero*, this novel was "marketed to the opposition against the moderate regime (1844–1845) then in power" ("Marketing et édition au XIXe siècle," 34).

28. "As if newspapers (we generalize) had not done enough damage by using the weapon of politics, which has completely disrupted our unfortunate kingdom, they have sought to increase their harmful influence with the addition of the *folletín*" ("Folletines de los periódicos," 267). We should remember here that only 4.32 percent of the Spanish population was eligible to vote in 1843. See Miguel Artola, *La burguesía revolucionaria (1808–1874)* (Madrid: Alianza, 1973), 197.

29. The idea of the nonexistence of a nineteenth-century Spanish "middle class"—considered as the social basis of the new hegemonic genre—has been refuted by Raymond Carr as a well-spread but false "axiom of the historical interpretation" (*Spain (1808–1939)* [Oxford: Oxford University Press, 1966], 61). For the affirmation of the nonexistence of a bourgeois society in Spain prior to 1868 as explanation for the absence of the novel in Spain until late in the nineteenth century see Vicente Llorens Castillo, *El romanticismo español* (Madrid: Castalia, 1989), 588.

30. Wadda C. Ríos-Font, *Rewriting Melodrama: The Hidden Paradigm in Modern Spanish Theater* (Lewisburg, Pa.: Bucknell University Press, 1997), 11; and Peter Brooks, *Reading for the Plot: Design and Intention in Narrative* (London and Cambridge: Harvard University Press, 1992), 153.

31. Montesinos, *Introducción a una historia de la novela*, 95, 98. "Influence," said André Gide, "is regarded as something terrible, a sort of attack on oneself, a crime of lese personality" ("De l'influence en littérature," in *Prétextes: Réflections sur quelques points de littérature et de morale* [Paris: Mercure de France, 1945], 16). For a reflection on the issues involved in the discipline of literary history see Edward Baker, "Introducción: La problemática de la historia literaria," in *Texto y sociedad: Problemas de historia literaria*, ed. Bridget Aldaraca, Edward Baker, and John Beverley (Amsterdam and Atlanta: Rodopi, 1990), 12–18.

32. Roberto Schwarz, *Misplaced Ideas: Essays on Brazilian Culture* (London and New York: Verso, 1992), 11; and Blanco, "Gender and National identity," 123.

33. According to Alda Blanco, women were seen "as the producers and reproducers of imitation," and their works were associated with "fashion, barbarism, and the loss of national consciousness" for the first time by Menéndez Pelayo and other late-century neocatholic critics ("Gender and National Identity," 131, 125). See also Nancy Amstrong, *Desire and Domestic Fiction: A Political History of the Novel* (New York: Oxford University Press, 1987); Lou Charnon-Deutsch, *Gender and Representation: Women in Nineteenth-Century Spanish Realist Fiction* (Amsterdam and Philadelphia: John Benjamins, 1990); Lou Charnon-Deutsch and Jo Labanyi, eds., *Culture and Genre in Nineteenth-Century Spain* (Oxford: Clarendon Press, 1995); Helen Graham and Jo Labanyi, "Culture and Modernity: The Case of Spain," in *Spanish Cultural Studies: An Introduction*, ed. Helen Graham and Jo Labanyi (Oxford: Oxford University Press, 1995), 1–19; Noami Schor, "Idealism in the Novel: Recanonizing Sand," in *Displacements: Women, Tradition, Literatures in French*, ed. Joan DeJean and Nancy K. Miller (Baltimore: Johns Hopkins University Press, 1991), 55–73; and Valis and Maier, eds., *In the Feminine Mode*.

34. See José Lambert, "In Quest of Literary World Maps," in *Interculturality and the Historical Study of Literary Translations*, ed. Harald Kittel and Armin Paul Frank (Berlin: Erich Schmidt, 1991), 133–44. On the romantic notion sustaining our understanding of literature as sacred see André Lefevere, "Théorie littéraire et littérature traduite," *Canadian Review of*

Comparative Literature 9.2 (June 1982): 144. For a criticism of the nationalistic foundations and purposes of literary history see René Wellek, "The Crisis of Comparative Literature," in *Concepts of Criticism* (New Haven: Yale University Press, 1963), 282–95. The exclusion of translations from literary histories is based on similar values. The authority awarded to *original* writing is mirrored by the authority given to *original* reading. Thus, to the discredit of being a derivative writing, translation adds that of fomenting a mediated reading. Consequently, the repudiation of translation is determined by both the perceived dependent character of its writing and the supposed lack of literary competence—and autonomy—of its reader. Even-Zohar reflects about the thin line separating translated texts from other works considered adaptations or imitations (see "Translation and Transfer," *Poetics Today* 11.1 [spring 1990]: 79–84). For a critical revision of this traditional understanding of translation see Lefevere, ed., *Translation/History/Culture: A Sourcebook* (London and New York: Routledge, 1992); James S. Holmes et al., *Literature and Translation: New Perspectives in Literary Studies* (Leuven: Acco, 1978); Gideon Toury, *In Search of a Theory of Translation* (Tel Aviv: University of Tel Aviv Press, 1981); Edwin Gentzler, *Contemporary Translation Theories* (London and New York: Routledge, 1993); Susan Bassnett-McGuire, *Translation Studies* (London: Methuen, 1980); and Lawrence Venuti, *The Translator's Invisibility: A History of Translation* (London and New York: Routledge, 1995).

35. Romero Tobar, *La novela popular*, 37, 50.

36. Thomas Mallon, *Stolen Words: Forays Into the Origins and Ravages of Plagiarism* (New York: Ticknor, 1989), 5–8. See also Walter Benjamin, "The Author as Producer," in *Reflections: Essays, Aphorisms, Autobiographical Writings*, ed. Peter Demetz (New York: Schocken, 1978), 220–38, and "The Work of Art in the Age of Mechanical Reproduction," in *Illuminations*, ed. Hannah Arendt (New York: Schocken, 1968), 217–51.

37. Roland Barthes, "The Death of the Author," in *Image, Music, Text* (New York: Hill and Wang, 1977), 142–48; and "Histoire ou littérature," in *Sur Racine* (Paris: Seuil, 1963), 143.

38. Walter J. Bate, *The Burden of the Past and the English Poet* (Cambridge: Harvard University Press, 1970), 107.

39. T. S. Eliot, "Philip Massinger," in *Selected Essays, 1917–1932* (New York: Harcourt, 1932), 182.

40. See Harold Bloom, *The Anxiety of Influence* (New York: Oxford University Press, 1973), 6–14. See also Robert Escarpit, " 'Creative Treason' as a Key to Literature," *Yearbook of Comparative and General Literature* 10 (1961): 16–21.

41. Mallon, *Stolen Words*, 25. See, for example, Gómez de Baquero's comments on Fernán Caballero (*El renacimiento de la novela española*, 40), and Llorens's comment on the crucial borrowings carried out by major mid-nineteenth-century Spanish literary figures (*El romanticismo español*, 598).

42. Claudio Guillén, *The Challenge of Comparative Literature*, trans. Cola Franzen (Cambridge: Harvard University Press, 1993), 300; and Barthes, "The Death of the Author," 146.

43. Franco Moretti, *Atlas of the European Novel (1800–1900)* (London and New York: Verso, 1998), 190–91.

44. Schwarz, *Misplaced Ideas*, 17. Commenting on the "list of 'imitations' " that characterize nineteenth-century Brazilian life (from fashions and patterns of behavior to laws and novels), he points out how "judged separately against the social reality" these imports were superfluous, but that in their combination "they entered into the formation and equipping of the new nation-state, as well as laying the ground for the participation of new elites in contemporary culture" (13). Despite the specificity of the cultural dynamics framing the nineteenth-century Brazilian novel, I find Schwarz's analysis relevant to the Spanish case. As he says, "We didn't invent Romanticism [or] Naturalism. . . . None of which

prevented us adopting them" (34). Carlos J. Alonso, analyzing autochthonous processes of cultural formation in Latin America, talks about modern culture being "the province of another society" (*The Spanish American Regional Novel: Modernity and Autochthony* [Cambridge: Cambridge University Press, 1990], 28).

45. Mikhail Bakhtin, *The Dialogic Imagination*, ed. Michael Holquist, trans. Caryl Emerson and Michael Holquist (Austin: University of Texas Press, 1981), 347, 274. Similarly, Raoul Granqvist says that imitation is "a multifaceted artifact" that embeds "both the 'local' and the 'far away' ": "Imitation, despite common belief, does not function as the antithesis of originality; it does not materialize without permitting and stimulating reciprocity on many levels" (*Imitation as Resistance: Appropriations of English Literature in Nineteenth-Century America* [Madison, Wis.: Teaneck, 1995], 20).

46. Foucault, "What Is an Author?," 132.

47. See George Steiner, *After Babel: Aspects of Language and Translation* (New York and London: Oxford University Press, 1975), 296–413. André Lefevere refers to appropriation as "refraction," and the resulting writing as "refracted texts": "Refractions are texts that have been adapted to a certain audience . . . to a certain poetics or ideology" ("Théorie littéraire et littérature traduite," 148).

48. André Gide, "De l'influence en littérature," 20, 28, 14. Anna Balakian talks about "false influences": "a deviation, which stemmed from a desire to be influenced" ("Influence and Literary Fortune," *Yearbook of Comparative and General Literature* 7 [1958]: 28). Similarly, Barbara Herrnstein Smith considers the "*appropriability* of one's judgements for other people" as dependent on "the extent to which they share one's particular perspective" ("Value/Evaluation," in *Critical Terms for Literary Study*, ed. Frank Lentricchia and Thomas McLaughlin [Chicago: University of Chicago Press, 1990], 184). See also Steiner on the issue of "alternality" (*After Babel*, 333–34).

49. Bakhtin, *The Dialogic Imagination*, 345, 62. About the internally persuasive word he further comments: "Its creativity and productiveness consist precisely in the fact that such a word awakens new and independent words, that it organizes masses of our words from within, and does not remain in an isolated and static condition. It is not so much interpreted by us as it is further, that is, freely, developed, applied to new material, new conditions; it enters into interanimating relationships with new contexts. More than that, it enters into an intense interaction, a *struggle* with other internally persuasive discourses" (345–46).

50. For Schwarz's ideas on imitation summarized here see *Misplaced Ideas*, 25–64.

51. Antonio Elorza talks about "refraction" as one type of ideological relationship between the French referent and the Spanish political and cultural trends for the period before 1848; see "El tema de Francia en el primer republicanismo español," in *L'image de France en Espagne (1808–1850)*, ed. Jean-René Aymes and Javier Fernández Sebastián (Bilbao: Universidad del País Vasco, 1997), 111.

52. Schwarz, *Misplaced Ideas*, 62–66. He also reminds us that "it was inevitable that [Brazilian literature] should stumble in its own fashion, in a way that French works did not, since the social history upon which the latter were based could be thoroughly explored in them by means of those very same plots" (46). See Carlos Alonso's criticism of the subject/object model of history characteristic of the dependency theory applied to processes of cultural affirmation in nineteenth-century Latin America (*The Spanish American Regional Novel*, 32). For imitation as instances of master narratives in the Spanish novel see Valis's "Clarín y la vida cultural del extranjero: Tres artículos desconocidos," *Boletín del Real Instituto de Estudios Asturianos* 47 (1993): 157–78, and "The Perfect Copy: Clarín's *Su único hijo* and the Flaubertian Connection," *PMLA* 104.5 (1989): 856–967.

53. Schwarz, *Misplaced Ideas*, 66.

54. See Lambert, "L'éternelle question des frontières: Littératures nationales et systèmes

littéraires," in *Langue, dialecte, littérature: Etudes romanes à la mémoire de Hugo Plomteux*, ed. C. Angelet et al. (Leuven: Leuven University Press, 1983), 355–70; and Santana, *Foreigners in the Homeland: The Spanish American New Novel in Spain* (Lewisburg, Pa.: Bucknell University Press, 2000), 17–32.

55. Bakhtin, *The Dialogic Imagination*, 61, 63.

56. Derek Flitter's position in this regard is exemplary: "After the demise in Spain of French Romantic drama, attacked both by Classicist and Conservative critics, Spanish literature continued to follow the direction suggested by the ideas of the Schlegels and of Chateaubriand" (*Spanish Romantic Literary Theory and Criticism* [Cambridge: Cambridge University Press, 1992], 127). Similarly, José A. Valero says: "Universalist individualism— or other forms of autonomous identification with groups other than the nation, or national identification according to non-monarchical or religious criteria—disappear from the spectrum of possibilities" ("Historia literaria y articulación de identidades en la transición a la España liberal," *Journal of Interdisciplinary Literary Studies* 6.2 [1994]: 122). Scholars are still debating the extent and nature of the hegemonic role played by Schlegelian Romanticism in both the aesthetics and national discourses of mid-nineteenth-century Spain. For some of the critical—and sometimes polemical—turning points on the discussion of Schlegelian Romanticism see also David T. Gies, *Romanticismo* (Madrid: Taurus, 1989); Edmund L. King, "What Is Spanish Romanticism?" *Studies in Romanticism* 2 (1962): 1–11; Susan Kirkpatrick, "Spanish Romanticism," in *Romanticism in National Context*, ed. Roy Porter and Mikulás Teich (Cambridge: Cambridge University Press, 1988), 260–83; E. Allison Peers, *A History of the Romantic Movement in Spain* (New York and London: Hafner, 1964); Russell P. Sebold, *Cadalso: El primer romántico "europeo" de España* (Madrid: Gredos, 1974); Donald Shaw, "The Anti-Romantic Reaction in Spain," *Modern Language Review* (1968): 606–11; and Phillip Silver, "Toward a Revisionary Theory of Spanish Romanticism," *Revista de Estudios Hispánicos* 28 (1994): 293–302.

57. Wlad Godzich and Nicholas Spadaccini, "Introduction: The Course of Literature in Nineteenth-Century Spain," in *The Institutionalization of Literature in Spain*, ed. Wlad Godzich and Nicholas Spadaccini (Minneapolis, Minn.: Prisma Institute, 1988), 18.

58. Claudio Guillén emphasizes the importance of synchronic rivalries—"the rivalry . . . with the Brothers, that is, the contemporaries" over diachronic rivalries—rivalry with "the Father"—for literary creation (*The Challenge of Comparative Literature*, 300).

59. Marco, "Prólogo," 22.

Chapter 1. The Market Conditions in a Peripheral Literary Space

1. Moretti, *Atlas of the European Novel*, 187.

2. Boris M. Ejxenbaum, "Literary Environment," in *Readings in Russian Poetics: Formalist and Structuralist Views*, ed. Ladislaw Matejka and Krystyna Pomorska (Cambridge: MIT Press, 1971), 58. See also Christopher Charle, "Le champ de la production littéraire," in *Le temps des éditeurs: Du Romanticisme à la Belle Epoque*, ed. Henri-Jean Martin and Roger Chartier (Paris: Promodis, 1985), 126–57.

3. Contrary to the French trend, only a few English novels were translated into Spanish during the first half of the nineteenth century. The presence of the English novel is practically limited to the works by Walter Scott, who is the only non-French author to achieve an important commercial success among Spanish readers. During the 1840s and 1850s there are almost no Spanish translations of Dickens, whose works did not receive the attention of readers or critics until much later. For the different reception in Spain and Europe of the

French and English novels see Montesinos, *Introducción a una historia de la novela*; and Moretti, *Atlas of the European Novel*, 174–85.

4. Besides the aforementioned studies by Botrel, Carrillo, Duran i Sampere, and Marrast, see Santiago Luxán Meléndez, *La industria tipográfica en Canarias (1750–1900): Balance de la producción impresa* (Gran Canaria: Cabildo Insular de Gran Canaria, 1994); Martí-López, "El mercado editorial en la España de mediados del siglo XIX," *Cuadernos Hispanoamericanos* 565–66 (July–August 1997): 177–88; Manuel Núñez de Arenas, "Impresos españoles en Burdeos hasta 1850," *Revue Hispanique* 81 (1933): 5–46; and Aline Vauchelle-Haquet, *Les Ouvrages en langue espagnole publiées en France entre 1814 et 1833 (présentation et catalogue)* (Aix-en-Provence: Presses Universitaires de Provence, 1985).

5. As Leopoldo A. de Cueto said in 1843: "The novel of manners, which does not require profound preliminary studies and thus accords well with both the character of French writers and the taste of the society to which they address their work, has been and still is cultivated in France with such extreme profusion that it has managed to inundate Europe, and most particularly Spain" ("Crítica literaria: *Creencias y engaños*, novela original de D. Ramón de Navarrete," *Revista de Madrid* 1 [1843]: 100–106; rpt. in Zavala, 242).

6. "Until now I had only seen the competition in certain practices. I knew that men with special commissions were in Paris, a kind of plenipotentiaries, resident ministers, or chargés d'affaires . . . whose only task and responsibility was to keep watch . . . waiting for some new play or novel to come to light, so it could be immediately mailed to Madrid and translated without delay before someone else could beat them to it" (Modesto Lafuente, "Pleito ruidoso," *Teatro Social del siglo XIX* II [1846]: 146–50; rpt. in Zavala, 254–55; hereafter page citations are to Zavala).

7. The simultaneous publication of a work in different national markets was a fairly common practice during those days. See Lyons, *Le triomphe du livre*, 135.

8. Lafuente, "Pleito ruidoso," 255.

9. "So far I had seen the translating rivalry of the publishing houses and the eagerness to get adoption rights over that which was still to be born. But what I had never seen before was this curious and edifying dispute now very seriously launched between the two most serious Spanish newspapers [*El Español* and *El Heraldo*] about which of them first had the intention of publishing the translation of a French novel" (Lafuente, "Pleito ruidoso," 256).

10. The 1812 copyright legislation was not revised until 1847. The new law established the authors' right to their intellectual work as well as that of their heirs for a period, depending on the kind of work, between twenty-five and fifty years after the author's death. The first copyright agreement between France and Spain dates from 1853–54 and was due to Eugenio de Ochoa's efforts. See María Cruz Seoane, *Oratoria y periodismo en la España del siglo XIX* (Madrid: Castalia, 1977).

11. "They pulled all the appropriate strings, and by means of ingenuity and diplomacy they were able to extract from the author the important promise that he would send the original of his novel to this Spanish house before any other . . . as soon as the author wrote it" (Lafuente, "Pleito ruidoso," 256).

12. Ibid., 256–57.

13. The "Esbozo" is included in Montesinos's *Introducción a una historia de la novela*, 153–269.

14. "Revista Literaria," *Revista de Madrid* 4 (1844): 402–13; rpt. in Zavala, 248. Similarly, Carlos Rubio said in 1857, "Since newspapers need to have a *folletín* everyday, they will make up for the lack of Spanish novels with French ones, and the public, whose taste is rather tainted by these novels, will continue to become accustomed to the French genre" ("Sección Doctrinal," *La Iberia* [22 August 1857]; rpt. in Romero Tobar, *La novela popular*, 255). Similarly, Ayguals de Izco complained in the epilogue to his *La marquesa de*

Bellaflor that the first Spanish essays in the new genre had gone unnoticed as a consequence of the deluge of translations (*La marquesa de Bellaflor o El niño de la inclusa* [Madrid: Wenceslao Ayguals de Izco, 1847–48], 2:508).

15. As Leopoldo A. de Cueto said in 1843, the French novel "proves enough to satisfy the curiosity of our public" ("Críticia literaria," 242).

16. Ángel Fernández de los Ríos, "Prólogo," to *La casa de Pero-Hernández*, by Miguel Agustín Príncipe (Madrid: Baltasar González, 1848), xi–xii.

17. Francisco Javier Moya, "La novela nacional," *El Espectador* (9 May 1848); rpt. in Zavala, 275. Similarly, Fernández de los Ríos commented: "The preference of the public for foreign novels is simply the result of that same abuse of translations, which familiarizes readers with outside works and practically makes them regard with contempt the work of Spaniards" ("Prólogo," xi).

18. Quoted in Fernández de los Ríos, "Prólogo," xiii–xiv. To these words by Príncipe, Fernández de los Ríos added: "To the misfortunes mentioned in this novel we should add another one that it encountered. The novel was expected to be somewhat shorter, but then it became clear that it required a greater breadth, to the extent that it could not find comfortable room within the confines of the newspaper in which it was once more being published, and it was suspended again. Subscribers were duly compensated, and those who subscribe to the *Semana Pintoresca* now get the complete legend as a gift with the announcement of this publication. Such is the history of this work, so many times initiated and so worthy of being concluded" (xiii–xiv).

19. The combination of the functions of artist, publisher, and bookseller characteristic of the mid-nineteenth-century Spanish novelist was still quite common at the end of the century: "It is first the authors themselves who, being often their own publishers, logically ensure on their own the diffusion of their works. It is not rare to find in the press announcements inviting possible clients to come to the author's house and acquire such and such book, wholesale or retail. Thus, for instance, in May 1878, it was possible to buy *Las Nacionalidades* directly at Pi y Margall's" (Jean-François Botrel, *La diffusion du livre en Espagne (1868–1914): Les libraires* [Madrid: Casa de Velázquez, 1988], 27).

20. The exception is Ayguals de Izco who was also a successful publisher.

21. "The poet, once decided, writes a historical novel or one of those so-called of social manners. He goes to meet with the publishers, but they are practical and know very well how little profit they will get from the novel and scorn him with frivolous apologies, adding that always shameful clause . . . 'If it were a translation.' . . . [Then the poet] goes in search of money for the publication, but here new difficulties arise" (Mariano Noriega, *La fisiología de un poeta* [Madrid: Imprenta y Casa de la Unión Comercial, 1843], 37–38).

22. Ibid., 39.

23. Ibid., 39–40.

24. Alfonso García Tejero, *El pilluelo de Madrid* (Madrid: Sociedad Literaria, 1844), 1:9.

25. José Nicasio Milá de la Roca, *Los misterios de Barcelona* (Barcelona: Imprenta y Librería Española y Extranjera, 1844), iv.

26. Fernández de los Ríos, "Prólogo," x. See also the biographical notes on nineteenth-century Catalan writers compiled by Antonio Elías de Molins in *Diccionario biográfico y bibliográfico de escritores y artistas catalanes del siglo XIX* (Barcelona, 1889).

27. Ayguals managed La Sociedad Literaria (1843–44) and later became the chair and owner of La Imprenta de Wenceslao Ayguals de Izco (known in its last years as "Ayguals de Izco, Hermanos"). For the history of Ayguals de Izco's publishing enterprises and the editions of *María* see Carrillo, "Marketing et édition au XIXe siècle." For the catalogue of works published by Ayguals see Blas María Araque, *Biografía del Señor Don Wenceslao*

Ayguals de Izco, appendix to *Pobres y ricos o La bruja de Madrid*, by W. Ayguals de Izco (Madrid: Sociedad Literaria, 1850).

28. Ayguals, *La marquesa de Bellaflor*, 2:509.

29. Fernán Caballero often wrote to her supporters reminding them of their promises and commitments. See, for instance, her letter to Eugenio de Ochoa (28 August 1852) in *Cartas de Fernán Caballero*, ed. Diego de Valencina (Madrid: Librería de los Sucesores de Hernando, 1919), 35.

30. Javier Herrero, *Fernán Caballero: Un nuevo planteamiento* (Madrid: Gredos, 1963), 254. This same conservative newspaper, *El Heraldo*, would immediately publish three more of Caballero's novels: *La familia de Alvareda* (1849), *Lágrimas* (1850), and *No transige la conciencia* (1850).

31. José F. Montesinos, *Fernán Caballero: Ensayo de justificación* (Berkeley: University of California Press, 1961), 24.

32. Donald A. Randolph, *Eugenio de Ochoa y el romanticismo español* (Berkeley: University of California Press, 1966), 155–56; and *Don Manuel Cañete, cronista literario del romanticismo y del posromanticismo en España* (Chapel Hill: North Carolina University Press, 1972), 181–84, 192–93. The protection Fernán Caballero received from the Duchess of Montpensier (the sister of the queen) is at the origin of the article dedicated to her work published in *Le Correspondant* (25 August 1857) by Antoine de Latour (secretary of the duke and duchess). For more reviews and articles on Fernán Caballero's works see Randolph, *Eugenio de Ochoa*, 154–57.

Chapter 2. The Preoccupation with Autochthony

1. Franco Moretti, "Modern European Literature: A Geographical Sketch," *New Left Review* 206 (1994): 98–101.

2. Edward W. Said, *Orientalism* (New York: Vintage, 1979), 43. It seems pertinent to remember here that only a few years after the Napoleonic troops had engaged in the plundering of Egyptian historical and cultural objects, taking them from their original location and transporting them to France, the same army not only would repeat its territorial aggression in Spain but would treat the Spanish legacy similarly. This parallelism, though, is hardly unique. As Moretti says: "The great nineteenth-century museums are located in London, Paris, Berlin, and are filled with objects taken from Greece, from the Roman Empire; Mediterranean Europe, taken by force to the north" ("Modern European Literature," 108).

3. See Arturo Farinelli, *Il romanticismo del mondo latino* (Torino: Fratelli Bocca, 1927), 2:97.

4. Denys Hay, *Europe: The Emergence of an Idea* (Edinburgh: Edinburgh University Press, 1968), 122.

5. Said, *Orientalism*, 119. In this respect, it is also interesting to mention the discussions that took place at the time on whether the northern European countries were truly Romantic; see, for example, Philarète Chasles, "Des auteurs espagnols contemporains," *Revue des Deux Mondes* 3 (1841): 630–47.

6. For specific titles see the bibliography in Léon-François Hoffman, *Romantique Espagne: L'image de l'Espagne en France entre 1800 et 1850* (Paris: Presses Universitaires de France, 1961).

7. Jean-François Bourgoing, *Tableau de l'Espagne moderne* (1788; Paris: Levrault Frères, 1803), v.

8. George Sand, *Un hiver à Majorque* (1841; Paris: Michel Levy Frères, 1867), 182.

9. It would be necessary to compare the nineteenth-century production of oriental texts that had Spain as the main object with Spain's own recovery of its Muslim past. See the studies in Martine Baruch et al., *Nationalisme et cosmopolitisme dans les littératures ibèriques au XIXème siècle* (Paris: Presses Universitaires de Lille III, 1975).

10. Hoffman, *Romantique Espagne*, 40, 36. A similar gesture of imitation is found in both France (the cultural center) and Spain (one of its peripheries) during those years. However, and as important as the fact that the French are not imitating any contemporary author, is that the French recourse to Spanish texts does not entail an overall dependency on Spanish literary production. As Even-Zohar points out, "Whereas richer or stronger literatures may have the *option* to adopt novelties from some periphery within their indigenous borders, 'weak' literatures in such situations often depend on import alone" ("The Position of Translated Literature Within the Literary Polysystem," *Poetics Today* 11.1 [spring 1990]: 48; italics mine). He also distinguishes between "disguising appropriations" (by richer literary systems) and "conspicuous appropriations" (by dependent systems). For a further analysis on the option/necessity distinction, see also "Laws of Literary Interference," *Poetics Today* 11.1 (spring 1990): 53–72. On the Romantic myth of Carmen, see Carlos Serrano, *El nacimiento de Carmen: Símbolos, mitos y nación* (Madrid: Taurus, 1999).

11. As Hoffman notes in regard to the French theater listings: "Without pretending to give complete statistics, we should note that hardly a theater season between 1800 and 1850 was without at least one play in which Spain was being depicted on the stage. At least sixteen such plays ran between August 1823 and January 1824. In the decade 1830–1840, we find about fifty, twelve of them in the year 1836 alone" (*Romantique Espagne*, 39). In regard to the *roman noir*, he points out: "When a French writer wants to compose a story in which an all-consuming passion leads to the most horrifying crimes, more often than not he sets the action in Spain" (37); for specific titles see 167–78).

12. Ibid., 80.

13. Honoré Balzac, *Les Parisiens comme ils sont* (Genève: La Palatine, 1947), 12.

14. "[Identities] are constructed through, not outside, difference. This entails the radically disturbing recognition that it is only through the relation to the Other, the relation to what it is not, to precisely what it lacks, to what has been called its *constitutive outside*, that the 'positive' meaning of any term—and thus its 'identity'—can be constructed" (Stuart Hall, "Introduction: Who Needs 'Identity'?" in *Questions of Cultural Identity*, ed. Stuart Hall and Paul du Gay [London: Sage, 1996], 4–5).

15. Arturo Farinelli, in his 1927 book on Romanticism in the Latin world, discussed the European inner spaces of this "Orient of the imagination": "It is absurd to mark the boundaries and limits of this Orient envisioned by the most fervid imagination, to fix its lands and dominions. It was bound to include all those blissful and remote shores—the East and the West, from China to Spain. Spaniards and Orientals were thus regarded as identical by many romantics. And the most fantastic mental geography was undoubtedly the one which exercised a greater power: Iberia, Italy, Greece, Turkey, Palestine, Persia, Egypt, India, Florida, China, the Mississippi River, the whole East—all of that lay in that imaginary terrestrial paradise, everything according to the 'Kennst du das Land' sung by the poets" (*Il Romanticismo del mondo latino*, 2:97).

16. For approaches to this issue see Hugo Dyserinck et al., coords., *Europa en España: España en Europa: Actas del simposio internacional de literatura comparada* (Barcelona: PPU, 1990); Geoffrey Ribbans, *Catalunya i València vistes pels viatgers anglesos del segle XVIIIè* (Barcelona: Barcino, 1993); and Elena Echevarría Pereda, "La imagen de España en Francia: Viajeras francesas decimonónicas" (Ph.D. diss., Universidad de Málaga, 1994).

17. Stendhal, *Mémoires d'un touriste*, vols. 45–47 of *Oeuvres complètes* (Paris: A. Dupont, 1838), 47:185.

18. "Algunas palabras sobre la obra que en francés y con título de *Estudios sobre España*

ha dado a la luz el Sr. D. Antonio de Latour," *Revista de Ciencias, Literatura y Artes* II (1856): 638.

19. Ramón de Mesonero Romanos, "Los viajeros franceses en España," in *Recuerdos de viaje por Francia y Bélgica en 1840–1841*, vol. 5 of *Obras de Don Ramón de Mesonero Romanos*, ed. Carlos Seco Serrano (Madrid: Atlas, 1967), 253, 254. The literatos' resentment of the French discourse on Spain can be found in most mid-nineteenth-century texts. In his *La maravilla del siglo* (1852) Ayguals de Izco complains about Dumas's characterization of Spain (*La maravilla del siglo: Cartas a María Enriqueta o sea Una visita a París y Londres durante la famosa exhibición de la Industria Universal de 1851* [Madrid: Ayguals de Izco, 1852], 124). Juan Martínez Villergas had this to say about the perception of Spain by foreign travelers: "Bullfighting and fandango. Both have excited the curiosity of many foreigners and the admiration of some of them, but they have also allowed our enemies to sink their teeth into our glories, convinced that, because of our crimes of fighting bulls and dancing fandangos, we are lagging far behind in the civilization race" ("Introducción" to *El Fandango* [Madrid: Sociedad Literaria, 1845–46], 1–2). Similarly, Eugenio de Ochoa writes in 1841 to Federico Madrazo about Gauthier's negative depiction of Spaniards: "You have probably heard by now that upon his return from Spain he wrote a series of articles in which he censures us very harshly" (qtd. in Randolph, *Eugenio de Ochoa*, 54–55). See also Enrique Gil y Carrasco, "Literatura extranjera: Bosquejos de España por el Capitán S. E. Cook, de la marina real inglesa," *El Laberinto* 10 (16 March 1844): 128. On Spain's imperial status, Alejandro Oliván said in 1839: "Spain has no reason to be envious of other nations for their overseas colonies" (untitled article, *Revista de Madrid* 3 [1839]: 279).

20. Chasles, "Des auteurs espagnols contemporains," 638.

21. El Pobre Diablo, "De la importancia de las novelas o historias y de las razones por qué no prevalece en España este ramo de literatura," *Eco del Comercio* (7 January 1838); rpt. in Zavala, 229.

22. Mariano José de Larra, "Espagne poétique: Choix de poésies castillanes depuis Charles-Quint jusqu'à nos jours mises en vers français par Don Juan María Maury," in *Obras completas* (Barcelona: Montaner y Simón, 1886), 335. Larra repeats his denunciation of the European belief of the death of Spanish letters in an 1836 article: "We are not like those who, like foreigners, think that the end of our golden age marked also the end of love for fine letters in Spain" ("Literatura: Rápida ojeada sobre la historia e índole de la nuestra," *El Español* [18 January 1836]; rpt. in *Las palabras: Artículos y ensayos*, ed. José Luis Varela (Madrid: Espasa-Calpe, 1982), 259. See also his "Carta al editor Delgado (20 de agosto de 1835)," in Carmen de Burgos, *"Fígaro": Revelaciones, "Ella" descubierta, epistolario inédito* (Madrid: Alrededor del Mundo, 1919), 179–80.

23. Juan Martínez Villergas said in his 1854 *Juicio crítico de los poetas españoles contemporáneos* (París: Rosa y Bouret, 1854): "On the other hand, when those foreigners have deigned to talk about modern Spanish literature or have depicted our customs, they have not been genuine interpreters. On the contrary, being always badly informed about everything related to our peninsula, they appear to have set out to echo the most outdated and crude concerns. For them, Spain has produced nothing of value since the time of Calderón and Lope de Vega . . . which is as true as that anecdote related by Alexandre Dumas, who insists that he could not find in Madrid a hatter who could fix him an opera hat" (7–8). Similarly, the first fifteen issues (from April 1844 to June 1845) of the monthly periodical *El Dómine Lucas* (1844–46), founded by Ayguals de Izco and Martínez Villergas, opened with the long and serialized article "España y los Extranjeros"—a denunciation of the foreign construction of Spain and a vindication of its contribution to the civilization of Europe. Ayguals also published his *Galería regia y vindicación de los ultrajes extranjeros* (Madrid: Ayguals de Izco, 1843–45) as an "apology of Spain" (1:3). Susan Kirkpatrick also mentions the project conceived by Larra, Ramón Ceruti, and the Duke of Frías to found a

magazine "that would serve to improve the image of Spain in France" (*Larra: El laberinto inextricable de un romántico liberal* [Madrid: Gredos, 1977], 56).

24. As Hoffman points out, "These [French] books . . . drew the attention of Europe and the whole world toward Spain" (*Romantique Espagne*, 15).

25. The author of an article published in 1844 said in the *Revista de Madrid*: "The literary public is usually more willing to favor works written in the most civilized country in Europe than those made in a nation lagging behind in sciences and literature. Let us cover the distance that separates us from them, and you will see how the opposite will be true" ("Revista literaria," 248). See also Larra, "Horas de invierno," *El Español* (25 December 1836); rpt. in *Las palabras*, 324, and "Literatura: Rápida ojeada," 263–64.

26. Larra, "Literatura: Poesías de don Juan Bautista Alonso," in *Obras completas* (Barcelona: Montaner y Simón, 1886), 395.

27. "In Spain," said Luis González Bravo, "the vague character that these current agitations will impress upon us is still uncertain" ("De la crítica," rpt. in *El Alba (Madrid, 1838–1839)*, ed. José Simón Díaz [Madrid: CSIC, 1946], 27).

28. Juan Eugenio Hartzenbusch, "Estudios literarios: Apuntes sobre el carácter de la literatura contemporánea leídos en el Ateneo científico y literario de Madrid," *Siglo Pintoresco* 3 (1847): 152.

29. Salvador Bermúdez de Castro, "De la novela moderna," *Semanario Pintoresco Español* 19 (10 May 1840): 150. Larra also said, referring to the large number of translations of foreign works: "This derives naturally from our decadence . . . from the position Spanish society holds in the hierarchy of Europe" ("Horas de invierno," 320). Similarly, the author of "Revista Literaria" said: "Thus, no matter how difficult it is for us to admit, a neighboring nation provides us with the works we need for our own instruction and recreation, and there is hardly a writer who, even as he tries to be original, does not take from foreign sources the substance for his doctrine. This is a deplorable necessity, but one we do not condemn. As good patricians, we would like to see Spain leading the civilized nations, imposing her rule over the intellectual progress of the rest of Europe. But since this is not the case, it is preferable to follow in the footsteps of other civilized nations than to remain stagnant and look down on their accomplishments for the sake of some misguided patriotism. We would be extremely pleased if our bookstores would only advertise original works in their catalogues; but, given that this is not possible, it is better to see our printing presses sweat copious translations" (248). See also García Tejero, *El pilluelo de Madrid*, 1: 17–18; and Buenaventura Carlos Aribau, "Crítica literaria," *Semanario Pintoresco* (1846): 302.

30. Larra, "Literatura: Rápida ojeada," 259.

31. Philarète Chasles said in this respect: "Americans in the United States do not have a literature yet; Spaniards no longer have one. For the former, the era of originality has not arrived; for the others, it has already ended" ("Des auteurs espagnols contemporains," 75).

32. Larra, "Horas de invierno," 323.

33. Juan Bautista Alonso, "Cuál debe ser el carácter de la literatura en el siglo XIX," *El Alba* 6 (1838): 1–2; rpt. in *El Alba (Madrid, 1838–1839)*, 7. Similarly, Gabino Tejado said: "Literature is part of a civilization, and the history of our civilization has barely begun" ("De la crítica contemporánea," *El Laberinto* 17 [9 June 1845]: 239). See also Moya, "La novela nacional," 275.

34. "Local causes blocked intellectual progress in Spain, and thus necessarily any literary advancement. The death of national freedom, which had already received a disastrous blow with the collapse of the Communities, added political oppression to the already existing religious tyranny. While we had been able to preserve literary preeminence for a century, this was no more than the necessary effect of a previous impulse, and our literature lacked any inquiring, systematic, and philosophical character—that is, it was neither useful nor

progressive" (Larra, "Literatura: Rápida ojeada," 260–61). See also Ángel Fernández de los Ríos, *La España del siglo XIX* (Madrid, 1879).

35. Larra, "Literatura: Rápida ojeada," 265. See Kirkpatrick, "Spanish Romanticism," 267.

36. Carlos J. Alonso has identified this conviction as characteristic of all agendas of cultural redemption: "Since the autochthonous cultural order is judged consubstantial with the community, its recoverability can always be portrayed as an imminent achievement, that is, as the effective realization of an immanent potentiality. Therefore, accession to it is conceived as a matter of collective volition, as a momentous project to be undertaken by the community in its entirety" (*The Spanish American Regional Novel*, 12).

37. "We are happy to report the progress made in Spanish literature. An industrious youth brightly shows everywhere the glorious elements that will soon place this nation on a par with, or perhaps even at the front of, the most developed in Europe" (Ayguals, "Movimiento literario," *El Dómine Lucas* 15 [1 June 1845]: 118). Similarly, Gabino Tejado said in 1845: "We are doing with the history of our literature as we have done with our nation: prepare it by gathering, classifying, and defining as much as possible the materials that will determine its form" ("De la crítica contemporánea," 239). See also Larra, "Literatura: Rápida ojeada," 264; and Ayguals de Izco, *La marquesa de Bellaflor*, 2: 508–9.

38. Larra, "Horas de invierno," 323–24.

39. See Larra, "Literatura: Rápida ojeada," 263.

40. Leonardo Romero Tobar, "Españoles en París: Contactos de románticos españoles y escritores franceses contemporáneos," in *L'image de France en Espagne (1808–1850)*, 216. Fernán Caballero, *Cartas inéditas de Fernán Caballero*, ed. Santiago Montoto (Madrid: S. Aguirre Torre, n.d.), 108.

41. Ayguals de Izco reproached the Spaniards for their "shameful apathy" and encouraged them to confront the "ignominious tutelage" the French had over Spanish culture (*La marquesa de Bellaflor*, 2: 508).

42. Luis González Bravo asked his contemporaries: "Since when do nations look so much alike and so uniform, no matter how powerful the central drive towards identification?" ("De la crítica," 27).

43. El Pobre Diablo, "De la importancia de las novelas," 228–29. We recognize in the literary activity of those years an investigation about the causes of Spain's cultural predicament similar to the inquiry that occupied the Spanish American regional novelists: the investigation that "quickly becomes an historical indictment" on the motives—events, circumstances, and deviant practices—that initiated "the descent into cultural fallenness" (Alonso, *The Spanish American Regional Novel*, 11).

44. Cueto, "Crítica literaria," 242. Moya talked about the boredom—*tedio*—one felt when reading the old Spanish novels ("La novela nacional," 276). For the criticism of Golden Age narratives by mid-nineteenth-century literatos see also Fernández de los Ríos, "Apuntes biográficos: Eugenio Sue," *El Siglo Pintoresco* 9 (September 1846): 209–12; and J. Guillén Buzarán, "Sobre las novelas en España," *Semanario Pintoresco Español* 43 (27 October 1844): 338–40.

45. "Carta de Fernán Caballero al Dr. Julius," in *Fernán Caballero: Algo más que una biografía*, by Santiago Montoto (Sevilla: Gráficas del Sur, 1969), 366.

46. Noriega, *La fisiología de un poeta*, 36–37.

47. Larra, "Literatura: Rápida ojeada," 262. Similarly, Fernández de los Ríos stated a few years later: "Unfortunately, no national novel presently exists in Spain. And although there have been times when our writers, among the immense accumulation of translations, have published books belonging to that genre, all of them have always reflected the taste dominant abroad. Thus, once the genius of Walter Scott liberated the novel from the timidity, monotony, and coldness that were its distinguishing features, and as soon as Hugo followed

in the steps of the Scottish Homer, Espronceda, Villalta, Larra, and Escosura embarked upon the publication of a series of chronicles wrapped in the forms introduced by those celebrated masters" ("Crítica literaria: *María o La hija de un jornalero*, novela original de D. Wenceslao Ayguals de Izco," *Semanario Pintoresco* 36 [6 September 1846] [Madrid: Baltasar Gómez, 1846], 285).

48. Larra, "Carta al editor Delgado," 179.

49. Blas María Araque reproduces numerous positive reviews on the French translation of *María* published in French periodicals: *La Gazette des Tribunaux, Le National, L'Époque, Le Courrier Français, Le Journal des Débats, La Presse, Le Constitutionnel, Le Chirivari,* and *Le Siècle* (*Biografía*, 46–49). As an example, here is the review that appeared in *Le Journal des Débats*: "The writer Mr. Ayguals de Izco . . . has greatly succeeded in representing the intrigues, the political activities that have recently troubled Spain, and in exhibiting this country's customs, habits, majestic sites, and main artistic monuments" (rpt. in Araque, *Biografía*, 38). For the number of editions in Spanish and French of *María* see Carrillo, "Marketing et édition au XIXe siècle," 36.

50. Bakhtin, *The Dialogic Imagination*, 376–77.

51. Rpt. in Araque, *Biografía*, 47.

52. Moretti, *Atlas of the European Novel*, 166.

53. Hoffman has pointed out that the French literary construction of Spain, translated in turn by the literatos, had to leave—and did leave—its mark on the Spaniards' own perception of themselves: "Moreover, are not the Spaniards rushing to translate most of the French works for which their country has supplied the setting or the characters?" (*Romantique Espagne*, 137). Also Elorza, referring to Ayguals de Izco's decision to make the protagonist of *María, el marquesito,* an accomplished *torero,* comments: "Curiously, despite rejecting the stereotype, Ayguals accepts some of its fundamental elements" ("El tema de Francia en el primer republicanismo español," 121).

54. Fernán Caballero, *La Gaviota*, ed. Carmen Bravo-Villasante (Madrid: Castalia, 1982), 39. On the influence of French Idealism in Spain see Jagoe, "Disinheriting the Feminine."

55. As Schwarz has commented: "From afar, this substitution of one pastiche for another is so obvious it makes us smile. But it is also dramatic, since it points out to what extent our desire for authenticity had to express itself in an alien language" (*Misplaced Ideas*, 27).

56. See Ibid., 42.

57. As Ayguals de Izco said, "Since we do not have the honor of counting him [Eugène Sue] as a Spaniard, we can at least consider him a universal man" ("Introducción: Eugenio Sue," *El Fandango* 7 [15 June 1845]: 98). Similarly, Fernán Caballero wrote to a friend: "I now write always in French to portray the contemporary condition of society, this time of transition" ("Carta de Fernán Caballero al Dr. Julius," 366–67).

58. Jesús Torrecilla, *El tiempo y los márgenes* (Chapel Hill: North Carolina Studies in the Romance Languages and Literatures, 1996), 55–56. For Torrecilla's analysis of the process of imitation and appropriation in nineteenth-century Spain see *La imitación colectiva: Modernidad vs. autenticidad en la literatura española* (Madrid: Gredos, 1996), 11–45. See also Paul Ilie, "Antrophagous Spain and the European Other," *Hispania* 67.1 (March 1984): 28–35; and "Self-Images in the Mirror of Otherness," in *Iberian Identity: Essays on the Nature of Identity in Portugal and Spain,* ed. Richard Herr and John H. R. Polt (Berkeley: University of California Press, 1989), 156–80.

59. Larra, "Dos palabras," in *El pobrecito hablador* (Madrid: Ibero-Africano-Americana, 1927), 24–25.

60. Steiner, *After Babel*, 298.

61. Larra, "Los amigos," *Revista Española* 107 (20 October 1833): 40.

62. Larra, "Vindicación," *Revista Española* (23 March 1834); rpt. in Carmen de Burgos, "Figaro," 78–79; and "Dos palabras," 25.

63. Reprinted in Araque, *Biografía*, 46–47. See also several reviews of *María* published in different Spanish newspapers and reprinted under the title "Triunfo de la novela española," *El Dómine Lucas* (1846): 178–81.

64. See Schwarz, *Misplaced Ideas*, 43. Eugenio Ochoa pointed out the literary difficulties the literatos had when they tried to write a novel: "Our writers fail to appeal with their novels, because none of them has written enough to gain possession, so to speak, of all the artistic resources; their productions are no more than trials, and these trials are seldom perfect or even good" ("La Gaviota. Juicio crítico," in Caballero, *La Gaviota*, 326).

65. "Revista Literaria," 248. Similarly, Fernández de los Ríos commented: "Readers have suddenly decided to demand [from Spanish writers] that which they have come to expect from foreign works and which is the result of many years of experience" ("Prólogo," xi).

66. El Pobre Diablo reminded his contemporaries that "novels are a powerful means to transmit that word which Spain needs to recognize rather than to appease herself" ("De la importancia de las novelas," 228).

67. Fernández de los Ríos, "Prólogo," xi.

68. Martínez Villergas, *Los misterios de Madrid* (Madrid: Manini, 1844–45), 316.

69. Moya, "La novela nacional," 276; Milá de la Roca, *Los misterios de Barcelona*, iv; Ayguals de Izco, *La marquesa de Bellaflor*, 2: 508.

70. Fernández de los Ríos, "Prólogo," vii.

71. Martínez Villergas, *Los misterios de Madrid*, 316–17. Similarly, Fernández de los Ríos insisted on the political legitimation of the literatos' insistent undertaking of the novel ("Prólogo," viii–xii).

72. Ayguals, *María o La hija de un jornalero* (Madrid: Ayguals de Izco, 1845–46), 1:6. He insists more dramatically on the same idea in the epilogue of *La marquesa de Bellaflor* (the continuation of *María*): "Overwhelmed by the sublime desire to avenge my homeland for the insults some foreigners—out of ignorance, bad faith, or stupidity—have had the nerve to hurl at her, and eager to demonstrate the true state of civilization in Spain by describing the customs in her capital . . . I entered the literary arena with the publication of *María*" (2:507). Ayguals de Izco tells us also that he decided to publish the periodical *El Fandango* (1845) in order to avenge Spain for the misrepresentations it was subjected to, "with no other intention than to avenge *the country of the castanets* for the insults commonly divulged by those tedious foreigners" ("Introducción: Eugenio Sue," 97–98).

73. Caballero, *La Gaviota*, 41.

74. Art, and particularly literature, is said to be the highest expression of the unique soul of a nation. It brings a nation's collective being to the higher level of aesthetic accomplishments which reveal the ultimate apolitical nature of its culture and, consequently, its contribution to human history (A. W. Schlegel's *Kunstgeist*).

75. I agree with Tom Lewis's assertion that it is "the phenomenon of the cultural articulation and coexistence (for a time) of rival romanticisms that most vividly stands out as characteristic of Spanish cultural history from the mid-1830s through the early 1840s" ("Religious Subject-Forms: Nationalism, Literature, and the Consolidation of *Moderantismo* in Spain during the 1840s," in *Culture and the State in Spain: 1550–1850*, ed. Tom Lewis and Francisco J. Sánchez [New York and London: Garland, 1999], 260).

76. A few years earlier Larra had captured less enthusiastically the "real" (and backward) customs of Spain and contraposed them to a foreigner's expectations in "Vuelva usted mañana."

77. The term *language* is used as understood by Bakhtin: not simply a system of words but also a worldview (*The Dialogic Imagination*, 60–63).

78. For the eighteenth-century roots of the Spanish liberals' stand on national identity and

the role of foreign influence see Albert Dérozier, "L'esprit national et les apports étrangers: Une harmonieuse conciliation?" in *Nation et Nationalites en Espagne: XIXe–XXe siècles* (Paris: Fondation Singer-Polignac, 1985), 123–38.

CHAPTER 3. THE CRITICAL RECEPTION OF THE FRENCH NOVEL

1. Elorza, "El tema de Francia en el primer republicanismo español," 110.

2. "Revista Literaria," 247. The reliance of the literatos on foreign works for both critical considerations and practical exercises is attested to already in 1838 by El Pobre Diablo: "Incapable of mentioning a single Spanish novel that represents any kind of progress in our literature since the restitution of Gil Blas by Father Isla, I will necessarily have to resort to the examination of foreign works to show the level of excellence achieved by the novelistic genius" ("De la importancia de las novelas," 226). The notion of a literary life determined more by reception than by origin has been applied to the study of the Spanish novel in the 1960s by Mario Santana in *Foreigners in the Homeland*.

3. "With regard to novels," wrote Fernán Caballero in 1855, the French "are the masters" (*Cartas de Fernán Caballero*, 80–81).

4. "We promised in this article to examine the genre cultivated and the system followed by the main French novelists, and to see which of them is more adaptable to the demands of our public and which is more suitable to its customs, sympathies, and instincts" (Navarrete, "La novela española," 258–59). Even-Zohar reminds us that "the [imported] texts are chosen according to their compatibility with the new approaches and the supposedly innovatory role they may assume within the target literature" ("The Position of Translated Literature Within the Literary Polysystem," 47).

5. Lafuente, "Pleito ruidoso," 257.

6. Jean-René Aymes has pointed out that in this period literary debates were ideological contentions—"a combat of ideas which, broadly speaking, pits liberals against conservatives" ("L'image de George Sand en Espagne [1836–1850]," in *L'image de France en Espagne [1808–1850]*, 245). Similarly, Hazel Gold has commented on the openly ideological stand—"the little attempt to disguise . . . local, parochial motivations"—that characterized value judgments on the novel in Spain since the earliest moments ("Back to the Future," 185).

7. Fernández de los Ríos, "Crítica literaria: *María o La hija de un jornalero*," 285.

8. Fernández de los Ríos, "Apuntes biográficos: Eugenio Sue," 210.

9. For the reception of other aspects of George Sand's novels in mid-nineteenth-century Spain see Aymes, "L'Image de George Sand en Espagne (1836–1850)." For an analysis of the reception of Sand's works and its implications for the formation of the Spanish canon see Jagoe, "Disinheriting the Feminine"; see also Kirkpatrick, *Las Románticas*,133–202; and Colette Rabaté, "Deux 'modèles' français de la Avellaneda: Madame de Staël et George Sand," in *L'image de France en Espagne (1808–1850)*, 263–81.

10. Ramón de Navarrete, "La novela española" (1847); rpt. in Zavala, 259–60; hereafter page citations are to Zavala. The conservative literato Eugenio de Ochoa talked about Sand's "elegant follies" (qtd. in Randolph, *Eugenio de Ochoa* 39). See also Mesonero Romanos, "Las novelitas francesas," *Semanario Pintoresco Español* (28 June 1840): 261–63; rpt. in Zavala, 232–35.

11. Larra, "Panorama matritense," in *Obras completas de D. Mariano José de Larra (Fígaro)*, ed. Carlos Seco Serrano (Madrid: Atlas, 1960), 2:240.

12. Fernández de los Ríos, "Crítica literaria: *María o La hija de un jornalero*," 285. Balzac's moral detachment when representing French society was also highly problematic for conservatives such as Fernán Caballero who, despite her great admiration for his

novelistic mastery, considered that the indifference toward "principles" shown by his writing was detrimental to the literary quality of his works: "The problem with these and other eminent men is that they have ideas, but no convictions; opinions, but no principles. Therefore they cannot be endorsed or condemned in moral terms, since their beliefs are so variegated that in one page they appear religious and spiritual, and then skeptical, materialistic and rationalist in the next. This discredits their works among people of good faith. . . . Were they were less cynical in their affections, more moral in their affairs, and firmer in their good convictions, they would be admirable in their novels" (*Cartas de Fernán Caballero*, 81). See also Mesonero Romanos, "Las novelitas francesas."

13. Moretti has commented on the European reception of Balzac's and Stendhal's works: "All of Europe unified by a desire, not for 'realism' (the mediocre fortune of Stendhal and Balzac leaves no doubts on this point)—but for what Peter Brooks has called 'the melodramatic imagination': a rhetoric of stark contrasts that is present a bit everywhere, and is perfected by Dumas and Sue (and Verdi), who are the most popular writers of the age" (*Atlas of the European Novel*, 176–77).

14. Navarrete, "La novela española," 261. As Diego de Valenciana reminds us, the novels by Balzac were forbidden by the Sagrada Congregación del Índice on September 16, 1841; the ban was repeated on June 20, 1864 (in Caballero, *Cartas de Fernán Caballero*, 81–82).

15. Valenciana also records the ban of the novels written by both Dumas (father and son) by the Sagrada Congregación del Índice, first, on 22 June 1863, and later, on 21 June 1880 (in Caballero, *Cartas de Fernán Caballero*, 81–82).

16. Navarrete, "La novela española," 258–59. Francisco Javier Moya, a Spanish Fourierist, is more lenient when he comments on Dumas's novels: his works "do not go so far as [to pulverize social vices], but they do crush old concerns and present the events in the story with all the charms of popular activity. Dumas does not reflect about the future, does not display any aspiration for a more perfect condition, nor does he seem to be very concerned about the misfortunes and ordeals of contemporary society; rather, he mercilessly criticizes the rubble of the past, makes the story more captivating, and teaches by pleasing" ("La novela nacional," 276). See also Mesonero Romanos, "Las novelitas francesas."

17. The first Spanish translations of *Les mystères* were published in 1843 in Cádiz (by the press of *El Comercio*) and in Havana, Cuba (by D. R. Oliva). Many translations appeared from 1844 to 1850. See Montesinos, *Introducción a una historia de la novela*, 249–54.

18. Fernández de los Ríos, "Apuntes biográficos: Eugenio Sue," 210.

19. Guillén Buzarán, "Sobre las novelas en España," 339.

20. Fernández de los Ríos, "Crítica literaria: *María o La hija de un jornalero*," 285. In his 1847 article "La novela española," Ramón de Navarrate says: "Many may believe that the novel should not serve a higher purpose but should be content with being what it has been before—an occupation for women and an entertainment for men. We strongly object to that idea" (265). Similarly, Martínez Villergas speaks about the "social leaning" of the novel (*El cancionero del pueblo* [Madrid: 1844–45], viii). See also Moya, "La novela nacional."

21. El Pobre Diablo, "De la importancia de las novelas," 227. As Larra had already pointed out in 1836: "At a time like this, when the main obstacle to carry out the regeneration of the country lies in attracting the interest of the popular masses, . . . it is admirable that every Spaniard who thinks himself capable of forming an opinion rushes to announce it through the press" ("El ministerio Mendizábal," in *Obras completas de D. Mariano José de Larra (Fígaro)*, 2:214).

22. Benedict Anderson has pointed out the responsibility shared by the novel and the newspaper in processes of national consciousness formation: "These forms," he tells us, "provided the technical means for 're-presenting' the *kind* of imagined community that is

the nation" (*Imagined Communities: Reflections on the Origin and Spread of Nationalism* [London and New York: Verso, 1993], 25).

23. Ceferino Tressera—one of Sue's late Spanish imitators—in his *Los misterios del Saladero* (Barcelona: Manero, 1860), for instance, following in Sue's and Ayguals's footsteps, uses statistics, maps, and salary and demographic tables to illustrate the political arguments he is making. Furthermore, he not only discusses and quotes extensively the political thought of utopian socialist authors, but also mentions Hegel and Darwin.

24. Navarrete, "La novela española," 262. Sue, Fernández de los Ríos commented, delivered his critical message on the causes and possible political solutions of social injustice "to all ears" ("Apuntes biográficos: Eugenio Sue," 211). See also Moya, "La novela nacional"; "Revista Literaria"; and R. de Carvajal, "Sobre la traducción que hace del *Judío Errante* D. Wenceslao Ayguals de Izco," *El Fénix* (Valencia, 19 January 1845); rpt. in *El Dómine Lucas* 11 (1845): 83. This new socially unified and politically aware readership addressed by *Les mystères* was criticized by conservative literatos; see Duke de Rivas, "Discurso de contestación a Don Cándido Nocedal, del Excmo Sr. Duque de Rivas"; rpt. in Zavala, 310; García Tejero, *El Pilluelo de Madrid*, 1: 23–24; and Bretón de los Herreros, *El editor responsable*. For a defense of the traditional categories of readership in the mid nineteenth century see Joaquín Roca y Cornet, *Ensayo crítico sobre las lecturas de la época* (Barcelona, 1847).

25. Gary Saul Morson, *The Boundaries of Genre: Dostoevsky's "Diary of a Writer" and the Traditions of Literary Utopia* (Austin: University of Texas Press, 1981), 17. On the boundary character of *feuilleton*, Morson says: "A feuilleton is everything. . . . 'Everything' often included not only the author's chatter about the 'news,' but also documents from the daily press or from everyday life which the author had collected" (16).

26. Nicodemes Pastor Díaz, "Review: *Sab*," *El conservador* (19 December 1841): 440. Peter Brooks comments in this regard: "It may be significant that the publication of *Les Mystères de Paris* in the *Journal des Débats* ended . . . with an open letter from Sue to the paper's editor-in-chief, drawing attention of readers to a new periodical, *La Ruche Populaire*. . . . Sue, that is, closes his *novel* with announcement of a *newspaper* that will continue his work; and he ends his letter to the editor by recapitulating a four-point legislative program aimed toward the relief of social misery. The novel passes on into the world of the readers, whom it has defined and who have defined it, becoming part of the movement toward reform and social justice, putting itself at the service of a political world discovered by way of the melodramatic fiction" (*Reading for the Plot*, 166–67).

27. Armand Lanoux reminds us about the effect of the folletín on newspaper sales and journalism: "If Émile de Girardin's journalistic revolution has succeeded, it is thanks to the serial. . . . These processes may be accused of mercantilism, but the serial flourishes with Frédéric Soulié, Alexandre Dumas, Eugène Sue. The latter made the fortune of the *Débats*" ("Introduction," 3).

28. Martínez Villergas, *Los misterios de Madrid*, 313–14. For laws regulating censorship on printed materials see Seoane, *Oratoria y periodismo*. It is also interesting to note here that Sue's feuilleton, *Les mystères de Paris*, first published in *Le Journal des Débats*, appeared on the same page that reported on the sessions of the French Parliament.

29. As José Valero says, referring to Gil y Zárate's conception of "good literature": "It must be popular (having the 'indispensable spirit of nationality') but not the product of the people (since it must have 'literary merit'). The people are the passive recipient of good popular literature. In conclusion, a good literary work is characterized by its patriotic value (the movement 'toward' the people) and its literary value (warranty that only the selected minority will fully experience it)" ("Historia literaria," 125).

30. Donald E. Pease, "Author," in *Critical Terms for Literary Study*, ed. Frank Lentricchia and Thomas McLaughlin (Chicago and London: University of Chicago Press, 1990), 108–9.

31. For the analysis of the ultimate reactionary quality of *Les mystères de Paris,* despite its social critique and its support of utopian socialism, see Karl Marx and Frederick Engels, "The Earthly Course and Transfiguration of 'Critical Criticism,' or 'Critical Criticism' as Rudolph, Prince of Geroldstein," in *Collected Works* (New York: International Publishers, 1976), 4:162–209; and V. G. Belinski, *"Los misterios de París,"* in *Socialismo y consolación: Reflexiones en torno a "Los misterios de París" de Eugène Sue* (Barcelona: Tusquets, 1970), 39–48.

32. Fernández de los Ríos, "Apuntes biográficos: Eugenio Sue," 211.

33. Eco, "Socialismo y consolación," 36.

34. Albert Ghamine comments on the conservative literatos' interest in *Les mystères de Paris:* "To speak of myopia, ignorance or confusion of the bourgeoisie seems to me rather questionable, if not impossible. I would favor a more tactical interpretation: the conservative bourgeoisie was trying to appropriate the arguments of progressives and democrats in order to halt the criticism against the dogmatic liberal system, and thus to tame progress" *(Joan Cortada: Catalunya i els catalans als segle XIX* [Barcelona: Abadia de Montserrat, 1995], 87).

35. For Spanish translations of *Le juif errant* in the 1840s see Montesinos, *Introducción a una historia de la novela,* 249–52.

36. Oblivious to the literatos' reaction to *Le juif,* readers continued to enjoy Sue's narrative formula. As the author of "Revista literaria" points out, "The reader imagines that the Jew will save his family from the traps the Society of Jesus has apparently set for them, but does not anticipate either the means he will use to do that or the difficulties this family will have to go through before getting rid of such powerful enemy. Who can read *The Wandering Jew* without wanting to uncover the mystery behind the summons received by that cosmopolitan family to be in Paris on the thirteenth of February? Who does not want to know the motivation the Jesuits have to persecute this unfortunate family so fiercely?" (253–54).

37. Moya, "La novela nacional," 276.

38. As Kirkpatrick commented, only a few "scattered groups of utopians" had a proposal to enhance women's political rights *(Las Románticas,* 51).

39. Fernández de los Ríos, "Apuntes biográficos: Eugenio Sue," 211–12.

40. See Ayguals de Izco, "Introducción," 99.

41. Navarrete, "La novela española," 262.

42. Carvajal, "Sobre la traducción que hace del *Judío Errante* D. Wenceslao Ayguals de Izco."

43. For the differences between *Les mystères de Paris* and *Le juif errant,* and their critical reception in France, see Jean-Louis Bory, *Eugène Sue: Le roi du roman populaire* (Paris: Hachette, 1962), 230–322; and Francis Lacassin, "Preface," in *Le juif errant,* by Eugène Sue (Paris: Robert Laffont, 1983), 1–7.

44. Joaquín Rubió y Ors, *Memoria crítica literaria sobre "El Judío Errante"* (Barcelona: José Rubió, 1845), 17–18.

45. Ibid., 13, 11.

46. "The systems of Saint-Simon, Fourier, and Owen, born today and modified the following day, are worth more than all of Christ's precepts" (Rubió y Ors, *Memoria crítica,* 14). He also added: "As far as religion is concerned, Eugène Sue believes only in the natural one, that religion whose final consequence is pantheism, and whose only cult is that of the passions" (17). See also "Folletines de los periódicos," 267.

47. "Revista Dramática," *La España* (18 de mayo 1851), qtd. in Randolph, *Eugenio de Ochoa,* 144–45. For many literatos *Le juif errant* was an open invitation to the "abyss" that ruins both people and civilizations with the "force of vertigo" (Rubió y Ors, *Memoria crítica,* 20): society, said this critic, is "like a lake that is very easy to disturb [and] the

novel *The Wandering Jew* . . . could in the meantime increase the already heavy swell of this lake" (23–24). Sue's novels were listed in the "Índice" of forbidden works.

48. Ayguals de Izco, "A Mr. Eugenio Sue," preface to *María o La hija de un jornalero*, 1:5–8.

49. José Coll y Vehí, *Diálogos literarios* (1868; Barcelona: A. J. Bastinos, 1896), 3. See also Mesonero Romanos, "Las novelitas francesas," 233–34; Bermúdez de Castro, "De la novela moderna"; and Eugenio de Ochoa, *Miscellania de literatura, viajes y novelas* (Madrid, 1867), 375–76.

50. Rubió y Ors, *Memoria crítica*, 4–5.

51. Qtd. in Randolph, *Eugenio de Ochoa*, 39.

52. "This eagerness of modern writers to attach so much importance to their task . . . finds an explanation in . . . the feverish craving for philosophical and social fodder that plagues the nations. . . . The ignorance of the masses is constantly surprised by issues that should only be within reach of highly educated people; and these issues, vulgarized to the point of degradation, handled until they become dirty, and debated in squares, cafés, and even taverns, fall into the hands of writers who imprudently paint our customs and look to gain popularity with whatever is in fashion" (Duke de Rivas, "Discurso de contestación," 311). Jürgen Habermas notes that public opinion was considered at the time "the reign of the many and the mediocre," a "pressure of the street," a "coercive force" (*The Structural Transformation of the Public Sphere: An Inquiry into a Category of Bourgeois Society*, trans. Thomas Burger [Cambridge: MIT Press, 1989], 132–33).

53. "The novel does not conceal its ambition to educate readers. It teaches without the airs of the philosopher . . . within the reach of weak and frivolous minds" (José Fernández Espino, "Discurso leído ante la Real Academia sevillana de Buenas Letras" [1857], rpt. in Zavala, 300).

54. For the role of religious sentiment in the imaginative writing of moderado literatos and national formation see Lewis, "Religious Subject-Forms."

55. Jagoe, "Disinheriting the Feminine," 229.

56. See also Blanco, "The Moral Imperative for Women Writers," 95.

57. Fernández Espino, "Discurso leído ante la Real Academia sevillana de Buenas Letras," 307.

58. Ochoa, "La Gaviota," 340; italics mine. Similarly, Vicente Barrantes said: "Your books have lifted just the veil of anonymity a little bit, clearly and obviously revealing—as if under the light of a lantern—the heart of a woman" ("Carta a Fernán Caballero" [1853], rpt. in Zavala, 284–85). I disagree here with Charnon-Deutsch's assertion that if a nineteenth-century woman writer "made a mark in the literary world, it was for her *virile* style" (*Narratives of Desire: Nineteenth-Century Spanish Fiction by Women* [University Park: Pennsylvania State University Press, 1994], 8).

59. Stephen Gilman, *Galdós and the Art of the European Novel: 1867–1887* (Princeton, N.J.: Princeton University Press, 1981), 31, italics mine; and Fernández Espino, "Discurso leído ante la Real Academia sevillana de Buenas Letras," 300. As domestic novels, the *novelas morales y recreativas* received also the acquiescence of the conservatives, but as works written by women for a mostly female audience, they never succeeded in obtaining institutional recognition. Cecilia Böhl de Faber's male *nom de plume*, Fernán Caballero, hiding her true gender and supplanting it with that of a man, secured for her, although not uncontestedly, the institutional recognition awarded only to male authors, and a socially diverse audience. See Kirkpatrick, *Las Románticas*, 248.

60. Ayguals referred to his writing as an exercise in the subversion of social power (*La marquesa de Bellaflor*, 1:6). Caballero, *Cartas de Fernán Caballero*, 45. On Fernán Caballero's novels as a "corrective" of French—or French inspired—folletín see Montesinos,

Fernán Caballero, 2; Goldman, "Toward a Sociology of the Modern Spanish Novel, Part II," 191; and Shaw, "The Anti-Romantic Reaction in Spain."

61. Fernández Espino, "Discurso leído ante la Real Academia sevillana de Buenas Letras," 307.

62. "Costumbres: Biografía de una novela contemporánea" (qtd. in Romero Tobar, *La novela popular*, 68).

63. Fernández Espino, "Discurso leído ante la Real Academia sevillana de Buenas Letras," 307.

64. José Joaquín de Mora, qtd. in Carmen Bravo-Villasante, "Introducción bibliográfica y crítica," in Caballero, *La Gaviota*, 16–17. The attack by conservative literatos on the French novels and their Spanish imitators, and their support of the feminine writing of Fernán Caballero, help explain the strength of idealism in mid-nineteenth-century Spain. Idealism was still widely defended by the literary establishment as late as 1875 as the authentic writing of the Spanish novel. For idealism in Spain and Pérez Galdós's contentious literary position against Valera see Gifford Davis, "The Spanish Debate over Idealism and Realism before the Impact of Zola's Naturalism," *PMLA* 84 (1969): 1649–56; and Vernon A. Chamberlin, "*Doña Perfecta*: Galdós' Reply to *Pepita Jiménez*," *Anales Galdosianos* 15 (1980): 11–21.

CHAPTER 4. FROM TRANSLATION TO IMITATION

1. Romero Tobar, *La novela popular*, 35. Montesinos briefly mentions the positive effect of translations for Spanish letters in general: "Such a bustle of translations, even if some but not all of them were bad, proved to be eventually beneficial, and the language, far from being bastardized, came out enriched" (*Introducción a una historia de la novela*, 31). However, for him, the presence of the French novel did not have any impact on, or encourage the development of, the Spanish novel: "[b]ut the sensitive issue was not that there were too many translations . . . or that they were badly chosen, which is not necessarily true—the best sellers are the same here and there. The problem was that nothing of value was being produced within Spain herself, that she was not using those contributions as a point of departure for a new and vigorous national art. What we find strange is that, given the cravings of readers, the Spanish novel had such a late coming" (96).

2. The "Esbozo de una bibliografía española de traducciones de novelas (1800–1850)" compiled by Montesinos provides some examples of the generalized translating activity among the literatos in the 1840s: José María Anduenza translated George Sand (1846); Ayguals de Izco, Eugène Sue (1844 and 1845); Vicente Barrantes, Balzac (1854); Juan Cortada, Sand (1837) and Sue (1844); Patricio de la Escosura, Leclerc d'Aubigny (1843); A. Fernández de los Ríos, Sue (1846) and Dumas (1848); Antonio Flores, Sue (1844); Antoni Gironella, Soulié (1845 and 1848) and Dumas (1849); Pere Mata, Scott (1840, 1842, and 1843); F. Navarro Villoslada, Dumas (1847); A. Neira de Mosqueira, Paul de Kock (1845); José Orellana, Dumas (1848); Pau Piferrer, Scott (1843); T. Trueba y Cossío, Soulié (1849); and G. Romero Larrañaga, Paul de Kock (1839). Eugenio de Ochoa was the most prolific translator of French novels in the 1830s; he translated, among other authors, Scott (1840, 1841, 1842, 1843, and 1846). In the 1840s it was Victor Balaguer, who translated works by Bourgon, Cottin, Achard, Arlincourt, Dumas, Féval, Genlis, Sand, Hoffman, Houssaye, Hugo, Lamartine, Méry, Scribe, Soulié, and Sue. See also Montesinos, *Introducción a una historia de la novela*, 137–38.

3. Mañé y Flaquer wrote: "We have been thinking for some time about organizing a Literary Society like the one in Madrid, which has become increasingly famous and has done so much good for Spanish literature. Our goal in conceiving such project is no other

than to restore Barcelonese literature to the prestige it has shamefully lost with its dreadful translations.... Since these were printed in this city there are some who ... have presented us with the gift of calling these grotesque productions our literary works" (qtd. in Elías de Molins, *Diccionario biográfico y bibliográfico*, 2:80). Mañé was voicing the opinion of the group that published the journal *El Genio* (1844–45), which was founded by Víctor Balaguer. Besides Mañé y Flaquer, Coll y Vehí, Llausás, Aguiló, and Permanyer y Duran wrote for *El Genio*.

4. "Amid the overflow of dreadful translations of this novel that is deluging us ... we find consolation in seeing that some justly renowned writers, among them Mr. Ayguals de Izco, have assumed responsibility for vindicating our literature and translated *The Wandering Jew* into Castilian" (qtd. in Araque, *Biografía*, 22–23). The literary prestige—or disprestige—a translation could confer on its author is shown also in Larra's determination to decide which of his translations were to bear his name: "I warn you that in my translations for the stage and the press I will require—for those I will indicate—the most severe secret and anonimity; otherwise, I will not give you a single one. I will put my name only to those I may deem convenient. This is all my fortune and it is necessary to manage it carefully" ("Carta al editor Delgado," 180).

5. According to Brown, "Spanish novelists at the time would characterize their adaptations as 'original Spanish novels,' and it would be wrong to think of the word 'original' in this generic subtitle as opposed to 'translation.' It was meant rather to point in part to the understanding, present since the seventeenth century, of the literary word as something 'invented, created anew' " (*La novela española 1700–1850*, 10). Octavio Paz makes a similar, although more general, statement when talking about the nature of translation: "Each translation is, to some extent, an invention, and therefore represents a unique text.... A translation ... is always a literary operation" ("Traducción, imitación, originalidad," *Cuadernos Hispanoamericanos* 253–54 [January–February 1971]: 9). For him, the history of Western literature is the history of a series of crossings—*entrecruzamientos*—of styles and trends that often adopt the form of an imitation or a translation. In this sense, he rejects the term *influence* as being equivocal (14).

6. Larra, "De las traducciones," *El Español* (11 March 1836), rpt. in *Obras completas*, 497. Octavio Paz has said that "to learn to speak is to learn to translate" ("Traducción, imitación, originalidad," 7). The significance of translation for modern Spanish literature is just starting to be acknowledged. See, for example, Valentín García Yebra, "Opinión: Derechos morales del traductor," *ABC* (19 May 1999); Jacqueline A. Hurtley, "Translation in Postwar Spain: Twixt Survival and Interior Exile," *Journal of Interdisciplinary Literary Studies* 1.2 (fall 1989): 265–76; Francisco Lafarga, *La traducción en España (1750–1830): Lengua, literatura, cultura* (Lleida: University of Lleida, 1999); and Jordi Llovet, "Els vostres clàssics: El crèdit de la literatura," *El País* (20 May 1999), sec. "Quadern," 5.

7. Juan Cortada's translation follows the text of *Les mystères de Paris* published in *Le Journal des Débats* (19 June 1842 – 15 October 1843). All references in this book to the French text are from the edition of *Les mystères de Paris*, published by Robert Laffont, that reproduces that of *Le Journal*. According to Albert Ghamine, Cortada's translation was published simultaneously in a deluxe edition (5 volumes), and in a more affordable one in 4 volumes (*Joan Cortada*, 86). I have consulted this last one.

8. Steiner, *After Babel*, 379, 361. A. San Martín, another translator of *Les mystères de Paris*, mentions in his prologue the "intelligibility" of Sue's style and concepts and, consequently, his reliance on a word-for-word transfer of the French text (*Los misterios de París* [Barcelona: Saurí and Gaspar y Berdaguer, 1845], ix).

9. See Steiner for the notions of "elective affinity" and "resistant difference" (*After Babel*, 379–95). For an analysis on general strategies used by translators see also André Lefevere,

Translation, Rewriting, and the Manipulation of Literary Fame (London and New York: Routledge, 1992).

10. Ayguals de Izco's *María o La hija de un jornalero* (1845–46) is an example of an imitation of *Les mystères de Paris* that shows also the influence of *Le juif errant*. For other translations of these and other novels by Sue see Montesinos, "Esbozo de una bibliografía española de traducciones de novelas (1800–1850)," *Introducción a una historia de la novela*, 249–53.

11. See, for instance, Bory, *Eugène Sue*, 230–322; and Brooks, *Reading for the Plot*, 143–70. While it is true that many of the French readers of the novel were unfamiliar with Paris and, in general, with the social geography of the new industrial cities, Sue's text had an unequivocal immediacy to its French audience that Cortada could not ignore (Sue's novel referred to specific French social configurations and institutions and discussed French laws and customs).

12. Following Sue's own conversion to utopian socialism, the novel was conceived as a political appeal to its reader. According to Bory, socialist tendencies appear in *Les mystères de Paris* for the first time with the description of the model farm of Bouqueval in the third part of the novel (*Eugène Sue*, 250).

13. *Les mystères de Paris*, 563, *Los misterios de París*, 2:256; and *Les mystères de Paris*, 646, *Los misterios de París*, 2:355.

14. Friedrich Schleiermacher, "On the Different Methods of Translating," in *Theories of Translation: An Anthology of Essays from Dryden to Derrida*, ed. Rainer Schulte and John Biguenet (Chicago and London: University of Chicago Press, 1992), 40, 41. For other definitions see Schulte and Biguenet, eds., *Theories of Translation*. Steiner has criticized these distinctions, but his analysis is driven mostly by aesthetic considerations, while my study is not (*After Babel*, 303).

15. In the following example, Cortada omits a quotation from the *Traité d'éducation pour le Dauphin* by Cygne de Cambrai (*Les mystères de Paris*, 1081, *Los misterios de París*, 3:144). Probably due to the lack of Spanish translations for most of the books quoted by Sue, Cortada suppresses also all specific bibliographical references provided by the original. Cortada, however, gives the bibliographical information referred to in Stendhal's *Histoire de la peinture en Italie* for which a contemporary Spanish translation did exist (*Les mystères de Paris*, 1124, *Los misterios de París*, 4:196).

16. *Les mystères de Paris*, 922, *Los misterios de París*, 3:308. The translation's motion toward and away from literalness reflects sometimes in a contradictory manner the tension between affinity and difference with respect to the French original. Thus, and for example, Cortada suppresses the specific Parisian location of the French prison for men where part of the story takes place—promoting, consequently, the naturalization of the foreign text—while, and at the same time, he keeps the original French name of the prison and italicizes it, stressing, then, the otherness of the description:

Entrons à la Force.
   Rien de sombre, rien de sinistre dans l'aspect de cette maison de détention, située rue du Roi-de-Sicile, au Marais. (956)
Entremos pues en la *Force*.
   El aspecto de esta cárcel nada tiene de funesto ni de sombrío. (3:350)

Similarly, Cortada does not translate the word "*maire*" [mayor] (2:21 and 4:211), both implying the reader's familiarity with the French word and marking its otherness, while his untranslated reference to the very Parisian "Boulevards" or "passages" is accompanied by a footnote that naturalizes them by way of a description based on familiar references (3:17).

17. *Les mystères*, 1240.

18. In relation to Cortada's use of *caló* as the language of low-class violence, it is important to mention the highly visible participation of gypsies in Barcelona's riots of August 1835. See Anna M. Garcia Rovira, *La revolució liberal a Espanya i les classes populars* (Vic: Eumo, 1989), 360–61.

19. *Les mystères de Paris*, 76–77, *Los misterios de París*, 1:55. See also in *Los misterios de París*, 4:32. He identifies low and evil instincts with being a gypsy in 3:133. A. San Martín resorts to the same metonymic motion in his translation of *Les mystères de Paris*. In the prologue he talks about the obvious convenience of relying on *caló* to translate the French *argot*, relying exclusively on the prejudices of his readers against gypsies to justify his decision (ix). André Lefevere says in regard to this kind of substitution: "Dialects and idiolects tend to reveal the translator's ideological stance toward certain groups thought of as 'inferior' or 'ridiculous,' both inside their culture and outside" (*Translation, Rewriting*, 58).

20. Cortada resorts to footnotes only four times to translate the characters' words for his readers, in comparison to Sue's 162.

21. *Les mystères de Paris*, 72, *Los misterios de París*, 1:50.

22. *Les mystères de Paris*, 69, *Los misterios de París*, 1:47.

23. See Steiner, *After Babel*, 298.

24. The centralist policies that successive Spanish governments had dictated since 1714 are well known.

25. Steiner, *After Babel*, 33.

26. An example of the translation tendency to abbreviate is Cortada's summary of Juana (Jeanne) Duport's relation of her troubles to a friend—troubles already known to the reader: "Aquí Juana refirió a su compañera lo que había relatado a su hermano en la cárcel" [At this point Juana related to her friend what she had told his brother in prison] (4:220–21). See also the lengthy cut on the issue of phrenology (*Les mystères de Paris*, 1135, *Los misterios de París*, 4:210).

27. The following lines, found at the beginning of the chapter entitled "Cecilia," exemplify the compensatory function of most of Cortada's additions. They follow the omission already mentioned of the chapter entitled "Une intimité forcée": "El orden de nuestro relato exige que el lector se traslade a la habitación del portero Pipelet, quien acababa de salir dejando en casa a su esposa acompañada de la señora Serafina, ama de gobierno del notario Ferrand" [The order of our narrative demands that the reader move now to doorman Pipelet's room, who has just gone out, leaving his wife at home with madam Serafina, notary Ferrand's housekeeper] (3:3). We find few instances of censorship in Cortada's translation, and they do not affect the most morally audacious passages of the novel, such as the highly eroticized tale of Cécily's sexual manipulation of Jacques Ferrand, the episode that narrates the infanticide of Luise Morel's newborn baby, or the story of La Louve's passionate—almost brutal—love for Martial. They do not affect Sue's harsh criticism of the treatment of poor people in municipal hospitals, the high interests imposed by *Monts de Pieté* on the financially strained working class, or other similar, politically charged issues.

28. The complete omission of those footnotes that in Sue's text function as a reminder of previous aspects of the plot (addressed to an audience who is reading a lengthy and winding story by installments) is most probably due to the fact that Cortada's translation was published as a book.

29. The episode is part of the chapter entitled "Amitié" (*Les mystères de Paris*, 691–92, *Los misterios de París*, 3:33). The omission of episodes like this in the translation may be due to Cortada's desire to avoid comic digressions that distract the attention of the readers from the sociopolitical incursions and moral reflections of the main story line.

30. *Les mystères de Paris*, 1163, *Los misterios de París*, 4:244. Compare, also, *Les mystères de Paris*, 706, *Los misterios de París*, 3:50.

31. See Steiner, *After Babel*, 6.

32. *Les mystères de Paris*, 1077.

33. *Los misterios de París*, 4:140.

34. *Les mystères de Paris*, 69, *Los misterios de París*, 1:46.

35. *Los misterios de París*, 3:111.

36. Some decisive intrusions of the translator into Sue's text require simply a small, sometimes imperceptible, omission, like the suppression of just one word at the end of a long digression by Sue where he defends, against tradition and belief, the need for a divorce law:

[L'homme] impose, consacre, perpétue ses plus redoutables infirmités en les mettant sous la sauvegarde de l'immutabilité des lois divines et humaines. (*Les mystères de Paris*, 410)
[El hombre] consagra y perpetúa sus más temibles enfermedades, dándoles por salvaguardia la inmutabilidad de las leyes. (*Los misterios de París*, 2:68)

The omission of "divines" avoids a reading where human and divine laws are equally under attack and equally given an historical origin. Consequently, the authority of the Church is protected from Sue's criticism. Compare also Cortada's suppression of a reference to the marriages of priests during the French Revolution (*Les mystères de Paris*, 221, *Los misterios de París*, 1:216).

37. *Les mystères de Paris*, 525–27, *Los misterios de París*, 2:212–13.

38. *Los misterios de París*, 1:32, 1:340, 1:162. Cortada's resort to these footnotes is limited throughout the four volumes of his translations since their effect is somehow contradictory to the translation's main motion toward naturalization: on the one hand, they compensate for the alien elements, but on the other, they are ostensible marks of the text's foreignness.

39. See, for example, *Los misterios de París*, 1:153, 2:217, 3:31, 4:36.

40. "Hemos resumido en pocas palabras el último tercio de este capítulo, en primer lugar porque en él hay cosas que hubieran lastimado los oídos de nuestros lectores; en segundo porque la pintura que hace el autor nos parece muy exagerada, aunque no nos gloriamos de estar en los ápices de la legislación francesa" [We have summarized in a few words the last third of this chapter: first, because it contains things that would have hurt our readers' ears, and, secondly, because the author's depiction seems to be very extravagant—although we cannot claim to be experts in French legislation] (*Los misterios de París*, 2:212).

41. After ambiguously talking of low-class "hommes, femmes, enfants," Sue moves immediately to avoid an indiscriminate identification of that mob with the proletariat in general: "Écume fangeuse et fétide de la population de Paris, cette immense cohue se composait de bandits et de femmes perdues qui demandent chaque jour au crime le pain de la journée" [The foul and fetid scum of the population of Paris—this vast mob was formed of thieves and licentious women, who everyday tax crime for their daily bread] (*Les mystères de Paris*, 1236).

42. *Los misterios de París*, 4:327–28.

43. "Por fortuna," says Cortada in another of those defiant translator's notes, "nuestras costumbres están muy lejos del estado de corrupción [de las francesa].... En el corazón de los españoles existe siempre un fondo de virtud, de moral y de delicadeza que no bastan a extinguirlo transtornos, revoluciones, ni malas enseñanzas que de otras partes nos vienen" [Fortunately, our customs are very distant from the state of corruption [of the French ones].... In the heart of the Spanish people there is always an element of virtue,

morality, and kindness that cannot be extinguished by the disruptions, revolutions, and bad teachings coming from abroad] (*Los misterios de París*, 2:213).

44. Steiner, *After Babel*, 299.

45. Larra, "De las traducciones," 496–97. In the same article, referring to Ventura de la Vega's translations of French plays, Larra said: "The translation is so well done that it can be called original" (498). He seems to have a different position when poetry is the object of translation. The task of translating Spanish poetry into French seemed to him difficult: "This idea had to confront, however, an insurmountable hurdle: the nature of French language and poetry, so contrary to the Spanish" ("Espagne Poétique," 335).

46. Even-Zohar, "The Position of Translated Literature," 47. In the same article, Even-Zohar comments on the role of translation in peripheral literatures: "Such literatures often do not develop the same full range of literary activities (organized in a variety of systems) observable in adjacent larger literatures (which in consequence may create a feeling that they are indispensable). They may also 'lack' a repertoire which is felt to be badly needed vis-à-vis, and in terms of the presence of, that adjacent literature. This lack may then be filled, wholly or partly, by translated literature" (47). See "The Position of Translated Literature" also for the conditions that give rise to the centrality of translation within a national literary system and, in particular, for the hierarchical relations that are established among European literatures. For the analysis of interference between different national literatures see Even-Zohar, "Laws of Literary Interference."

47. In this respect Bakhtin says about the primordial moment of the European novel: "Translating and assimilating alien material is completed here not in the individual consciousness of the creators of novels: this process, lengthy and multi-staged, is accomplished in the literary-language consciousness of the epoch. Individual consciousness neither begins it nor ends it, but is part of its progress" (*The Dialogic Imagination*, 378, note 47).

48. It is well known that *La Gaviota* was translated from the French by José Joaquín de Mora. Julio Cejador y Frauca, however, expressing commonly held views, said: "Fernán Caballero no tiene ni pizca de francés" (*Historia de la lengua y literatura castellana* [Madrid: Tipografía de la "Revista de Archivos, Bibliotecas, y Museos," 1915–22], 8:24).

49. In 1846, for instance, the literato E. de C. resorted to the translation of a text by Amadée Achard entitled "Decadencia de la literatura francesa" to vent his frustration and anger at French cultural hegemony (*Revista Semanal del Avisador Malagueño* 44 [1846]: 344–49).

50. Ramón de Mesonero Romanos, "Las traducciones," in *Obras de Don Ramón de Mesonero y Romanos*, ed. Carlos Seco Serrano, 2:277 (Madrid: Atlas, 1967).

Chapter 5. Imitation and the Autochthonous Novel: *Los misterios de Barcelona*

1. As the case of the publishers "Hermanos Manini" analyzed by Botrel shows, imitation (even when it involves the material and mechanical aspects of book production) produces "hybridization"—the realignment of original forms and meanings by new social conditions: "an 'original' product adapted to the needs of the moment—those of the new readers" ("L'Espagne et les modèles éditoriaux français [1830–1850]," in *L'image de France en Espagne (1808–1850)*, 235–36). As Botrel tells us, the Spanish publishers not only imported the French novel but also all the publishing techniques involved in the making of a book. They imitated everything: typography, format, illustrations, distribution methods, etc.—all the formal aspects that were at the time helping to create a new form of reading and a new readership. According to Botrel, imitation imposed an "inauthentic" identity to Spaniards, but it represented also a form of national affirmation: "That what we tend to regard as a

form of imitation can be at the same time a sign of dependency and an element of nationalist reaction" (236).

2. *Los misterios de Barcelona* (Barcelona: Imprenta y Librería Española y Extranjera, 1844) was published in book form (in one volume of 308 pages).

3. *Los misterios de Barcelona*, iv.

4. Schwarz, *Misplaced Ideas*, 60.

5. See Ibid., 65.

6. See Schwarz's analysis of Machado de Assis' novels (*Misplaced Ideas*, 78–99).

7. Bory, *Eugène Sue*, 265. In the *misterios* the city replaces the rural and foreign sceneries so common in other forms of melodramatic writing. In this sense, Ríos-Font states a different situation in the Spanish theater: "The plots of melodramas are usually set in rural France, or in culturally French locales (Brussels, Geneva). Spanish writers of melodrama also adopt exotic locales the majority of the time, and in consequence Spanish audiences see melodrama's contents as foreign" (*Rewriting Melodrama*, 33).

8. Bory, *Eugène Sue*, 266. Steiner talks about a "climate of feeling" (*After Babel*, 457).

9. Sue, *Les mystères de Paris*, 31.

10. *Los misterios de Barcelona*, 5–6.

11. See *Los misterios de Barcelona*, 24. "El cazador" [The Hunter] is the title of the first chapter (5).

12. The progressive and radical liberals arrested the night of 18–19 August 1836 were held in the "brigantine schooner Isabel II" (Josep Maria Ollé Romeu, *Les bullangues de Barcelona durant la Primera Guerra Carlista (1835–1837)* [Tarragona: El Mèdol, 1994], 1:412).

13. Roger Chartier and Daniel Roche, "Livres et presse: Véhicules des idées," in *Seventh International Congress on the Enlightenment: Introductory Papers* (Oxford: Voltaire Foundation, 1987), 101. We should remember here Stephen Gilman's comments on the importance of journalistic writing in Pérez Galdós's *La Fontana de Oro* (*Galdós and the Art of the European Novel*, 29–48).

14. Ayguals, *María*, 2:384. In the epilogue to *La marquesa de Bellaflor*, Ayguals de Izco compares again his task as a novelist to that of an historian: "I have tried to be an exact, meticulous, and impartial historian in relating historical events" (2:510). For the close relationship between journalism and history in nineteenth-century Spain see Paloma Cirujano Marín et al., *Historiografía y nacionalismo español, 1834–1868* (Madrid: CSIC, 1985), 51.

15. In this respect, Milá's narrative strategies differ from the ones used by Ayguals de Izco in *María o La hija de un jornalero*. Umberto Eco is right when he points out that the use of footnotes by Sue signals the inability of the narrative to express all it wants to say ("Socialismo y consolación," 27).

16. Antoni Jutglar explains the events of July 1835 as follows: "[The events] did not constitute . . . an advanced, progressive movement, but . . . a common attempt by all the bourgeois groups—the typical and traditional middle class—to implement the basic demands of the political and legal revolution advocated by liberalism" against both urban workers and absolutists (*Ideologías y clases en la España contemporánea: Aproximaciones a la historia social de las ideas* [Madrid: Edicusa, 1972], 77).

17. The alliance between the city's bourgeoisie and the new Capitán de Catalunya, Barón de Meer, began in March 1837 and culminated in October of that same year when the Junta de Comercio of Barcelona and Meer met to discuss, among other things, the need to restore social order in the city. The conservative hold over the city's political institutions and the repression of the city's progressive liberal forces were to last until 1839. See Ollé Romeu, *Les bullangues de Barcelona*, 2:275–86.

18. Ollé remarks on the class character of these riots: "The continuous efforts to regulate

salaries were no more than a false solution to a real problem—the difficult situation of the proletarian classes, who wanted also to benefit from the changes taking place in order to improve their standard of living. Thus, in the Summer of 1835 there was in Barcelona a strong social element of class conflict that—sometimes in a more or less covert manner, others openly, without false appearances—profoundly marks the city's collective behavior" (*Les bullangues de Barcelona*, 1:76). Barcelona's social unrest returned with increased violence in 1842 and lasted until 1844.

19. Erich Auerbach comments on the eruption of the political and the social into the bourgeois sentimental novels: "The touching and, in essence, wholly personal love-alliance now no longer clashed with the opposition of ill-willed relatives, parents, and guardians or with private moral obstacles, but instead with a public enemy, with the unnatural class structure of society" (*Mimesis: The Representation of Reality in Western Literature* [Princeton: Princeton University Press, 1953], 441).

20. Sue, *Les mystères de Paris*, 1240.

21. *Los misterios de Barcelona*, 298.

22. Other secondary characters associated with morally perverse behavior and evil actions, such as Lagarza, are given an absolutist affiliation (*Los misterios de Barcelona*, 307). Francisco Piló, the evil character responsible for Carolina's loss of identity and fortune, is described as a hypocritical pietist.

23. Ollé has described the three moments that characterized the uprising on August 5th: "Thematically, during the first phase, the riots were dominated by violent actions of what we see as an essentially political nature. . . . In the second phase most actions were directed against the tax system and corporations or institutions that, because of their monopoly or regulations, increased the cost of living for the whole population and, most particularly, worsened the conditions of survival among the popular classes. Finally, the third phase was characterized by the charges against new forms of technological production" (*Les bullangues de Barcelona*, 1:122).

24. *Los misterios de Barcelona*, 129–30.

25. For an historical account of the third *bullanga* see Ollé, *Les bullangues de Barcelona*, 1:307.

26. On the Romantic theme of *la vierge souillé* see Eco, "Socialismo y consolación"; and Mario Praz, *The Romantic Agony* (Oxford: Oxford University Press, 1970).

27. Brooks, *Reading for the Plot*, 148.

28. For the dependency of the commercial and manufacturing Catalan bourgeoisie of the time upon the Spanish American market see Josep M. Fradera, *Indústria i mercat: Les bases comercials de la indústria catalana moderna (1841–1845)* (Barcelona: Crítica, 1987).

29. *Los misterios de Barcelona*, 307.

30. Brooks, *Reading for the Plot*, 150.

31. *Los misterios de Barcelona*, 16.

32. Ibid., 291.

33. Ibid., 9.

34. Schwarz, *Misplaced Ideas*, 59.

35. *Los misterios de Barcelona*, 32.

36. Ibid., 38–39, 40–43; italics mine.

37. On the function of enigma see Roland Barthes, *S/Z: An Essay*, trans. Richard Miller (New York: Noonday Press, 1974), 18–20, 209–10.

38. I do not completely agree, however, with Romero Tobar's analysis of the temporal structure that organizes the misterios: "The rigidity and awkwardness that halt the course of 'historical time' as it is translated into 'fictional time' result in the fact that this temporal perspective is of very little consequence as an element of novelistic technique" (*La novela popular*, 160). In the same manner Edward Baker insists on Ayguals's essentialist notion of

time: "The present is . . . a deception, a lie; and therefore it is unreal, since only the truth is real" ("Espacio urbano y representación literaria: Madrid de la Ilustración a la Gloriosa," in *Texto y sociedad: Problemas de historia literaria*, ed. Bridget Aldaraca, Edward Baker, and John Beverley [Amsterdam and Atlanta: Rodopi, 1990], 211). See also Valeriano Bozal Fernández, "La novela en España en el siglo XIX," *Cuadernos Hispanoamericanos* 219 (March 1968): 578–84.

39. *Los misterios de Barcelona*, 211–12, 208–10.

40. Ibid., 212–13, 209.

41. For a definition of the main notions of genealogy see José Ferrater Mora, *Diccionario de filosofía* (Madrid: Alianza, 1979), 2:1334.

42. Josep Termes pointed out, in regard to the idealization of the social order of the guilds: "Mid-century Romantic medievalism represented neither a nostalgic view nor a concealment of feudalism, but on the contrary, it was rather the emblem of a nationalism . . . in search of the lost nation" (*La immigració a Catalunya i altres estudies d'història del nacionalisme català* [Barcelona: Empúries, 1984], 118).

43. See Barthes, *S/Z*, 39–41.

44. *Los misterios de Barcelona*, 52–53.

45. Ibid., 306.

46. Ibid., 306–7.

47. Schwarz talks about the "measure of Río" in the novels of Alencar (*Misplaced Ideas*, 64).

48. *Los misterios de Barcelona*, 198–99.

49. Ibid., 204.

50. Ibid., 125. The tenant building on *la rue du Temple* is occupied as follows: on the ground floor, the doorman and his wife (the Pipelets); on the first floor, the military officer who tries to seduce Mme. d'Harville; on the second, Mère Burette, a moneylender and fortune-teller; on the third, César Bramandi (or Polidori), a sacrilegious priest; on the fourth, representatives of the working class and employees such as Rigolette (a *grissette*) or François Germain, and poor artists like Cabrion; finally, in the attic, the fragment of the working class that lives under miserable conditions: the Morels.

51. Ibid., 125–27.

52. Beltrán is the character who appears always associated with different legal contentions involving either the ambitious middle class or the economic policy of the government in Madrid. See, for example, the chapters "El juicio de conciliación" [The Conciliation Trial] and "Los cigarros" [Cigars].

53. *Los misterios de Barcelona*, 200. Don Cristóbal justifies his dealings with doña Mercedes as follows: "No soy ningún joven y . . . no tengo genio de andar buscando conquistas; soy frágil como todos los hombres y como los demás tengo mis necesidades" [I am not a young man and . . . don't have the energy to go searching for conquests; I am weak like any other man, and like any other man I have my own needs] (204). We should notice here the resonance of Sue's trial of the young seducer and his acquittal by a bourgeois jury of *pro-hommes*.

54. Leo Bersani, "Realism and the Fear of Desire," in *A Future for Astyanax: Character and Desire in Literature* (New York: Columbia University Press, 1984), 74.

55. *Los misterios de Barcelona*, 18–19.

56. On the lack of work for Barcelona's laborers in the late 1830s see Ollé, *Les bullangues de Barcelona*, 1:204, 221, 390.

57. *Los misterios de Barcelona*, 43. As Ollé puts it, talking of that summer of 1835, "There were too many people and very few jobs" (*Les bullangues de Barcelona*, 1:204).

58. *Los misterios de Barcelona*, 44.

59. Ibid., 51, 226.

60. The threat and fear of ruin is played out around the story of the old, rich, merchant Basny family whose businesses and fortune are usurped by Bardisa using immoral but legal means (Ibid., 57–68).

61. It is interesting to point out here that some historical sources blame mostly the sailors and fishermen from la Barceloneta for Barcelona's riot on August 5th (see Ollé, *Les bullangues de Barcelona*, 1:121).

62. *Los misterios de Barcelona*, 226, 228.

63. "Muy ajeno estaba el moderno don Miguel, de que siendo capitán de milicia, alcalde de barrio, propietario y rico, fuese demandado a juicio de condenación; admirado y colérico leyó a su cara mitad la papeleta de aplazamiento para el día siguiente a las nueve de la mañana a instancias de don José Bardisa" [Being captain of the militia, borough mayor, landowner, and rich, the modern don Miguel certainly did not anticipate the possibility of being sued in court. Amazed and furious, he read to his better half the citation for the next day at nine in the morning at the request of don José Bardisa] (Ibid., 230–31).

64. Ibid., 229.

65. Ibid., 37–38.

66. Ibid., 48–55, 129, 39. Milá describes the popular manifestations of the old town as follows: "Eran para [Francisco] acontecimientos de gran importancia y de sumo placer . . . la feria de Santo Domingo, por cuya solemnidad, en aquellos tiempos calmosos y pacíficos, en que el torbellino del espíritu de partido y de la política no había aun envuelto a los españoles, se engalanaba la calle de la Boria y las demás immediatas al vecino templo de santa Catalina. . . . Otro de los objetos predilectos de nuestro joven y que formaban época en su vida, eran las procesiones del Corpus y de la Semana Santa: no faltaba a las primeras Francisco con su abanico de paja ribeteado de badana plateada acompañando la bandera de su gremio, y haciendo otro tanto con su hacha y hábito penitencial con el *misterio* en las de Semana Santa" [For Francisco, those events were of great importance and pleasure. . . . In those calm and peaceful times when Spaniards had not been besieged by the turmoil of partisanship and politics, the solemnity of the Santo Domingo fair was celebrated with the decoration of the Boria street and those around the nearby temple of Santa Catalina. . . . Another element informing this period in the life of our young man was his predilection for the processions of Corpus Christi and Holy Week: he would always participate in the first, with his straw fan trimmed with a silver band, walking next to his guild's flag; and he would do the same, with the torch and penance robes during the Holy Week] (50–52).

67. Ibid., 85. Nemesio Torrellas repeats the narrator's moral condemnation of the taverns: "Hace ya tres noches que las pasamos de taberna en taberna y de cafetín en cafetín y en todas partes vemos lo mismo que aquí [el Café de Levante], juegos, borracheras, inmoralidad y blasfemias" [For three nights we have been going from tavern to tavern, from coffee bar to coffee bar, and everywhere is the same as here [the Café de Levante]: gambling, drunks, immorality, and blasphemy] (88).

68. The narrator describes a character named Diego Valido "(alias) el Chato" as a "antiguo cabo de la brigada de marina, hombre audaz y travieso, que había trocado la casaca militar por la levita de tahur de café" [a former corporal of a navy unit, a daring and mischievous man, who had traded the military jacket for a sharper's frock coat at a gambling café] (Ibid., 275). We recognize Cortada's mention of the presence in the "Salón Maville" of "empleados de la policía y guardias municiples" [members of the police] and the disturbing presence of soldiers and workers in "El Café de Levante."

69. It would be interesting to trace the literary evolution of the tavern in the Spanish novelistic imaginary from "El Café de Levante" to the "patriotic club" or "revolutionary café" of *La Fontana de Oro*.

70. Ibid., 85. Sue's tavern represents a typical inn in la Cité and, as such, his description relies on linguistic signs to replicate the geographical boundaries that confine its clients not

only to a specific area—l'île de la Cité—but, more important, to a social group—that of thieves and assassins. The description is punctuated by the use of *argot*, and, marking the sociolinguistic otherness of the space depicted, the narrator mediates between his description and his reader adopting the style and tone of a translator.

71. Ibid., 112–13.

72. "[A]llí verá V. capitanes, sargentos, soldados, tenderos y artesanos, carreteros y labradores, en suma, todas las clases de la alta y baja sociedad" [There you will see captains, sergeants, soldiers, shopkeepers and craftsmen, cart drivers and farmworkers—in short, all classes of high and low society] (Ibid., 134).

73. Ibid., 135–36.

74. Barthes, *S/Z*, 40.

75. Schwarz, *Misplaced Ideas*, 53.

Afterword

1. Two more examples of this type of narrative are *El cancionero del pueblo* and, in spite of its title, *Los misterios de Madrid* by Juan Martínez Villergas. It would be necessary to study these kinds of works—pretty popular at the time—in relation to the construction of a national imaginary and as parallel narrative forms of the novel.

2. García Tejero, *El Pilluelo de Madrid*, 1:19–20.

3. Ibid.

4. In another context, Vicente Llorens makes a somewhat similar statement when reflecting on the 1830–40 generation: "The fact is that the three Spanish writers of the first half of the nineteenth century with a more modern and personal style—Larra, Donoso Cortés, and Fernán Caballero—are the ones who received the most intense French education" (*El romanticismo español*, 599).

5. Moretti, "Modern European Literature," 103.

6. Gómez de Baquero, *El renacimiento de la novela española*, 46.

7. Mariano Baquero Goyanes, *Proceso de la novela actual* (Madrid: Rialp, 1963), 178, 181. As Romero Tobar has put it, "Although they rejected the *folletín*, the great novelists of the Restoration could not ignore the stimulus of the formula, and this made possible a special form of literary contamination, best represented in the narrative of Pérez Galdós" ("Folletín," in *Diccionario de la Literatura Española e Hispanoamericana*, Ed. Ricardo Gullón [Madrid: Alianza, 1993], 1:570).

8. Moretti, "Modern European Literature," 103. In this sense, it is appropriate to remember here Walter Benjamin's assertion on the need to "rethink" our conceptions of literary forms and genres in view of the new and changing conditions of production, "if we are to identify the forms of expression that channel the literary energies of the present" and, we can add, of the recent past ("The Author as Producer," 224).

Bibliography

"Algunas palabras sobre la obra que en francés y con título de *Estudios sobre España* ha dado a la luz el Sr. D. Antonio de Latour." *Revista de Ciencias, Literatura y Artes* II (1856): 637–44, 689–97.

Alonso, Carlos J. *The Spanish American Regional Novel: Modernity and Autochthony.* Cambridge: Cambridge University Press, 1990.

Alonso, Juan Bautista. "Cuál debe ser el carácter de la literatura en el siglo XIX." *El Alba* 6 (1838): 1–2. Rpt. in *El Alba (Madrid, 1838–1839)*, ed. José Simón Díaz, 7. Madrid: CSIC, 1946.

Amstrong, Nancy. *Desire and Domestic Fiction: A Political History of the Novel.* New York: Oxford University Press, 1987.

Anderson, Benedict. *Imagined Communities: Reflections on the Origin and Spread of Nationalism.* London and New York: Verso, 1993.

Andreu, Alicia. "Maternal Discourse in *La Cruz del Olivar* by Faustina Sáez de Melgar." *Revista Canadiense de Estudios Hispánicos* 19.2 (winter 1995): 229–40.

Aparici, Pilar, and Isabel Gimeno, eds. *La literatura menor del siglo XIX: Una antología de la novela de folletín (1840–1870)*, vol. 1. Barcelona: Anthropos, 1996.

Araque, Blas María. *Biografía del Señor Don Wenceslao Ayguals de Izco.* Appendix to W. Ayguals de Izco, *Pobres y ricos o La bruja de Madrid.* Madrid: Sociedad Literaria, 1850.

Arendt, Hannah. "What Is Authority." *Between Past and Present*, 91–141. London: Penguin, 1983.

Aribau, Buenaventura Carlos. "Crítica literaria: Biblioteca de autores españoles, desde la formación del lenguaje hasta nuestros días, ordenada e ilustrada por Don Buenaventura Carlos Aribau." *Semanario Pintoresco* (1846): 302–3.

Ariza, Juan. *Un viaje al infierno.* Madrid, 1848.

Armada Losada, Juan. "Fernán Caballero y la novela de su tiempo." In *La España del siglo XIX: Colección de conferencias históricas (curso de 1885–86)*, 2:297–323. Madrid: Ateneo de Madrid, 1887.

Artola, Miguel. *La burguesía revolucionaria (1808–1874).* Madrid: Alianza, 1973.

Auerbach, Erich. *Mimesis: The Representation of Reality in Western Literature.* Princeton: Princeton University Press, 1953.

Ayguals de Izco, Wenceslao. "Introducción: Eugenio Sue." *El Fandango* 7 (15 June 1845): 97–100.

———. *Galería regia y vindicación de los ultrajes extranjeros.* 3 vols. Madrid: Wenceslao Ayguals de Izco, 1843–45.

———. *La maravilla del siglo: Cartas a María Enriqueta o sea Una visita a París y Londres durante la famosa exhibición de la Industria Universal de 1851.* Madrid: Ayguals de Izco, 1852.

———. *María o La hija de un jornalero*. 2 vols. Madrid: Wenceslao Ayguals de Izco, 1845–46.

———. *Marie l'Espagnole ou La victime d'un moine*. Paris: Librairie de Dutertre, 1846.

———. *La marquesa de Bellaflor o El niño de la inclusa*. 2 vols. Madrid: Wenceslao Ayguals de Izco, 1847–48.

———. "Movimiento literario." *El Dómine Lucas* 15 (1 June 1845): 118.

———. "A Mr. Eugenio Sue." Preface to *María o La hija de un jornalero*, 1:5–8.

Aymes, Jean-René. "L'image de George Sand en Espagne (1836–1850)." In *L'image de France en Espagne (1808–1850)*, ed. Jean-René Aymes and Javier Fernández Sebastián, 243–62. Bilbao: Universidad del País Vasco, 1997.

Baker, Edward. "Espacio urbano y representación literaria: Madrid de la Ilustración a la Gloriosa." In *Texto y sociedad: Problemas de historia literaria*, ed. Bridget Aldaraca, Edward Baker, and John Beverley, 203–13. Amsterdam and Atlanta: Rodopi, 1990.

———. "Introducción: La problemática de la historia literaria." In *Texto y sociedad: Problemas de historia literaria*, ed. Bridget Aldaraca, Edward Baker, and John Beverley, 12–18. Amsterdam and Atlanta: Rodopi, 1990.

Bakhtin, Mikhail. *The Dialogic Imagination*, ed. Michael Holquist. Translated by Caryl Emerson and Michael Holquist. Austin: University of Texas Press, 1981.

Balakian, Anna. "Influence and Literary Fortune." *Yearbook of Comparative and General Literature* 7 (1958): 30–37.

Balzac, Honoré. *Les Parisiens comme ils sont*. Genève: La Palatine, 1947.

Baquero Goyanes, Mariano. *Proceso de la novela actual*. Madrid: Rialp, 1963.

Barrantes, Vicente. "Carta a Fernán Caballero." 1853. Rpt. in Zavala, *Ideología y política en la novela española del siglo XIX*, 284–91.

Barthes, Roland. "The Death of the Author." In *Image, Music, Text*, ed. Stephen Heath, 142–48. New York: Hill and Wang, 1977.

———. "Histoire ou littérature." *Sur Racine*, 145–67. Paris: Seuil, 1963.

———. *S/Z: An Essay*. Translated by Richard Miller. New York: Noonday Press, 1974.

Baruch, Martine, et al. *Nationalisme et cosmopolitisme dans les littératures ibériques au XIXème siècle*. Paris: Presses Universitaires de Lille III, 1975.

Bassnett-McGuire, Susan. *Translation Studies*. London: Methuen, 1980.

Bate, Walter J. *The Burden of the Past and the English Poet*. Cambridge: Harvard University Press, 1970.

Belinski, V. G. "*Los misterios de París*." In *Socialismo y consolación: Reflexiones en torno a "Los misterios de París" de Eugène Sue*, 39–48. Barcelona: Tusquets, 1970.

Benítez, Rubén. *La ideología del folletín español: Wenceslao Ayguals de Izco (1801–1873)*. Madrid: José Porrúa Turanzas, 1979.

Benjamin, Walter. "The Author as Producer." In *Reflections: Essays, Aphorisms, Autobiographical Writings*, ed. Peter Demetz, 220–38. New York: Schocken, 1978.

———. "Paris, Capital of the Nineteenth Century." In *Reflections: Essays, Aphorisms, Autobiographical Writings*, ed. Peter Demetz, 146–62. New York: Schocken, 1978.

———. "The Work of Art in the Age of Mechanical Reproduction." In *Illuminations*, ed. Hannah Arendt, 217–51. New York: Schocken, 1968.

Bermúdez de Castro, Salvador. [S. B. de C.]. "De la novela moderna." *Semanario Pintoresco Español* 19 (10 May 1840): 150–51.

Bersani, Leo. "Realism and the Fear of Desire." *A Future for Astyanax: Character and Desire in Literature*, 51–88. New York: Columbia University Press, 1984.

Blanco, Alda. "Gender and National Identity: The Novel in Nineteenth-Century Spanish Literary History." In *Culture and Gender in Nineteenth-Century Spain*, ed. Lou Charnon-Deutsch and Jo Labanyi, 120–36. Oxford: Clarendon Press, 1995.

———. "The Moral Imperative for Women Writers." *Indiana Journal of Hispanic Literatures* 2.1 (fall 1993): 91–110.

Blanco Aguinaga, Carlos, Julio Rodríguez Puértolas, and Iris M. Zavala. *Historia social de la literatura española (en lengua castellana)*. 3 vols. Madrid: Castalia, 1978–79.

Bloom, Harold. *The Anxiety of Influence*. New York: Oxford University Press, 1973.

Bory, Jean-Louis. *Eugène Sue: Le roi du roman populaire*. Paris: Hachette, 1962.

Botrel, Jean-François. *La diffusion du livre en Espagne (1868–1914): Les libraires*. Madrid: Casa de Velázquez, 1988.

———. "L'Espagne et les modèles éditoriaux français (1830–1850)." In *L'image de France en Espagne (1808–1850)*, ed. Jean-René Aymes and Javier Fernández Sebastián, 227–42. Bilbao: Universidad del País Vasco, 1997.

———. "Narrativa y lecturas del pueblo en la España del siglo XIX." *Cuadernos Hispanoamericanos* 516 (June 1993): 69–91.

———. "Nationalisme et consolation dans la littérature populaire espagnole des années 1898." In *Nationalisme et littérature en Espagne et en Amérique Latine aux XIXè siécle*, ed. Claude Dumas, 63–98. Lille: Presses Universitaires de Lille III, 1982.

———. "La novela por entregas: Unidad de creación y público." In *Creación y público en la literatura española*, ed. J.-F. Botrel and S. Salaün, 111–55. Madrid: Castalia, 1974.

———. "Producción literaria y rentabilidad: El caso de Clarín." In *Hommage des hispanistes français à Noel Salomon*, ed. Henry Bonneville, 123–33. Barcelona: Laia, 1979.

Botrel, Jean-François, and Josette Blanquat, eds. *Clarín y sus editores: 65 cartas inéditas de Leopoldo Alas a Fernando Fe y Manuel Fernández Lasanta, 1884–1893*. Rennes: Université de Haute-Bretagne, 1981.

Bourgoing, Jean-François. *Tableau de l'Espagne moderne*. 1788. Paris: Levrault frères, 1803.

Bozal Fernández, Valeriano. "La novela en España en el siglo XIX." *Cuadernos Hispanoamericanos* 219 (March 1968): 578–84.

Bravo-Villasante, Carmen. "Introducción bibliográfica y crítica." In Caballero, *La Gaviota*, 7–30.

Bretón de los Herreros, Manuel. *El editor responsable*. Madrid: Repullés, 1842.

Brooks, Peter. *The Melodramatic Imagination: Balzac, Henry James, Melodrama, and the Mode of Excess*. New York: Columbia University Press, 1985.

———. *Reading for the Plot: Design and Intention in Narrative*. London and Cambridge: Harvard University Press, 1992.

Brown, Reginald F. *La novela española 1700–1850*. Madrid: Dirección General de Archivos y Bibliotecas, 1953.

Caballero, Fernán [Cecilia Böhl de Faber]. *Cartas de Fernán Caballero*, ed. Diego de Valencina. Madrid: Librería de los Sucesores de Hernando, 1919.

———. "Carta de Fernán Caballero al Dr. Julius." In Santiago Montoto, *Fernán Caballero: Algo más que una biografía*, 365–71. Sevilla: Gráficas del Sur, 1969.

———. *Cartas inéditas de Fernán Caballero*, ed. Santiago Montoto. Madrid: S. Aguirre Torre, n.d.

———. *La Gaviota*, ed. Carmen Bravo-Villasante. Madrid: Castalia, 1982.

Cañete, Manuel. "Literatura." *La Aureola* (3 octubre 1839).

Carr, Raymond. *Spain (1808–1939)*. Oxford: Oxford University Press, 1966.

Carrillo, Victor. "Marketing et édition au XIXe siècle: La Sociedad Literaria de Madrid (Etude d'approche)." *L'infra-littérature en Espagne au XIXe et XXe siècles: Du roman feuilleton au romancero de la guerre d'Espagne*, 7–101. Saint Martin d'Heres: Presses Universitaires de Grenoble, 1977.

———. "Radiografía de una colección de novelas a mediados del siglo XIX." In *Movimiento obrero, política y literatura en la España contemporánea*, ed. M. Tuñón de Lara and Jean-François Botrel, 159–77. Madrid: Cuadernos para el Diálogo, 1973.

Carvajal, R. de. "Sobre la traducción que hace del *Judío Errante* D. Wenceslao Ayguals de Izco." *El Fénix* (Valencia, 19 January 1845). Rpt. in *El Dómine Lucas* 11 (1845): 83.

Castillo, Rafael del. *Misterios catalanes o El obrero de Barcelona*. Barcelona: Font, 1862.

Cejador y Frauca, Julio. *Historia de la lengua y literatura castellana*. 14 vols. Madrid: Tipografía de la "Revista de Archivos, Bibliotecas, y Museos," 1915–22.

Chamberlin, Vernon A. "*Doña Perfecta*: Galdós' Reply to *Pepita Jiménez*." *Anales Galdosianos* 15 (1980): 11–21.

Charle, Christopher. "Le champ de la production littéraire." In *Le temps des éditeurs: Du Romanticisme à la Belle Epoque*, ed. Henri-Jean Martin and Roger Chartier, 126–57. Paris: Promodis, 1985.

Charnon-Deutsch, Lou. *Gender and Representation: Women in Nineteenth-Century Spanish Realist Fiction*. Amsterdam and Philadelphia: John Benjamins, 1990.

———. *Narratives of Desire: Nineteenth-Century Spanish Fiction by Women*. University Park: Pennsylvania State University Press, 1994.

Charnon-Deutsch, Lou, and Jo Labanyi, eds. *Culture and Genre in Nineteenth-Century Spain*. Oxford: Clarendon Press, 1995.

Chartier, Roger, and Daniel Roche. "Livres et presse: Véhicules des idées." In *Seventh International Congress on the Enlightenment: Introductory Papers* (Budapest, 26 July – 2 August 1987), 93–106. Oxford: Voltaire Foundation, 1987.

Chasles, Philarète. "Des auteurs espagnols contemporains." *Revue des Deux Mondes* 3 (1841): 630–47.

Cirujano Marín, Paloma, et al. *Historiografía y nacionalismo español, 1834–1868*. Madrid: CSIC, 1985.

Coll y Vehí, José. *Diálogos literarios*. 1868. Barcelona: A. J. Bastinos, 1896.

Cueto, Leopoldo Augusto de. "Crítica literaria: *Creencias y engaños*, novela original de D. Ramón de Navarrete." *Revista de Madrid* 1 (1843): 100–106. Rpt. in Zavala, *Ideología y política en la novela española del siglo XIX*, 241–46.

Davis, Gifford. "The Spanish Debate over Idealism and Realism Before the Impact of Zola's Naturalism." *PMLA* 84 (1969): 1649–56.

Dérozier, Albert. "L'esprit national et les apports étrangers: Une harmonieuse conciliation?" In *Nation et Nationalites en Espagne: XIXe–XXe siècles*, 123–38. Paris: Fondation Singer-Polignac, 1985.

Duke de Rivas. "Discurso de contestación a Don Cándido Nocedal, del Excmo Sr. Duque de Rivas." Rpt. in Zavala, *Ideología y política en la novela española del siglo XIX*, 308–14.

Duran i Sampere, Agustí. *Contribució a la història de la imprenta a Barcelona*. Barcelona, 1936.

———. *Editores y libreros de Barcelona: Estivill, Piferrer, Brusi Bastinas*. Barcelona: Bosch, 1952.

Dyserinck, Hugo, Enrique Banús, Angel R. Fernández, and Kurt Spang, coords. *Europa en España: España en Europa. Actas del simposio internacional de literatura comparada*. Barcelona: PPU, 1990.

E. de C. "Decadencia de la literatura francesa." *Revista Semanal del Avisador Malagueño* 44 (1846): 344–49.

Echevarría Pereda, Elena. "La imagen de España en Francia: Viajeras francesas decimonónicas." Ph.D. diss., Universidad de Málaga, 1994.

Eco, Umberto. "Socialismo y consolación." In *Socialismo y consolación: Reflexiones en torno a "Los misterios de París" de Eugène Sue*, 7–37. Barcelona: Tusquets, 1970.

Ejxenbaum, Boris M. "Literary Environment." In *Readings in Russian Poetics: Formalist and Structuralist Views*, ed. Ladislaw Matejka and Krystyna Pomorska, 56–65. Cambridge: MIT Press, 1971.

Elías de Molins, Antonio. *Diccionario biográfico y bibliográfico de escritores y artistas catalanes del siglo XIX*. 2 vols. Barcelona, 1889.

Eliot, T. S. "Philip Massinger." In *Selected Essays, 1917–1932*, 181–95. New York: Harcourt, 1932.

Elorza, Antonio. "El tema de Francia en el primer republicanismo español." In *L'image de France en Espagne (1808–1850)*, ed. Jean-René Aymes and Javier Fernández Sebastián, 107–25. Bilbao: Universidad del País Vasco, 1997.

Escarpit, Robert. " 'Creative Treason' as a Key to Literature." *Yearbook of Comparative and General Literature* 10 (1961): 16–21.

Escolano, Agustín, ed. *Leer y escribir en España: Doscientos años de alfabetización*. Madrid: Fundación Germán Sánchez Ruipérez, 1992.

Even-Zohar, Itamar. "Laws of Literary Interference." *Poetics Today* 11.1 (spring 1990): 53–72.

———. "The Position of Translated Literature Within the Literary Polysystem." *Poetics Today* 11.1 (spring 1990): 45–52.

———. "Translation and Transfer." *Poetics Today* 11.1 (spring 1990): 79–84.

Farinelli, Arturo. *Il romanticismo del mondo latino*. 3 vols. Torino: Fratelli Bocca, 1927.

Fernández Espino, José. "Discurso leído ante la Real Academia sevillana de Buenas Letras, en la solemne adjudicación del premio a la mejor memoria presentada sobre la influencia de la novela en las costumbres." 1857. Rpt. in Zavala, *Ideología y política en la novela española del siglo XIX*, 298–307.

Fernández de los Ríos, Ángel. "Apuntes biográficos: Eugenio Sue." *El Siglo Pintoresco* 9 (September 1846): 209–12.

———. "Crítica literaria: *María o La hija de un jornalero*, novela original de D. Wenceslao Ayguals de Izco." *Semanario Pintoresco* 36 (6 September 1846), 285–86. Madrid: Baltasar Gómez, 1846.

———. *La España del siglo XIX*. Madrid, 1879.

———. "Prólogo" to Miguel Agustín Príncipe, *La casa de Pero-Hernández*, i–xvi. Madrid: Baltasar González, 1848.

Ferrater Mora, José. *Diccionario de filosofía*. 4 vols. Madrid: Alianza, 1979.

Ferreras, Juan Ignacio. *Catálogo de novelas y novelistas españoles del siglo XIX*. Madrid: Cátedra, 1979.

———. *La novela española en el siglo XIX (h. 1868)*. Madrid: Taurus, 1987.

———. *La novela por entregas, 1840–1900: Concentración obrera y economía editorial*. Madrid: Taurus, 1972.

———. *Orígenes de la novela decimonónica (1830–1870)*. Madrid: Taurus, 1973.

Flitter, Derek. *Spanish Romantic Literary Theory and Criticism*. Cambridge: Cambridge University Press, 1992.

"Folletines de los periódicos." 1844. Rpt. in Zavala, *Ideología y política en la novela española del siglo XIX*, 266–68.

"Folletines: Literatura." 1850. Rpt. in Zavala, *Ideología y política en la novela española del siglo XIX*, 268–69.

Foucault, Michel. "What Is an Author?" In *Language, Counter-Memory, Practice: Selected Essays and Interviews*, 113–38, ed. Donald F. Bouchard. Ithaca: Cornell University Press, 1977.

Fradera, Josep M. *Indústria i mercat: Les bases comercials de la indústria catalana moderna (1841–1845)*. Barcelona: Crítica, 1987.

Galindo, Miguel. "Breves notas sobre el periodismo y el folletín en la prensa castellonense del XIX." *Boletín de la Sociedad Castellonense de Cultura* 46.2 (1970): 174–98.

García Canclini, Néstor. *Culturas híbridas: Estrategias para entrar y salir de la modernidad*. Mexico: Grijalbo, 1989.

García de Enterría, María Cruz. *Literaturas marginadas*. Madrid: Playor, 1983.

García Rovira, Anna M. *La revolució liberal a Espanya i les classes populars*. Vic: Eumo, 1989.

García Tejero, Alfonso. *El pilluelo de Madrid*. 2 vols. Madrid: Sociedad Literaria, 1844.

García Yebra, Valentín. "Opinión: Derechos morales del traductor." *ABC* (19 May 1999).

Gentzler, Edwin. *Contemporary Translation Theories*. London and New York: Routledge, 1993.

Ghamine, Albert. *Joan Cortada: Catalunya i els catalans als segle XIX*. Barcelona: Abadia de Montserrat, 1995.

Gide, André. "De l'influence en littérature." *Prétextes: Réflections sur quelques points de littérature et de morale*, 9–30. Paris: Mercure de France, 1945.

Gies, David T. *Romanticismo*. Madrid: Taurus, 1989.

Gil y Carrasco, Enrique. "Literatura extranjera: Bosquejos de España por el Capitán S. E. Cook, de la marina real inglesa." *El Laberinto* 10 (16 March 1844): 128–29, 11 (1 April 1844): 141–42, 12 (16 April 1844): 157–59.

Gilman, Stephen. *Galdós and the Art of the European Novel: 1867–1887*. Princeton: Princeton University Press, 1981.

Godzich, Wlad, and Nicholas Spadaccini. "Introduction: The Course of Literature in Nineteenth-Century Spain." In *The Institutionalization of Literature in Spain*, ed. W. Godzich and N. Spadaccini, 9–34. Minneapolis, Minn.: Prisma Institute, 1988.

Gold, Hazel. "Back to the Future: Criticism, the Canon, and the Nineteenth-Century Spanish Novel." *Hispanic Review* 58.2 (spring 1990): 179–204.

Goldman, Peter B. "Toward a Sociology of the Modern Spanish Novel: The Early Years. Part I." *MLN* 89 (January–April 1974): 173–90.

———. "Toward a Sociology of the Modern Spanish Novel: The Early Years. Part II." *MLN* 90 (January–April 1975): 183–211.

Gómez de Baquero, Eduardo [Andrenio]. *El renacimiento de la novela española en el siglo XIX*. Madrid: Mundo Latino, 1924.

González Bravo, Luis. "De la crítica." Rpt. in *El Alba (Madrid, 1838–1839)*, ed. José Simón Díaz, 25–28. Madrid: CSIC, 1946.

Graham, Helen, and Jo Labanyi. "Culture and Modernity: The Case of Spain." In *Spanish Cultural Studies: An Introduction*, ed. Helen Graham and Jo Labanyi, 1–19. Oxford: Oxford University Press, 1995.

Gramsci, Antonio. *Selections from Cultural Writings*, ed. David Frogacs and Geoffrey Nowell-Smith. Cambridge: Harvard University Press, 1985.

Granqvist, Raoul. *Imitation as Resistance: Appropriations of English Literature in Nineteenth-Century America*. Madison, Wis.: Teaneck, 1995.

Guillén, Claudio. *The Challenge of Comparative Literature*. Translated by Cola Franzen. Cambridge: Harvard University Press, 1993.

Guillén Buzarán, J. "Sobre las novelas en España." *Semanario Pintoresco Español* 43 (27 October 1844): 338–40.

Habermas, Jürgen. *The Structural Transformation of the Public Sphere: An Inquiry into a Category of Bourgeois Society*. Translated by Thomas Burger. Cambridge: MIT Press, 1989.

Hall, Stuart. "Introduction: Who Needs 'Identity'?" In *Questions of Cultural Identity*, ed. Stuart Hall and Paul du Gay, 1–17. London: Sage, 1996.

Hartzenbusch, Juan Eugenio. "Estudios literarios: Apuntes sobre el carácter de la literatura contemporánea leídos en el Ateneo científico y literario de Madrid." *Siglo Pintoresco* 3 (1847): 149–52.

Hay, Denys. *Europe: The Emergence of an Idea*. Edinburgh: Edinburgh University Press, 1968.

Herrero, Javier. *Fernán Caballero: Un nuevo planteamiento*. Madrid: Gredos, 1963.

Hoffman, Léon-François. *Romantique Espagne: L'image de l'Espagne en France entre 1800 et 1850*. Paris: Presses Universitaires de France, 1961.

Holmes, James S., et al. *Literature and Translation: New Perspectives in Literary Studies*. Leuven: Acco, 1978.

Hurtley, Jacqueline A. "Translation in Postwar Spain: Twixt Survival and Interior Exile." *Journal of Interdisciplinary Literary Studies* 1.2 (fall 1989): 265–76.

Ilie, Paul. "Antrophagous Spain and the European Other." *Hispania* 67.1 (March 1984): 28–35.

———. "Self-Images in the Mirror of Otherness." In *Iberian Identity: Essays on the Nature of Identity in Portugal and Spain*, ed. Richard Herr and John H. R. Polt, 156–80. Berkeley: University of California Press, 1989.

Jagoe, Catherine. "Disinheriting the Feminine: Galdós and the Rise of the Realist Novel in Spain." *Revista de Estudios Hispánicos* 27 (1993): 225–48.

Jutglar, Antoni. *Ideologías y clases en la España contemporánea: Aproximaciones a la historia social de las ideas*. Madrid: Edicusa, 1972.

King, Edmund L. "What Is Spanish Romanticism?" *Studies in Romanticism* 2 (1962): 1–11.

Kirkpatrick, Susan. *Larra: El laberinto inextricable de un romántico liberal*. Madrid: Gredos, 1977.

———. *Las Románticas: Women Writers and Subjectivity in Spain, 1835–1850*. Berkeley: University of California Press, 1989.

---. "Spanish Romanticism." In *Romanticism in National Context*, ed. Roy Porter and Mikulás Teich, 260–83. Cambridge: Cambridge University Press, 1988.
Lacassin, Francis. "Preface" to Eugène Sue, *Le juif errant*, 1–7. Paris: Robert Laffont, 1983.
Lafarga, Francisco. *La traducción en España (1750–1830): Lengua, literatura, cultura*. Lleida: Universitat de Lleida, 1999.
Lafuente, Modesto. "Pleito ruidoso." *Teatro Social del siglo XIX* II (1846): 146–50. Rpt. in Zavala, *Ideología y política en la novela española del siglo XIX*, 254–58.
Lambert, José. "L'éternelle question des frontières: Littératures nationales et systèmes littéraires." In *Langue, dialecte, littérature: Etudes romanes à la mémoire de Hugo Plomteux*, ed. C. Angelet, L. Melis, F. J. Merteens, and F. Musarra, 355–70. Leuven: Leuven University Press, 1983.

---. "In Quest of Literary World Maps." In *Interculturality and the Historical Study of Literary Translations*, ed. Harald Kittel and Armin Paul Frank, 133–44. Berlin: Erich Schmidt, 1991.

Lanoux, Armand. "Introduction" to Eugène Sue, *Les mystères de Paris*, 1–18. Paris: Robert Laffont, 1989.
Larra, Mariano José de. "Los amigos." *Revista Española* 107 (20 October 1833): 40.

---. "Carta al editor Delgado (20 de agosto de 1835)." Rpt. in Carmen de Burgos, *"Fígaro": Revelaciones, "Ella" descubierta, epistolario inédito*, 179–80. Madrid: Alrededor del Mundo, 1919.

---. "De las traducciones." *El Español* (11 March 1836). Rpt. in *Obras completas*, 496–99. Barcelona: Montaner y Simón, 1886.

---. "Dos palabras." In *El pobrecito hablador*, 23–25. Madrid: Ibero-Africano-Americana, 1927.

---. "Espagne Poétique: Choix de poésies Castillanes depuis Charles-Quint jusqu'à nos jours mises en vers Français par Don Juan Maria Maury." In *Obras completas*, 334–36. Barcelona: Montaner y Simón, 1886.

---. "Horas de invierno." *El Español* (25 December 1836). Rpt. in *Las palabras: Artículos y ensayos*, ed. José Luis Varela, 320–25. Madrid: Espasa-Calpe, 1982.

---. "Literatura: Poesías de don Juan Bautista Alonso." In *Obras Completas*, 395–97. Barcelona: Montaner y Simón, 1886.

---. "Literatura: Rápida ojeada sobre la historia e índole de la nuestra. Su estado actual. Su porvenir. Profesión de fe." *El Español* (18 January 1836). Rpt. in *Las palabras: Artículos y ensayos*, ed. José Luis Varela, 259–65. Madrid: Espasa-Calpe, 1982.

---. "El ministerio Mendizábal." In *Obras completas de D. Mariano José de Larra (Fígaro)*, ed. Carlos Seco Serrano, 4 vols., 2:214–16. Madrid: Atlas, 1960.

---. "Panorama matritense. Cuadros de costumbres de la capital observados y descritos por un curioso parlante. Articulo primero." In *Obras completas de D. Mariano José de Larra (Fígaro)*, ed. Carlos Seco Serrano, 4 vols., 2:238–41. Madrid: Atlas, 1960.

---. "Vindicación." *Revista Española* (23 March 1834). Rpt. in Carmen de Burgos, *"Fígaro": Revelaciones, "Ella" descubierta, epistolario inédito*, 78–79. Madrid: Alrededor del Mundo, 1919.

---. "Vuelva usted mañana." In *Artículos varios*, ed. Evaristo Correa Calderón, 324–36. Madrid: Castalia, 1984.

Lefevere, André. "Théorie littéraire et littérature traduite." *Canadian Review of Comparative Literature* 9.2 (June 1982): 137–56.

———. *Translation, Rewriting, and the Manipulation of Literary Fame*. London and New York: Routledge, 1992.

———, ed. *Translation/History/Culture: A Sourcebook*. London and New York: Routledge, 1992.

Lewis, Tom. "Religious Subject-Forms: Nationalism, Literature, and the Consolidation of *Moderantismo* in Spain during the 1840s." In *Culture and the State in Spain: 1550–1850*, ed. Tom Lewis and Francisco J. Sánchez, 252–77. New York and London: Garland, 1999.

Llorens Castillo, Vicente. *El romanticismo español*. Madrid: Castalia, 1989.

Llovet, Jordi. "Els vostres clàssics: El crèdit de la literatura." *El País* (20 May 1999), sec. "Quadern," 5.

Luxán Meléndez, Santiago. *La industria tipográfica en Canarias (1750–1900): Balance de la producción impresa*. Gran Canaria: Cabildo Insular de Gran Canaria, 1994.

Lyons, Martyn. *Le triomphe du livre: Une histoire sociologique de la lecture dans la France du XIXe siècle*. Mayenne: Promodis, 1987.

Mallon, Thomas. *Stolen Words: Forays into the Origins and Ravages of Plagiarism*. New York: Ticknor, 1989.

Mandelstam, Osip. "About the Nature of the Word." In *Osip Mandelstam: Selected Essays*, 65–79. Austin: University of Texas Press, 1977.

Marco, Joaquín. "Prólogo" to Wenceslao Ayguals de Izco, *La bruja de Madrid*, 7–22. Barcelona: Taber, 1969.

Marrast, Robert. "Libro y lectura en la España del siglo XIX." In *Movimiento obrero, política y literatura en la España contemporánea*, ed. M. Tuñón de Lara and Jean-François Botrel, 145–59. Madrid: Edicusa, 1974.

Martí-López, Elisa. "Historiografía literaria y folletín: Notas para un debate crítico sobre el siglo XIX español." *Siglo XIX (Literatura Hispánica)* 4 (1998): 109–30.

———. "El mercado editorial en la España de mediados del siglo XIX." *Cuadernos Hispanoamericanos* 565–66 (July–August 1997): 177–88.

———. "La orfandad de la novela española: Política editorial y creación literaria a mediados del siglo XIX." *Bulletin Hispanique* 98.2 (1996): 1–15.

Martínez Martín, Jesús. *Lectura y lectores en el Madrid del siglo XIX*. Madrid: CSIC, 1991.

Martínez Villergas, Juan. *El cancionero del pueblo*. Madrid, 1844–45.

———. *Juicio crítico de los poetas españoles contemporáneos*. París: Rosa y Bouret, 1854.

———. "Introducción" to *El Fandango*, 1–2. Madrid: Sociedad Literaria, 1845–46.

———. *Los misterios de madrid*. Madrid: Manini, 1844–45.

Marx, Karl, and Frederick Engels. "The Earthly Course and Transfiguration of 'Critical Criticism,' or 'Critical Criticism' as Rudolph, Prince of Geroldstein." In *Collected Works*. 48 vols., 4:162–209. New York: International Publishers, 1975.

Mayoral, Marina. "*La hija del mar*: Biografía, confesión lírica y folletín." In *Romanticismo 3–4. Atti del IV Congresso sul romanticismo spagnolo e ispanoamericano (Bordighera, 9–11 aprile 1987)*, ed. Ermanno Caldera, 80–89. Génova: Biblioteca di Lettere, 1988.

Mesonero Romanos, Ramón de. "Las novelitas francesas." *Semanario Pintoresco Español* (28 June 1840): 261–63. Rpt. in Zavala, *Ideología y política en la novela española del siglo XIX*, 232–35.

———. "Las traducciones." In *Obras de Don Ramón de Mesonero y Romanos*, ed. Carlos Seco Serrano, 5 vols., 2:277–78. Madrid: Atlas, 1967.

———. "Los viajeros franceses en España." In *Recuerdos de viaje por Francia y Bélgica en 1840–1841. Obras de Don Ramón de Mesonero Romanos*, ed. Carlos Seco Serrano, 5 vols., 5:250–55. Madrid: Atlas, 1967.

Milá de la Roca, José Nicasio. *Los misterios de Barcelona*. Barcelona: Imprenta y Librería Española y Extranjera, 1844.

Montesinos, José F. *Fernán Caballero: Ensayo de justificación*. Berkeley: University of California Press, 1961.

———. *Introducción a una historia de la novela en España en el siglo XIX; Seguida del esbozo de una bibliografía española de traducciones de novelas (1800–1850)*. Madrid: Castalia, 1980.

Moretti, Franco. *Atlas of the European Novel (1800–1900)*. London and New York: Verso, 1998.

———. "Modern European Literature: A Geographical Sketch." *New Left Review* 206 (1994): 86–109.

———. *Signs Taken for Wonders: Essays in the Sociology of Literary Forms*. London and New York: Verso, 1988.

Morson, Gary Saul. *The Boundaries of Genre: Dostoevsky's "Diary of a Writer" and the Traditions of Literary Utopia*. Austin: University of Texas Press, 1981.

Moya, Francisco Javier. "La novela nacional." *El Espectador* (9 May 1848). Rpt. in Zavala, *Ideología y política en la novela española del siglo XIX*, 274–78.

Navarrete, Ramón de. "La novela española." 1847. Rpt. in Zavala, *Ideología y política en la novela española del siglo XIX*, 258–66.

Navarro, Ana. "Historia editorial de *Pepita Jiménez*." *Cuadernos de Investigación de Literatura Hispánica* 10 (1988): 81–103.

Noriega, Mariano. *La fisiología de un poeta*. Madrid: Imprenta y Casa de la Unión Comercial, 1843.

Núñez de Arenas, Manuel. "Impresos españoles en Burdeos hasta 1850." *Revue Hispanique* 81 (1933): 5–46.

Ochoa, Eugenio de. "La Gaviota. Juicio crítico." In Caballero, *La Gaviota*, 325–40.

———. *Miscellania de literatura, viajes y novelas*. Madrid, 1867.

Oliván, Alejandro. Untitled article. *Revista de Madrid* III (1839): 279–91.

Ollé Romeu, Josep Maria. *Les bullangues de Barcelona durant la Primera Guerra Carlista (1835–1837)*. 2 vols. Tarragona: El Mèdol, 1994.

Ortega y Gasset, José. "Ideas sobre la novela." In *Teoría de la novela: Aproximaciones hispánicas*, ed. Germán Gullón and Agnes Gullón, 29–64. Madrid: Taurus, 1974.

Pastor Díaz, Nicodemes. "Review: *Sab*." *El conservador* (19 December 1841).

Paz, Octavio. "Traducción, imitación, originalidad." *Cuadernos Hispanoamericanos* 253–54 (January–February 1971): 7–16.

Pease, Donald E. "Author." In *Critical Terms for Literary Study*, ed. Frank Lentricchia and Thomas McLaughlin, 105–17. Chicago and London: University of Chicago Press, 1990.

Peers, E. Allison. *A History of the Romantic Movement in Spain*. 2 vols. New York and London: Hafner, 1964.

Pérez Galdós, Benito. "Observaciones sobre la novela contemporánea en España." In *Ensayos de crítica literaria*, ed. Laureano Bonet, 115–32. Barcelona: Península, 1972.

Pobre Diablo, El. "De la importancia de las novelas o historias y de las razones por qué no prevalece en España este ramo de literatura." *Eco del Comercio* (7 January 1838). Rpt. in Zavala, *Ideología y política en la novela española del siglo XIX*, 226–31.

Praz, Mario. *The Romantic Agony*. Oxford: Oxford University Press, 1970.

Rabaté, Colette. "Deux 'modèles' français de la Avellaneda: Madame de Staël et George Sand." In *L'image de France en Espagne (1808–1850)*, ed. Jean-René Aymes and Javier Fernández Sebastián, 263–81. Bilbao: Universidad del País Vasco, 1997.

Randolph, Donald A. *Don Manuel Cañete, cronista literario del romanticismo y del posromanticismo en España*. Chapel Hill: North Carolina University Press, 1972.

———. *Eugenio de Ochoa y el romanticismo español*. Berkeley: University of California Press, 1966.

"Revista literaria: *Los misterios de París*, traducidos por D. Antonio Flores.—*Madrid y sus misterios*, por un desconocido.—*Los misterios de Madrid*, por D. J. M. Villergas.—*El Judío errante*, por Eugenio Sue (traducción).—*Historia de Granada*, por don Miguel Lafuente Alcántara.—*Manual historiográfico-topográfico, administrativo y artístico de Madrid*, por don Ramón Mesonero Romanos.—*Sevilla Pintoresca*, por don José Amador de los Ríos." *Revista de Madrid* IV (1844): 402–13. Rpt. in Zavala, *Ideología y política en la novela española del siglo XIX*, 247–54.

Ribbans, Geoffrey. *Catalunya i València vistes pels viatgers anglesos del segle XVIIIè*. Barcelona: Barcino, 1993.

———. "*La Desheredada*, novela por entregas: Apuntes sobre su primera publicación." *Anales Galdosianos* 27–28 (1992–93): 69–75.

———. "*Doña Perfecta*: Yet Another Ending." *MLN* 105.2 (March 1990): 203–25.

Ríos-Font, Wadda C. *Rewriting Melodrama: The Hidden Paradigm in Modern Spanish Theater*. Lewisburg, Pa.: Bucknell University Press, 1997.

Roca y Cornet, Joaquín. *Ensayo crítico sobre las lecturas de la época*. Barcelona, 1847.

Román Gutiérrrez, Isabel. *Persona y forma: Una historia interna de la novela española del siglo XIX: Hacia el realismo*. Sevilla: Alfar, 1988.

Romero Tobar, Leonardo. "Españoles en París: Contactos de románticos españoles y escritores franceses contemporáneos." In *L'image de France en Espagne (1808–1850)*, ed. Jean-René Aymes and Javier Fernández Sebastián, 215–26. Bilbao: Universidad del País Vasco, 1997.

———. "Folletín." In *Diccionario de la literatura española e hispanoamericana*, dir. Ricardo Gullón, 2 vols., 1:568–70. Madrid: Alianza, 1993.

———. *La novela popular española del siglo XIX*. Madrid and Barcelona: Fundación Juan March/Ariel, 1975.

———. "*Pepita Jiménez* en folletín: La historia interminable de publicaciones efímeras." *Insula* 562 (October 1993): 4.

Rubio, Carlos. "Sección Doctrinal." *La Iberia* (22 August 1857). Rpt. in Romero Tobar, *La novela popular española del siglo XIX*, 252–57.

Rubió y Ors, Joaquín. *Memoria crítica literaria sobre "El Judío Errante."* Barcelona: José Rubió, 1845.

Said, Edward W. *Orientalism*. New York: Vintage, 1979.

Sand, George. *Un hiver à Majorque*. 1841. Paris: Michel Levy Frères, 1867.

Santana, Mario. "The Conflict of Narratives in Pérez Galdós' *Doña Perfecta*." *MLN* 113 (1998): 283–304.

———. *Foreigners in the Homeland: The Spanish American New Novel in Spain*. Lewisburg, Pa.: Bucknell University Press, 2000.

Schleiermacher, Friedrich. "On the Different Methods of Translating." In *Theories of Translation: An Anthology of Essays from Dryden to Derrida*, ed. Rainer Schulte and John Biguenet, 36–54. Chicago and London: University of Chicago Press, 1992.

Schor, Noami. "Idealism in the Novel: Recanonizing Sand." In *Displacements: Women, Tradition, Literatures in French*, ed. Joan DeJean and Nancy K. Miller, 55–73. Baltimore: Johns Hopkins University Press, 1991.

Schulte, Rainer, and John Biguenet, eds. *Theories of Translation: An Anthology of Essays from Dryden to Derrida*. Chicago: University of Chicago Press, 1992.

Schwarz, Roberto. *Misplaced Ideas: Essays on Brazilian Culture*. London and New York: Verso, 1992.

Sebold, Russell P. *Cadalso: El primer romántico "europeo" de España*. Madrid: Gredos, 1974.

Seoane, María Cruz. *Oratoria y periodismo en la España del siglo XIX*. Madrid: Castalia, 1977.

Serrano, Carlos. *El nacimiento de Carmen: Símbolos, mitos y nación*. Madrid: Taurus, 1999.

Shaw, Donald. "The Anti-Romantic Reaction in Spain." *Modern Language Review* (1968): 606–11.

Sieburth, Stephanie. *Inventing High and Low: Literature, Mass Culture, and Uneven Modernity in Spain*. Durham, N.C.: Duke University Press, 1994.

Silver, Phillip. "Toward a Revisionary Theory of Spanish Romanticism." *Revista de Estudios Hispánicos* 28 (1994): 293–302.

Smith, Barbara Herrnstein. "Value/Evaluation." In *Critical Terms for Literary Study*, ed. Frank Lentricchia and Thomas McLaughlin, 177–85. Chicago: University of Chicago Press, 1990.

Steiner, George. *After Babel: Aspects of Language and Translation*. New York and London: Oxford University Press, 1975.

Stendhal [Henri Beyle]. *Mémoires d'un touriste*. In *Oeuvres complètes*, vols. 45–47. Paris: A. Dupont, 1838.

Sue, Eugène. *Le juif errant*. 1844–45. Paris: Robert Laffont, 1983.

———. *Les mystères de Paris*. 1842–43. Paris: Robert Laffont, 1989.

———. *Los misterios de París*. Translated by Juan Cortada. 4 vols. Barcelona: Tomás Gorchs, 1845.

———. *Los misterios de París*. Translated by A. San Martín. 6 vols. Barcelona: Saurí, A. Gaspar y Berdaguer, 1845.

———. *Los misterios de París*. 5 vols. La Habana: D. R. Oliva, 1843.

Tejado, Gabino. "De la crítica contemporánea." *El Laberinto* 17 (9 June 1845): 238–40.

Termes, Josep. *La immigració a Catalunya i altres estudies d'història del nacionalisme català*. Barcelona: Empúries, 1984.

Torrecilla, Jesús. *El tiempo y los márgenes*. Chapel Hill, N.C.: North Carolina Studies in the Romance Languages and Literatures, 1996.

———. *La imitación colectiva: Modernidad vs. autenticidad en la literatura española*. Madrid: Gredos, 1996.

Toury, Gideon. *In Search of a Theory of Translation*. Tel Aviv: University of Tel Aviv Press, 1981.

Tressera, Ceferino. *Los misterios del Saladero*. 2 vols. Barcelona: Manero, 1860.

"Triunfo de la novela española." *El Dómine Lucas* (1846): 178–81.

Valero, José A. "Historia literaria y articulación de identidades en la transición a la España liberal." *Journal of Interdisciplinary Literary Studies* 6.2 (1994): 107–30.

Valis, Noël. "Clarín y la vida cultural del extranjero: Tres artículos desconocidos." *Boletín del Real Instituto de Estudios Asturianos* 47 (1993): 157–78.

———. "The Language of Treasure: Carolina Coronado, Casta Esteban, and Marina Romero." In Valis and Maier, eds., *In the Feminine Mode: Essays on Hispanic Woman Writers*, 246–72.

———. "The Perfect Copy: Clarín's *Su único hijo* and the Flaubertian Connection." *PMLA* 104.5 (1989): 856–967.

Valis, Noël, and Carol Maier, eds. *In the Feminine Mode: Essays on Hispanic Woman Writers*. London and Toronto: Associated University Presses, 1990.

Vauchelle-Haquet, Aline. *Les Ouvrages en langue espagnole publiées en France entre 1814 et 1833 (présentation et catalogue)*. Aix-en-Provence: Presses Universitaires de Provence, 1985.

Venuti, Lawrence. *The Translator's Invisibility: A History of Translation*. London and New York: Routledge, 1995.

Wellek, René. "The Crisis of Comparative Literature," ed. Stephen G. Nichols, Jr. In *Concepts of Criticism*, 282–95. New Haven: Yale University Press, 1963.

Zavala, Iris M. *Ideología y política en la novela española del siglo XIX*. Madrid: Anaya, 1971.

Index

Anderson, Benedict, 161n. 22
appropriation: concept of, 10, 28–32; as theft, 56–61. See also imitation; translation
Ariza, Juan, 63
Ayguals de Izco, Wenceslao, 18, 20, 21, 24, 32, 34, 40, 41–42, 45, 54, 55, 59–61, 69, 72, 75, 78, 98; *La marquesa de Bellaflor o El hijo de la inclusa,* 41; *El tigre del Maestrazgo,* 20; See also *María o La hija de un jornalero*

Bakhtin, M. M., 10, 28, 29, 54, 57
Balaguer, Víctor, 101
Balzac, Honoré, 47, 56, 64, 65, 66, 71, 135; *El verdugo* 47
Baquero Goyanes, Mariano, 137
Barthes, Roland, 26, 27
Bate, Walter J., 26
Benítez, Rubén, 20
Bermúdez de Castro, Salvador, 50
Blanco, Alda, 25
Blanco García, Francisco, 137
Bloom, Harold, 26, 57
Böhl de Faber, Cecilia. See Caballero, Fernán
book market, 11, 19, 21, 26, 27–28, 32, 33–43, 79
Bourgoing, Jean-François, 46; *Tableau de l'Espagne moderne,* 46
Brooks, Peter, 23
Brown, Reginald F., 78
bullangues, 106, 107, 108–9, 112–13, 128–31
Buzarán, Guillén, 66

Caballero, Fernán, 12, 25, 40, 41–42, 53, 54, 55, 60–61; *Elia,* 42, 99; *La familia de Alvareda,* 99; feminine novel, 74–76; and translation 98. See also *La Gaviota*

Calderón de la Barca, Pedro, 49
canon, formation of, 144 n. 7, 147 n. 34. See also *folletín,* imitation
Carr, Raymond, 23
Carvajal, R. de, 71
casticismo, 25
Castillo, Rafael del, 22
Chasles, Philarète, 49
Chateaubriand, François-René, 66, 135
consolation, literature of, 23, 80; and *Les mystères de Paris,* 69
Coronado, Carolina, 65
Cortada, Juan, 12, 13, 78–99, 114, 121, 131
Cueto, Leopoldo de, 53

D'Arlincourt, Charles-Victor Prévost, 66, 135
decadence, 49–53, 59–61. See also originality: and cultural hegemony; originality: and political hegemony
dependency theory, 149n. 52
Don Quijote, 47, 49
Dumas, Alexandre, père, 36, 37, 64, 66, 135; *Los cuarenta y cinco* 37; *Los Tres mosqueteros,* 36

Eco, Umberto, 23, 69
Eliot, T. S., 26
Elorza, Antonio, 63
Enlightenment, 31
Even-Zohar, Itamar, 98, 154 n. 10, 170n.46

Fernández Espino, José, 75
Fernández de los Ríos, Ángel, 37, 38, 41, 42, 59; and Balzac, 65–66; and French novel 64; and *Le juif errant,* 70; and *Les mystères de Paris,* 66; and Sue, 69
Fernández y González, Manuel, 41
Ferreras, Juan Ignacio, 19
Flaubert, Gustave, 22

192 INDEX

folletín, 10, 17–24, 145n.13; and newspaper, 162nn. 25, 26, 27, and 28; and prostitution, 75
folletinista, 20
Foucault, Michel, 20
Fourier, Charles, 72; and commune, 70
French novel: interference of, in Spain, 11–12, 49, 51, 53–54, 56; popularity of, 37–38, 53; as privileged referent, 63–64; progenitorship of, 12, 34–37, 64–76; social disorder, 72, 73–74, 75. *See also* originality: and cultural hegemony; translation 77–90

García Tejero, Alfonso, 40, 135–36; *El pilluelo de Madrid*, 40, 135–36
Gaviota, La, 25; and foreign imagination in, 55; nationalistic enterprise in 58–61; publication of, 42; translation into Spanish, 99. *See also* Caballero, Fernán
Gide, André, 29
Gilman, Stephen, 75
Godoy y Alcántara, José, 75
Godzich, Wlad, 31
Golden Age literature: European reception of, 49; French romantic adaptations of, 47; inadequacy of, 53–54, 135–36
Goldman, Peter B., 21
Gómez de Avellaneda, Gertrudis, 65
Gómez de Baquero, Eduardo, 137
Gramsci, Antonio, 19, 21–22
Guillén, Claudio, 27

Hartzenbusch, Juan Eugenio, 42, 50
Hay, Denis, 45
Herrero, Javier, 42
historia-novela, 106, 124, 129
Hoffman, Léon-François, 47
Hugo, Victor, 47, 66; *Hernani*, 47; *Notre-Dâme de Paris*, 22, 66; *Ruy Blas*, 47

imitation: and autochthonous novel, 101–134; concept of, 24–32, 81, 82; and Fernán Caballero, 55, 76; in hegemonic cultures, 154n. 10; of publishing techniques, 170n. 1; and women, 25, 147n. 33. *See also* appropriation; influence; French novel; translation
influence, 26, 28, 29

Jagoe, Catherine, 18, 21, 74
juif errant, Le, 12, 22, 37, 69–73, 78, 79

Lafuente, Modesto, 34–37, 64
Larra, Mariano José de Larra, 27, 32, 49, 136; and Balzac, 65; on cultural decadence, 50–52, 54, 55; on literature as theft 56–57; and translation, 78, 97, 98; and *Un Voyage Pintoresque par l'Espagne* 54

Mallon, Thomas, 26, 27
Mandelstam, Osip, 18, 27
Mañé y Flaquer, Juan, 77
Marco, Joaquín, 18, 20, 32
María o La hija de un jornalero, 22, 34, 41, 72, 146n. 19, 147n. 27; editions of, 152n. 27; foreign imagination in, 55; international success of, 54–55, 58; nationalistic enterprise in 59–61; French translation, 98. *See also* Ayguals de Izco
Martínez de la Rosa, Francisco, 47; *Aben Humeya*, 47
Martínez Villergas, Juan, 59, 60, 68
Marx, Karl, 23
Mellado, Francisco, 42
melodrama, 17, 19, 23, 66, 70, 73, 136–37. *See also folletín*
Menéndez y Pelayo, Marcelino, 18
Merimée, Prosper, 47; *Carmen*, 47
Mesonero Romanos, Ramón de, 48, 77, 99
Milá de la Roca, Nicasio José, 13, 40, 59, 69, 79, 101–34
Misterios, Los, 10, 17–24, 72; and imitation, 24–32
Misterios catalanes o El obrero de Barcelona, 22
Misterios de Barcelona, Los, 13, 40, 61, 79, 101–34; plot summary, 139–42
Misterios de Madrid, Los, 22, 68
Misterios de París, Los, 9, 12, 22, 77–99
Misterios del Saladero, Los, 72
mode espagnole, 47–48
Montesinos, José Fernández, 25, 36, 42
Mora, José Joaquín, 25, 42
Moretti, Franco, 17, 27–28, 33, 55, 136, 137
Moya, Francisco José, 38, 59, 70
Mystères de Paris, Les, 9, 12,13, 17, 22, 23, 54, 55, 63–73, 77–99, 101–3, 105–6, 107, 110, 111, 114, 122, 123, 126, 129,

INDEX

131, 136. *See also* Sue; *Los misterios de Barcelona*

Navarrete, Ramón de, 63, 66, 65, 67–68, 70–71

Nombela, Julio, 41

Noriega, Mariano, 39–40, 54; *La fisiología de un poeta*, 39–40

novela original, 37, 41; vs. translation, 77, 78, 98–99. *See also* originality; Spanish novel

novelas morales y recreativas, 41; and the French novel, 74

Ochoa, Eugenio de, 72, 73, 74

Orientalism: and Spain, 45–49. *See also* travelers

Originality: and authorship, 26; concept of, 26–27; and cultural hegemony 54–55; and cultural redemption, 51- 52, 157n. 36; and political hegemony 50–51. *See also* decadence; novela original

Ortega y Gasset, José, 18–19

Pastor Díaz, Nicodemes, 68

Pease, Donald E., 68

Pérez Escrich, Enrique, 41

Pérez Galdós, Benito, 18–19, 41, 137

plagiarism, 27, 98

"Pleito ruidoso," 34–37, 64

Pobre diablo, El, 49, 53, 67

popular novel, 18, 20, 21, 136–37

Príncipe, Miguel Agustín, 37–40; *La casa de Pero-Hernández*, 37–39

prostitution, 114–16

Puente, Fermín, 42

Randolph, Donald A., 42

readers, 21–23; and woman, 22; and translation 80, 81, 82, 87

realism: and idealism, 76; *juvenalia* of, 18; limits of, 137; and rules of good taste, 73

Renaixença, 88

Ribot, Antonio, 54–55, 58

Ríos-Font, Wadda, 23

romance, 79–88, 102–20

Romero Tobar, Leonardo, 17, 25, 52, 77,137

Rubió y Ors, Joaquín, 71–72

Said, Edward, 46–47

Sand, George, 46, 64, 65, 66, 135; *Un hiver à Majorque*, 46

Schleiermacher, Friedrich, 81

Schwarz, Roberto, 25n. 32, 28, 29–30, 33, 102, 112, 121, 134

Scott, Walter, 66, 74

serial novels, 20, 33. See also *folletín*

Sieburth, Stephanie, 21

Sinués, María del Pilar, 41

Sociedad Literaria, La, 152n. 27

Soulié, Frédréric, 66

Spadaccini, Nicholas, 31

Spanish novel: publication of, 37–43, 144n.10

Steiner, George, 77, 78, 89, 97

Stendhal, 48

subliterature, 20

Sue, Eugène, 9, 12, 13, 17, 21, 22, 28, 41, 64–74, 78–79, 101, 105–6, 107, 114, 120, 122, 123, 124, 125, 126, 129, 131, 132, 146n. 26. See also *Los misterios de Barcelona*; *Les mystères de Paris*; *Le juif errant*; translation, 77–90

Torrecilla, Jesús, 56

translation, 12–13, 35–37, 147n. 34, 150n. 3; authorship in, 88–98; and copyright legislation, 151n. 10; and cultural hegemony, 54, 57; and decadence, 156 n. 29; and paraphrase, 81–82; in peripheral literatures, 77–99, 170n. 46; translators, 165n. 2. *See also* originality: and political hegemony; *Los misterios de París*

travelers: foreign, in Spain, 48

Tressera, Ceferino, 24, 72

utopian socialism, 23, 72, 89

verisimilitude, 143n. 5